CAPITAL CITY ANTHOLOGY

Writings on Washington D.C. from the Founding Era to the Civil War

EDITED AND INTRODUCED BY CHRISTOPHER LEE PHILIPS

Pierre Charles L'Enfant, Thomas Jefferson, George Washington, Abigail Adams, Thomas Moore, Paul Jennings, Francis Hall, Auguste Levasseur, Harriet Martineau, Captain Marryat, Philip Hone, Solomon Northup, Charles Dickens, Fredrika Bremer, Casimir Bohn, Rose O'Neal Greenhow, Louisa May Alcott, Walt Whitman, Noah Brooks, and Many Others

ETHER EDITIONS

Copyright © 2024 by ETHER EDITIONS

All rights reserved. No part of this book may be reproduced in any manner whatsoever without written permission except in the case of brief quotations embodied in critical articles and reviews.

Several excerpts in the present volume originally appeared in slightly different format in *A View of the Swamp* (2020) by Christopher Lee Philips.

Cover illustration, "View of Washington," by Edward Sachse, circa 1852.

First Ether Editions Printing, 2024

CONTENTS

Introduction	xi
The Constitution	1
The President	2
Pierre Charles L'Enfant	5
Thomas Jefferson	8
George Washington	10
Isaac Weld, Jr.	13
John Harriott	21
Duke Rochefoucauld-Liancourt	25
Oliver Wolcott, Jr.	31

CONTENTS

Abigail Adams	35
Thomas Moore	38
John Melish	42
Paul Jennings	47
George Robert Gleig	52
Francis Hall	63
Henry Bradshaw Fearon	69
George Watterston	76
Auguste Levasseur	84
Captain Basil Hall	96
James Fenimore Cooper	102
Benjamin Perley Poore	108
Thomas Hamilton	111

District of Columbia	115
Francis Trollope	117
Tyrone Power	133
Theodore Dwight, Jr.	139
Harriet Martineau	143
Captain Frederick Marryat	148
Philip Hone	154
Adolphe Fourier de Bacourt	164
Solomon Northup	170
Charles Dickens	175
Caleb Atwater	183
Daniel Drayton	189
Fredrika Bremer	193

John F. Weishampel	199
Casimir Bohn	206
Anthony Trollope	219
Rose O'Neal Greenhow	229
Louisa May Alcott	235
James J. Williamson	244
Walt Whitman	253
Lafayette C. Baker	260
Francis Bicknell Carpenter	266
Noah Brooks	274
Sources	283

CAPITAL CITY ANTHOLOGY

INTRODUCTION

Washington, D.C., the "District of Columbia," has served as the permanent capital of the United States since 1800. From its post-revolutionary era founding through the American Civil War, the fledgling capital city evolved from an ambitious plan conceived on paper into a rapidly expanding national metropolis. During this formative era, domestic and international observers captured the city's growth and development in their personal and published writings. Among these observers were journalists, novelists, poets, politicians, social activists, soldiers, spies, tourists, and travel writers. They came to the city from different states among the former English colonies. European visitors were often critical of the new capital city. Indeed, a few visitors came to the city with the expressed intention of writing about it. Some merely passed through the city as travelers enroute to other destinations, while others became brief, long-term, or even permanent residents. Those who stayed, however long, often had governmental duties to perform or business, diplomatic, and military affairs to administer. Although the capital city was first and foremost political in nature and purpose, a vibrant social life eventually flourished.

This *Capital City Anthology* presents excerpts from the writings of these contemporary observers as manifested in diaries, documents, histories, fiction, guidebooks, letters, memoirs, poetry, and travelogues. Taken together, they offer readers a chronologically arranged, first-person account of the early evolution of Washington, D.C.

Christopher Lee Philips

The Constitution

Article I, Section 8, Clause 17:

[Congress shall have the power . . .] To exercise exclusive Legislation in all Cases whatsoever, over such District (not exceeding ten Miles square) as may, by Cession of particular States, and the Acceptance of Congress, become the Seat of Government of the United States, and to exercise like Authority over all Places purchased by the Consent of the Legislature of the State in which the Same shall be, for the Erection of Forts, Magazines, Arsenals, dock-Yards, and other needful Buildings . . . .

The President

In January 1791, after a complex series of negotiations, compromises, and no small amount of arm-twisting, President of the United States George Washington issued a Proclamation that defined for and explained to the American people the intentions of the federal government with respect to the new capital of the United States.

"Ten Miles Square"

By the President of the U. S. of America, A Proclamation.

Whereas, the general assembly of the state of Maryland, by an act passed on the 23rd day of December, 1788, entitled, "An act to cede to Congress a district of ten miles square in this state, for the seat of the government of the U[nited] States," did enact, that the representatives of the said state, in the House of Representatives of the Congress of the United States, appointed to assemble at New York, on the first Wednesday of March then next ensuing, should be, and they were hereby authorized and required, on behalf of the said state, to cede to the Congress of the United States any district in the said state, not exceeding ten miles square, which the Congress might fix upon and accept for the seat of government of the United States.

And the general assembly of the commonwealth of Virginia, by an act passed on the third day of December, 1789, and entitled "An act for the cession of ten miles square, or any lesser quantity of territory within this state, to the United States in Congress assembled, for the permanent seat of the general government," did enact, that a tract of country not exceeding ten miles square or any lesser quantity, to be located within the limits of the said state, and in any part thereof, as Congress might by law direct, should be, and the same was thereby forever ceded and relinquished to the Congress and government of the United States, in full and absolute right, and exclusive jurisdiction, as well of soil as of persons residing, or to reside, thereon, pursuant to the tenor and effect of the eighth section of the first article of the constitution of government of the United States.

And the Congress of the United States, by their act passed the 16th day of July, 1790, and entitled "An act for establishing the temporary and permanent seat of the government of the United States," authorized the President of the United States to appoint three commissioners, to survey under his direction, and by proper metes and bounds, to limit a district of territory not exceeding ten miles square, on the river Potomac, at some place between the mouth of the Eastern Branch and Conococheague, which district, so to be located and limited, was accepted by the said act of Congress, as the district for the permanent seat of the government of the United States.

"Now, therefore, in pursuance of the powers to me confided, and after duly examining and weighing the advantages and disadvantages of the several situations within the limits aforesaid, I do hereby declare and make known, that the location of one part of the said district of ten miles square, shall be found by running four lines of experiment in the following manner, that is to say: running from the court house in Alexandria, in Virginia, due south-west half a mile, and thence a due south-east course, till it shall strike Hunting Creek, to fix the beginning of the said four lines of experiment:

"Then beginning the first of the said four lines of experiment at the point on Hunting Creek, where the said south-east course shall have struck the same, and running the said first line due northwest ten miles; thence the second line into Maryland, due north-east ten miles; thence the third line due south-east ten miles; and thence the fourth line due south-west ten miles, to the beginning on Hunting Creek.

"And the said four lines of experiment being to run, 1 do hereby declare and make known, that part within the said four lines of experiment which shall be within the state of Maryland, and above the Eastern Branch, and all that part within the same four lines of experiment which shall be within the commonwealth of Virginia, and above a line to be run from the point of land forming the Upper Cape of the mouth of the Eastern Branch due south-west. and no more, is now fixed upon and directed to be surveyed, defined, limited and located for a part of the said district accepted by the said act of Congress for the permanent seat of the government of the United States; hereby expressly reserving the direction of the survey and location of the remaining part of the said district, to be made hereafter contiguous to such part or parts of the present location as is or shall be agreeably to law.

"And I do accordingly direct the said commissioners, appointed agreeably to the tenor of the said act, to proceed forthwith to run the said lines of experiment, and the same being run, to survey, and by proper metes and bounds, to define and limit the part within the same, which is herein before directed for immediate location and acceptance; and thereof to make due report to me, under their hands and seals.

> *In testimony whereof, I have caused the seal of the U[nited] States to be affixed to these presents, and signed the same with my hand. Done at the City of Philadelphia, this 24th day of January, in the year of our Lord 1791, and of the Independence of the United States the fifteenth.*

GEORGE WASHINGTON.
By the President. Thomas Jefferson.

Pierre Charles L'Enfant

Pierre Charles L'Enfant (1754-1825) was born in Paris to an artistic family. He attended the Royal Academy of Painting and Sculpture during the 1770s until his fascination with the American Revolution brought him to the shores of his adoptive country. During the Revolution, L'Enfant served as an engineer under George Washington at Valley Forge. After the war, Washington commissioned L'Enfant to draw up a plan for the new capital city. Knowing who owned the best library among his acquaintances, L'Enfant, then in Georgetown, wrote [in his most formal if tortured English] to Secretary of State Thomas Jefferson on April 4th, 1791, to ask Jefferson for his assistance. Would the Secretary, then in Philadelphia, be willing to provide any materials from his personal collection to assist L'Enfant in devising his plan?

"A Grand Plan"

Mr. Jefferson, *Secretary of State.*

Sir.

I would have reproached myself for not having written to you as regularly as you had desired, I should were it not for circumstances, to which you will I doubt not attribute this seeming neglect in approving of the considerations which made me give the whole of my time to forwards as much as possibly could be the business I had to perform, great as were my endeavors to that end, it [a steel engraving of the

L'Enfant Plan] remained unfinished at the moment of the President's arrival at this place where I could present him no more but a rough drawing in pencil of the several surveys which I had been able to run. Nevertheless, the President, indulgent disposition making him account for the difficulties encountered, I had the satisfaction to see the little I had done agreeable to his wish, and the confidence with which he has been pleased since to honor me in ordering the survey to be continued and the delineation of a grand plan for the local distribution of the city to be done on principle conformable to the ideas which I took the liberty to hold before him at the proper [time] for the establishment being highly flattering to my ambition to . . . the best of my ability, it shall be from this moment my endeavor to answer the President's expectations in preparing those plans and having them ready for the time of his return from the southern tour.

I shall in the meanwhile, Sir, beg for every information respecting all what may in your judgment appear of most immediate importance to attend to as well as relating to every desirable establishment which it will be well to foresee although delaying or perhaps leaving the execution thereof to a natural succession of time to effect.

The number and nature of the public building with the necessary appendix I should be glad to have a statement of as speedily as possible, and I would be very much obliged to you in the meantime if you could procure for me whatever may fall within your reach of any of the different grand cities now existing; such as, for example, London, Madrid, Paris, Amsterdam, Naples, Venice, Genoa, Florence, together with particular maps of any such seaports or dock yards and arsenals as you may know to be the most complete in their improvement, for notwithstanding, I would reprobate the idea of imitating, and that contrary of having this intention, it is my wish and shall be my endeavor to delineate on a new and original way, the plan the contrivance of which the President has left to me without any restriction soever. yet the contemplation of what exists of well improved situation, given the parallel of these, with defective ones, may serve to suggest a variety of new Ideas and is necessary to refine and strengthen the judgment particularly in the present instance when having to unite the useful with the commodious and agreeable, viewing these will by offering means for comparing enable me the better to determine with a certainty the propriety of a locale which offers an extensive field for combinations.

I have the honor to be with great respect your most humble and most obedient servant,

P. C. L'Enfant.

Thomas Jefferson

Author of the Declaration of Independence and future President Thomas Jefferson (1743-1826) was serving as George Washington's Secretary of State in 1791 when Pierre Charles L'Enfant wrote to him to ask if there were materials in Jefferson's personal library that might assist in designing the plan for the new capital city. Jefferson was in Philadelphia at the time, along with the rest of the federal government, but was happy to assist, as his response of April 10th, 1791, indicates. True to form, Jefferson subsequently informed President Washington of his communications with L'Enfant in a letter written the same day.

"I Avoid Interfering . . . "

To Major L'Enfant.

Sir.

I am favored with your letter of the 4th instant, and in compliance with your request I have examined my papers and found the plans of Frankfort on the Mayne, Carlsruhe, Amsterdam, Strasburg, Paris, Orleans, Bordeaux, Lyons, Montpelier, Marseilles, Turin, and Milan, which I send in a roll by this Post. They are on large and accurate scales, having been procured by me while in those respective cities myself. As they are connected with the notes I made in my travels, and often necessary to explain them to myself, I will beg your care of them and to return them when no longer useful to you, leaving you absolutely free to keep them as long as useful. I am happy the President has left the planning of the Town in such hands and have no doubt it will be done to general satisfaction. Considering that the grounds to be reserved for the public are to be paid for by the acre, I think very liberal reservations should be made for them; and if this be about the Tiber on the back of the town, it will be of no injury to the commerce of the place, which will undoubtedly establish itself on the deep waters towards the Eastern branch and mouth of Rock Creek; the water about the mouth of the Tiber not being of any depth. Those connected with the Government will prefer fixing themselves near the public grounds, in the center, which will also be convenient to be resorted to as walks from the lower and upper town. Having communicated to the President, before he went away, such general ideas on the subject of the Town, as occurred to me, I make no doubt that, in explaining himself to you on the subject, he has interwoven with his own ideas, such of mine as he approved: for fear of repeating therefore, what he did not approve, and having more confidence in the unbiassed state of his mind, than in my own, I avoid interfering with what he may have expressed to you. Whenever it is proposed to prepare plans for the Capitol, I should prefer the adoption of some one of the models of antiquity, which have had the approbation of thousands of years, and for the President's House I should prefer the celebrated fronts of modern buildings, which have already received the approbation of all good judges. Such are the Galerie du Louvre, the Gardes meubles, and two fronts of the Hotel de Salm. But of this it is yet enough to consider, in the meantime I am with great esteem Sir &c.

Th: Jefferson.

George Washington

George Washington (1732-1799) had served his country well by the time a permanent location was chosen for the capital of the United States. The Virginia-born surveyor, soldier, plantation owner, Commander of the Continental Army during the American Revolution, President of the Constitutional Convention, and first President of the United States, was intimately involved in selecting the site for what he referred to as "Federal City." Washington is remembered for his generalship and his presidency, but his personal vision for the city that bears his name is less well-known. In the following letter, written as President, Washington addresses the "Commissioners," those men he had entrusted with guiding the development of the new capital.

"Ardent and Susceptible Minds"

TO THE COMMISSIONERS OF THE FEDERAL DISTRICT.
Philadelphia, 28 January, 1795.

Gentlemen,

A plan for the establishment of a university in the Federal City has frequently been the subject of conversation; but, in what manner it is proposed to commence this important institution, on how extensive a scale, the means by which it is to be effected, how it is to be supported, or what progress is made in it, are matters altogether unknown to me.

It has always been a source of serious reflection and sincere regret with me, that the youth of the United States should be sent to foreign countries for the purpose of education. Although there are doubtless many, under these circumstances, who escape the danger of contracting principles unfavorable to republican government, yet we ought to deprecate the hazard attending ardent and susceptible minds, from being too strongly and too early prepossessed in favor of other political systems, before they are capable of appreciating their own.

For this reason I have greatly wished to see a plan adopted, by which the arts, sciences, and belles-lettres could be taught in their fullest extent, thereby embracing all the advantages of European tuition, with the means of acquiring the liberal knowledge, which is necessary to qualify our citizens for the exigencies of public as well as private life; and (which with me is a consideration of great magnitude) by assembling the youth from the different parts of this rising republic, contributing from their intercourse and interchange of information to the removal of prejudices, which might perhaps sometimes arise from local circumstances.

The Federal City, from its centrality and the advantages, which in other respects it must have over any other place in the United States, ought to be preferred, as a proper site for such a university. And if a plan can be adopted upon a scale as extensive as I have described, and the execution of it should commence under favorable auspices in a reasonable time, with a fair prospect of success, I will grant in perpetuity fifty shares in the navigation of Potomac River towards the endowment of it.

What annuity will arise from these fifty shares, when the navigation is in full operation, can at this time be only conjectured; and those who are acquainted with the nature of it can form as good a judgment as myself.

As the design of this university has assumed no form with which I am acquainted, and as I am equally ignorant who the persons are, that have taken or are disposed to take the maturation of the plan upon themselves, I have been at a loss to whom I should make this communication of my intentions. If the Commissioners of the Federal City have any particular agency in bringing the matter forward, then the information I now give to them is in its proper course. If, on the other hand, they have no more to do in it than others, who may be desirous of seeing so important a measure carried into effect, they will be so good as to excuse my using them as the medium for disclosing these intentions; because it appears necessary, that the funds for the establishment and support of the institution should be known to the promoters of it; and I see no mode more eligible for announcing my purpose. For these reasons, I give you the trouble of this address, and the assurance of being, Gentlemen . . . .

[George Washington]

Isaac Weld, Jr.

The Irish traveler, topographical writer, and artist Isaac Weld, Jr. (1774-1856) set sail for the United States in 1795 with the intention of determining the merits of potential Irish emigration to the former English colonies. His voyage across the Atlantic was a difficult one, encompassing some fifty-nine days by his own account. After landing in Philadelphia in November 1795, Weld began an adventuresome two-year journey through the United States and Canada. Traveling south from Philadelphia, then the temporary capital of the United States, he reached the "City of Washington, or the Federal City," toward the end of the month.

"Drawn by a Frenchman"

The City of Washington, or the Federal City, as it is indiscriminately called, was laid out in the year 1792, and is expressly designed for being the metropolis of the United States, and the seat of the Federal Government. In the year 1800 the Congress is to meet there for the first time. As the foundation of this city has attracted the attention of so many people in Europe, and as such very different opinions are entertained about it, I shall, in the following pages, give you a brief account of its rise and progress.

Shortly after the close of the American war, considerable numbers of the Pennsylvanian line, or of the militia, with arms in their hands, surrounded the Hall in which the Congress was assembled at Philadelphia, and with vehement menaces insisted upon immediate appropriations of money being made to discharge the large arrears due to them for their past services. The Members, alarmed at such an outrage, resolved to quit a state in which they met with insult instead of protection, and quickly adjourned to New York, where the session was terminated. A short time afterwards, the propriety was strongly urged in Congress, of fixing upon some place for the meeting of the legislature, and for the seat of the general government, which should be subject to the laws and regulations of the Congress alone, in order that the Members, in future, might not have to depend for their personal safety, and for their freedom of deliberation, upon the good or bad police of any individual state. This idea of making the place, which should be chosen for the meeting of the legislature, independent of the particular state to which it might belong, was further corroborated by the following argument: That as the several states in the Union were in some measure rivals to each other, although connected together by certain ties, if any one of them, was fixed upon for the seat of the general government in preference, and thus raised to a state of pre-eminence, it might perhaps be the occasion of great jealousy amongst the others. Every person was convinced of the expediency of preserving the Union of the states entire; it was apparent, therefore, that the greatest precautions ought to be taken to remove every source of jealousy from amongst them, which might tend, though remotely, to produce a separation. It was absolutely necessary that the seat of government should be made permanent, as the removal of the public offices and the archives from place to place could not but be attended with many and very great inconveniences.

However, notwithstanding that this measure appeared to be beneficial to the interest of the Union at large, it was not until after the Revolution, by which the present Federal Constitution was established, that it was acceded to on the part of all the states. Pennsylvania in particular conscious of her being a principal and central state, and therefore likely to be made the seat of government if this new project was not carried into execution, was foremost in the opposition. At last, she complied; but it was only on condition that the Congress should meet at Philadelphia until the new city was ready for its reception, flattering herself that there would be so many objections afterwards to the removal of the seat of government, and so many difficulties in putting the project into execution, that it would finally be relinquished. To the discriminating judgment of General Washington, then President, it was left to determine upon the spot best calculated for the Federal City. After mature deliberation he fixed upon a situation on the banks of the Potomac River, a situation which seems to be marked out by nature, not only for a large city, but expressly for the seat of the metropolis of the United States.

In the choice of the spot there were two principal confederations: First, that it should be as central as possible in respect to every state in the Union; secondly, that it should be advantageously situated for commerce, without which it could not be expected that the city would ever be distinguished for size or for splendor; and it was to be supposed, that the people of the United States would be desirous of having the metropolis of the country as magnificent as it possibly could be. These two essential points are most happily combined in the spot which has been chosen.

The city is laid out on a neck of land between the forks formed by the eastern and western or main branch of Potomac River. This neck of land, together with an adjacent territory, which is in the whole ten miles square, was ceded to Congress by the states of Maryland and Virginia. The ground on which the city immediately stands was the property of private individuals, who readily relinquished their claim to one half of it in favor of Congress, conscious that the value of what was left to them would increase, and amply compensate them for their loss. The profits arising from the sale, that part of which has thus been ceded to Congress, will be sufficient, it is expected, to pay for the public buildings, for the watering of the city, and also for paving and lighting of the streets. The Plan of the city was drawn by a Frenchman of the name of L'Enfant and is on a scale well suited to the extent of the country, one thousand two hundred miles in length, and one thousand in breadth, of which it is to be the metropolis; for the ground already marked out for it is no less than fourteen miles in circumference. The streets run north, south, east, and west; but to prevent that sameness necessarily ensuing from the streets all crossing each other at right angles, a number of avenues are laid out in different parts of the city, which run transversely; and in several places, where these avenues intersect each other, are to be hollow squares. The streets, which cross each other at right angles, are from ninety to one hundred feet wide, the avenues one hundred and sixty feet. One of these is named after each state, and a hollow square also allotted to each, as a suitable place for statues, columns, &c., which, at a future period, the people of any one of these states may wish to erect to the memory of great men that may appear in the country. On a small eminence, due west of the Capitol, is to be an equestrian statue of General Washington.

The Capitol is now building upon the most elevated spot of ground in the city, which happens to be in a very central situation. From this spot there is a complete view of every part of the city, and also of the adjacent country. In the Capitol are to be spacious apartments for the accommodation of Congress; in it also are to be the principal public offices in the Executive Department of the government, together with the courts of justice. The plan on which this building is begun is grand and extensive; the expense of building it is estimated at a million dollars, equal to two hundred and twenty-five thousand pounds sterling.

The house for the residence of the President stands northwest of the Capitol, at the distance of about one mile and a half. It is situated upon a rising ground not far from the Potomac, and commands a most beautiful prospect of the river, and of the rich country beyond it. One hundred acres of ground, towards the river, are left adjoining to the house for pleasure grounds. South of this there is to be a large park or mall, which is to run in an easterly direction from the river to the Capitol. The buildings on either side of this mall are all to be elegant in their kind; amongst the number it is proposed to have houses built at the public expense for the accommodation of the foreign ministers, &c. On the Eastern Branch a large spot is laid out for a marine hospital and gardens. Various other parts are appointed for churches, theatres, colleges, &c. The ground in general, within the limits of the city, is agreeably undulated; but none of the risings are so great as to become objects of inconvenience in a town. The soil is chiefly of a yellowish clay mixed with gravel. There are numbers of excellent springs in the city, and water is readily had in most places by digging wells. Here are two streams likewise, which run through the city: Reedy Branch and Tiber Creek. The perpendicular height of the source of the latter, above the level of the tide, is two hundred and thirty-six feet.

By the regulations published, it was settled that all the houses should be built of brick or stone; the walls to be thirty feet high, and to be built parallel to the line of the street, but either upon it or withdrawn from it, as suited the taste of the builder. However, numbers of wooden habitations have been built; but the different owners have all been cautioned against considering them as permanent. They are to be allowed for a certain term only, and then destroyed. Three Commissioners, who reside on the spot, are appointed by the President, with a salary, for the purpose of superintending the public and other buildings and regulating everything pertaining to the city.

The only public buildings carrying on as yet are the President's House, the Capitol, and a large hotel. The President's House, which is nearly completed on the outside, is two stories high, and built of free stone. The principal room in it is of an oval form. This is undoubtedly the handsomest building in the country, and the architecture of it is much extolled by the people, who have never seen anything superior; but it will not bear critical examination. Many persons find fault with it as being too large and too splendid for the residence of any one person in a republican country; and certainly, it is a ridiculous habitation for a man who receives a salary that amounts to no more than £5,625 sterling per annum, and in a country where the expenses of living are far greater than they are even in London.

The hotel is a large building of brick, ornamented with stone; it stands between the President's House and the Capitol. In the beginning of the year 1796, when I last saw it, it was roofed in, and every exertion was being made to have it finished with the utmost expedition. It is anything but beautiful. The Capitol, at the same period, was raised only a very little way above the foundation.

The stone, which the President's House is built with, and such as will be used for all the public buildings, is very similar in appearance to that found at Portland in England; but I was informed by one of the sculptors, who had frequently worked the Portland stone in England, that it is of a much superior quality, as it will bear to be cut as fine as marble, and is not liable to be injured by rain or frost. On the banks of the Potomac, they have inexhaustible quarries of this stone; good specimens of common marble have also been found; and there is in various parts of the river abundance of excellent slate, paving stone, and limestone. Good coal may also be had.

The private houses are all plain buildings; most of them have been built on speculation and still remain empty. The greatest number, at any one place, is at Greenleaf's Point, on the main river, just above the entrance of the Eastern Branch. This spot has been looked upon by many as the most convenient one for trade; but others prefer the shore of the Eastern Branch, on account of the superiority of the harbor, and the great depth of the water near the shore. There are several other favorite situations, the choice of any one of which is a mere matter of speculation at present. Some build near the Capitol, as the most convenient place for the residence of Members of Congress, some near the President's House; others again prefer the west end of the city in the neighborhood of Georgetown, thinking that as trade is already established in that place, it must be from thence that it will extend into the city. Were the houses that have been built situated in one place all together, they would make a very respectable appearance, but scattered about as they are, a spectator can scarcely perceive anything like a town. Excepting the streets and avenues, and a small part of the ground adjoining the public buildings, the whole place is covered with trees. To be under the necessity of going through a deep wood for one or two miles, perhaps, in order to see a next-door neighbor, and in the same city, is a curious, and, I believe, a novel circumstance. The number of inhabitants in the city, in the spring of 1796, amounted to about five thousand, including artificers, who formed by far the largest part of that number. Numbers of strangers are continually passing and repassing through a place which affords such an extensive field for speculation.

In addition to what has already been said upon the subject, I have only to observe, that notwithstanding all that has been done at the city, and the large sums of money which have been expended, there are numbers of people in the United States, living to the north of the Potomac, particularly in Philadelphia, who are still very adverse to the removal of the seat of government thither, and are doing all in their power to check the progress of the buildings in the city, and to prevent the Congress from meeting there at the appointed time. In the spring of 1796, when I was last on the spot, the building of the Capitol was absolutely at a stand for want of money; the public lots were at a very low price, and the Commissioners were unwilling to dispose of them; in consequence they made an application to Congress, praying the House to guaranty a loan of three hundred thousand dollars, without which they could not go on with the public buildings, except they disposed of the lots to great disadvantage, and to the ultimate injury of the city; so strong, however, was the opposition, that the petition was suffered to lie on the table unattended to for many weeks; nor was the prayer of it complied with until a number of gentlemen, that were very deeply interested in the improvement of the city, went round to the different Members, and made interest with them in person to give their assent to the measure. These people who are opposed to the building of the City of Washington maintain that it can never become a town of any importance, and that all such as think to the contrary have been led astray by the representations of a few enthusiastic persons; they go so far even as to assert, that the people to the eastward will never submit to see the seat of government removed so far from them, and the Congress assembled in a place little better than a forest, where it will be impossible to procure information upon commercial points; finally, they insist, that if the removal from Philadelphia should take place, a separation of the states will inevitably follow. This is the language held forth; but their opposition in reality arises from that jealousy which narrow minded people in trade are but too apt to entertain of each other when their interests clash together. These people wish to crush the City of Washington while it is yet in its infancy, because they know, that if the seat of government is transferred thither, the place will thrive, and enjoy a considerable portion of that trade which is centered at present in Philadelphia, Baltimore, and New York. It is idle, however, to imagine that this will injure their different towns; on the contrary, although a portion of that trade which they enjoy at present should be drawn from them, yet the increase of population in that part of the country, which they must naturally supply, will be such, that their trade on the whole will, in all probability, be found far more extensive after the Federal City is established than it ever was before.

A large majority, however, of the people in the United States is desirous that the removal of the seat of government should take place; and there is little doubt that it will take place at the appointed time. The discontents indeed, which an opposite measure would give rise to in the south could not but be alarming and if they did not occasion a total separation of the southern from the northern states, yet they would certainly materially destroy that harmony which has hitherto existed between them.

John Harriott

The English adventurer and master mariner John Harriott (1745-1817) led a colorful and peripatetic life. As a youth, he served in the Royal Navy during the Seven Years War. Subsequent service with the merchant marine brought the young Harriott to the English Colonies in America in the 1760s. At twenty-three, he was awarded a military commission and joined the East India Company. During his India service Harriott suffered a leg wound which brought an end to his military career.

John Harriott was a practical man of little formal education, yet during his lifetime he was awarded patents for several maritime inventions and authored several books, including his memoir, *Struggles Through Life*, which proved to be a popular work. In this excerpt, Harriott reflects upon his visit to Washington, D.C., during which he observed a city in embryo, the growing capital of a new nation whose future was at that time far from certain.

"This Intended City"

We took several circuitous walks and rides to note all that was to be seen of Washington City, containing little besides open fields and large woods, with avenues cut through them, of miles in length, to show where the streets were intended to be.

The situation is pleasant, and I conceive healthy. The Potomac (between two branches of which the intended city is situated) is most certainly a grand river having a clear inland shipping navigation of 200 miles from the sea to this city; yet in my humble judgement of these great undertakings, I doubt whether they have not commenced at the wrong end. A place that is first established by trade and commerce may swell gradually or rapidly to a large city; but I doubt how far the building of a city to force commerce between two well-established powerful rivals, in a free country, will be likely to succeed. Neither Baltimore, in Maryland, nor Alexandria, in Virginia, seem to apprehend the smaller diminution of their trade, but were building and increasing faster than ever; while, respecting this intended city, I question much whether there ever will be a sufficient number of houses built to entitle it to the name of a great city. It is true, the public buildings are erected on a grand scale, possibly too much so for so young a country. A century hence, should the union of the states continue so long, they might correspond; at present, they do not. It is to be remembered that these remarks were made on the spot, in 1796.

The President's House is 180 feet in front and 88 deep, built of freestone of an excellent quality. Not more than a fourth part is built; but when finished, it promises to be an elegant building. The Capitol, building with the same materials, is 380 feet in front, by 120 in depth; of which one wing only is just raised high enough for the first scaffolding. But few men were at work either at the public or private buildings, and several of them told me they could get more work than money. Brickmaking was the principal business going forward; and for this purpose, the whole body of earth that I examined (where they had dug for cellars) seems well adapted, and the well-water good.

If any part of the whole might be said to have the appearance of a town, or rather a village, it is at the eastern point, nearly three miles from the President's House, and where Mr. Law and Mr. Duncason, two gentlemen of fortune from India, were the only individuals actually engaged in building private houses. The workmen told me that these gentlemen were the only people whom they could depend on for money; one or two others that had begun having left off. Here, again, (as I have before observed respecting the usual mistake of Englishmen),

I fear these gentlemen will find, to their cost, that they have calculated on English ideas unnecessarily magnified by Eastern habits.

In this part of the city, there are four or five groups of houses of four or six in a group, at no great distance from each other, in different stages of finishing, with but few that are inhabited; and reckoning up all the houses I could see or hear of as belonging to the new City of Washington, they did not amount to eighty. I was the more particular in remarking on this from the extravagant false accounts that had been sent to and published in the London papers, as before mentioned. Had they described them as house-lots, it might have passed, but would not have answered their purpose, as it was these lots to build houses on that they wished to sell by such puffs of the rapid progress which the new city was making.

Bad as I apprehend it is, and will turn out to be, to the purchasing speculators, it has proved of great advantage to the old proprietors of the land. When Congress first determined to build a Federal City, General Washington desired to fix on the most eligible spot. He chose the present, the land of which was not then worth more than five pounds an acre, Maryland money. In negotiating with the proprietors, it was agreed that all the streets, avenues, squares, grounds for public buildings and uses, should be paid for at twenty-five pounds an acre: the remainder of their respective lands to be divided into equal lots; one-half to be sold for the benefit of the public, by Commissioners, the other at the disposal of the original proprietor.

On average, an acre of ground is now estimated at 1,500£; and a Mr. B., whose estate of nearly 500 acres was not worth more than 3,000£, (more than which he was said to owe), has hereby realized a property of 80,000£.

Having seen and examined everything, and gained all the information I could concerning this so-much-talked-of city, I sat down between the President's House and the Capitol, and entered the following in my minute-book as my opinion, viz.

"Should the public buildings be completed, and enterprising individuals risk considerably in building houses; should the Union of the States continue undisturbed; should Congress assemble for a number of years, until the National Bank and other public offices necessarily draw the monied interests to it; the City of Washington, in the course of a century, may form a focus of attraction to mercantile and trading people, sufficient to make it a beautiful commercial city, deserving the name of its founder; but I apprehend so many hazards as to be most unwilling to venture any part of my property in the undertaking."

The price of provisions at Georgetown is much the same as at Baltimore. The good people in this town, as well as every other seaport I was at on the continent of North America, are remarkably fond of dress. At one chapel in Georgetown, I noticed Presbyterian service performed in the morning and Episcopal in the afternoon.

On our return from a short excursion in Virginia, back through Georgetown and Washington City, I was informed that Congress had guaranteed a loan, to enable them to go on with the public buildings, which renovated the hopes of the speculators. But I did then, and do still, recommend emigrants and foreign speculators to be on their guard against the delusive flattering accounts that for many years will be spread abroad.

Duke Rochefoucauld-Liancourt

François Alexandre Frédéric, duc de La Rochefoucauld-Liancourt (1747-1827) is remembered as a social reformer in his native France. A member of the French nobility, he supported the loyalists during the French Revolution. He fled Paris in 1792 and spent several years in exile, first in England and then in the United States, where he travelled extensively during the latter part of the decade. Upon his return to France in 1799, he published a reminiscence of his experiences in the United States and Canada. An English edition appeared in 1800.

In this excerpt from his *Travels*, he comments upon the rampant land speculation taking place in Washington, D.C. during its early years and identifies several of the major players in the game of boom and bust, including Robert Morris, John Nicholson and James Greenleaf, speculators who stood to make or lose a fortune in the local real estate market.

"A Handsome Tavern"

In America, where, more than in any other country in the world, a desire for wealth is the prevailing passion, there are few schemes which are not made the means of extensive speculations; and that of the erecting of Federal City presented irresistible temptations, which were not in fact neglected.

Mr. Morris was among the first to perceive the probability of immense gain in speculations in that quarter; and, in conjunction with Messrs. Nicholson and Greenleaf, a very short time after the adoption of the [L'Enfant] Plan purchased every lot he could lay hold on, either from the Commissioners or individual proprietors; that is to say, every lot that either one or the other would sell at that period. Of the Commissioners he bought six thousand lots at the price of eighty dollars per lot, each containing five thousand two hundred and sixty-five square feet. The conditions of his bargain with the Commissioners, which was concluded in 1793, were that fifteen hundred of the lots should be chosen by him in the northeast quarter of the city and the remaining four thousand five hundred wherever Mr. Morris and his partners chose to select them; that he should erect one hundred and twenty houses of brick, and with two stories, on these lots within the space of seven years; that he should not sell any lot before the first of January 1790, nor without the like condition of building; and finally, that the payment for the lots should be completed within seven years, to commence on the 1st of May 1794; a seventh part to be paid annually; that is to say, about sixty-eight thousand dollars yearly, the purchase money for the whole being four hundred and eighty thousand dollars.

The lots purchased by Mr. Morris from individuals amounted to nearly the same number and were bought at the same price. The periods for payment varied with the different proprietors and are not of importance in this general history of Federal City.

The sale made to Mr. Morris was the only one of like extent made either by the Commissioners or individuals. Expecting a higher price, the Commissioners waited for a time when demand for habitations would be more numerous. The private proprietors acted on the same principle, and both one and the other, in the sale made to Mr. Morris, considered it chiefly as the means of hastening the completion of the city, by the inducement he would have to sell part of his lots, and so augment the number of persons interested in the rapid progress of the undertaking. Mr. Morris, in fact, sold about a thousand of his lots within eighteen months of his purchase. The building of a house for the President, and a place for the sittings of the Congress, excited, in the purchasers of lots, the hope of a new influx of speculations. The public papers were filled with exaggerated praises of the new city;

accounts of the rapidity of its progress towards completion; in a word, with all the artifices which trading people in every part of the world are accustomed to employ in the disposal of their wares, and which are perfectly known, and amply practiced in this new world.

Mr. Law and Mr. Dickinson; two gentlemen that had lately arrived from India, and both with great wealth, General Howard, General Lee, and two or three wealthy Dutch merchants, were the persons who bought the greatest number of lots of Mr. Morris; but none more than Mr. Law, who purchased four hundred and forty-five lots. The lowest they gave was two hundred and ninety-three dollars per lot, or rather five pence for each square foot, of Maryland money; for all the lots were not absolutely of the same extent. Many of the lots sold for six, eight, and ten pence per square foot: the last comers constantly paying a higher price, and the situation of the lots also making a difference in their value. Some of the more recent purchasers, in order to have one or more of the entire squares into which the whole was divided, or for other purposes of their speculations, made their purchases from the Commissioners, paying at the same rate for them. The bargains were all clogged with the same conditions to build as those of Mr. Morris. The number of lots sold in this manner amounted to six hundred. Each of the purchasers chose his ground according to the opinion he had of its general advantages, and of its being in a neighborhood that would the most readily be filled with houses. The neighborhood of the President's House, of the Capitol, of Georgetown, the banks of the Potomac, [Greenleaf] Point, and the banks of the Eastern Branch, were the places chiefly chosen by the first purchasers.

The opinion that the ground marked out for the whole city would soon be filled was so general, and the President of the United States and the Commissioners were so much of the same opinion, that in their regulations they prohibited the cultivating any portion of the ground otherwise than for gardens; or to build houses with less than two stories, or even to build houses of wood.

These regulations were, however, speedily afterwards withdrawn; and the original proprietors had liberty to enclose and cultivate at their pleasure the ground they had not disposed of.

Mr. Blodget, one of the most considerable and intelligent speculators of Philadelphia, having purchased a large quantity of lots, under the pretense of forwarding the building of the city, but more probably with the real motive of disposing most securely and advantageously of his acquisitions, made two lotteries for the disposal of them. The principal lot of the first was a handsome tavern built between the Capitol and the President's House, valued at fifty thousand dollars; the three principal lots of the second were three houses to be erected near the Capitol, of the respective value of twenty-five thousand, fifteen thousand, and ten thousand, dollars. These lotteries were made before the prohibition of the State of Maryland to make private lotteries, without the authority of the legislature. They were powerfully patronized by the Commissioners, who considered them as the means of advancing the building of the city. It appears that these lotteries were attended with the effect proposed to himself by Mr. Blodget, that of gaining a large profit on the disposal of his lots, and that he was the only person not deceived in the transaction.

The speculations of Mr. Morris and the succeeding purchasers had not the same rapid success. After the Plan of the city had been for a while admired for its beauty and magnificence, people began to perceive that it was too extensive, too gigantic for the actual circumstances of the United States and even for those which must follow for a series of years, admitting that no intervening accidents arrested the progress of their prosperity. It was discovered that the immense extent of ground marked out for the city would not be so speedily covered with houses as was expected; and every proprietor of lots intrigued to get the neighborhood of his lots first inhabited. From that instant the common interest ceased, and the proprietors became rivals. Each began to build in his own quarter, with the hope of drawing thither the newcomers. Each vaunted of the advantages of that side of the city where his property lay, and depreciated others. The public papers were no longer filled with the excellencies of Federal City, but with those of one or other of its quarters.

The Commissioners were not altogether clear from this venal contest. Two of them possessed lots near Georgetown; and if that had not been the case, their habits and prejudices relative to the city would have determined their opinion as to the advantage of beginning to build in one quarter or another and would not have permitted them to remain indifferent spectators of the emulation of the several proprietors.

There were four principal quarters to which different interests had drawn the greatest number of houses. The inhabitants of Georgetown, who had purchased a great many lots in their neighborhood, maintained that a small town already built was the proper spot to begin the new city, by facilitating and augmenting its resources. They boasted of the port of Georgetown and represented the commerce already belonging to the place as a favorable opening to the general commerce of the city.

The proprietors of lots near the Point declared that situation to be the most airy, healthy, and beautiful in the city; advantageous to commerce, as it lay along the banks of both rivers, and as being a central situation between the Capitol and the President's House, from each of which it was equally distant.

The proprietors of the Eastern Branch contemned the port of Georgetown, and the banks of the Potomac, which are not secure in winter from shoals of ice; they decried the Point, which, placed between the two rivers, was far from being able completely to enjoy the advantage of either; and boasted of their own port, because of its great depth, and its security from ice, and from the most prevailing winds. They vaunted of their vicinity to the Capitol, which must be the common center of affairs, it being the place of the sittings of the Congress, and in which all the Members must meet at least once in the day, and from which their distance was not more than three quarters of a mile.

The proprietors in the neighborhood of the Capitol contended that Federal City was not necessarily a commercial town; that the essential point was to raise a city for the establishment of the Congress and government; that the natural progress was, first to build houses round the Capitol, and then to extend them towards the President's House, which, although of a secondary consideration, was nevertheless next in importance to the Capitol; and that every effort should be made, for the convenience of Congress and the facilitating of public affairs, to unite, by a continuation of streets and buildings, these two principal points of the government.

Thus, each proprietor supported with his arguments the interests of the quarter where the mass of his property lay; but he built notwithstanding with great caution, and with a constant fear of some of the opposite interests prevailing.

The Commissioners, to whom was entrusted the erection of public edifices, were accused by the proprietors that lay at a distance from Georgetown of paying an undue attention to the completion of the President's House, which was in their neighborhood; of designing to establish the public offices there, and, consequently, to neglect the capital; in a word, of being partial to Georgetown to the injury of the three other quarters of the town.

Each of these opinions relative to the spot at which they should begin to build the city might find advocates, even among disinterested people, regarding only the public advantage; but the public advantage was no motive of any of the rival parties.

Oliver Wolcott, Jr.

Oliver Wolcott, Jr. (1760-1833) was born to a prosperous and influential family in Litchfield, Connecticut. His father, Oliver Wolcott Sr., was a Signer of the Declaration of Independence. The younger Wolcott studied at Yale, attended law school, and served as Comptroller of Connecticut before succeeding Alexander Hamilton as Secretary of the Treasury in 1795.

According to architectural historian Pamela Scott, Wolcott was responsible for moving the Treasury Department from Philadelphia to Washington, D.C. in 1800. No small task. In a letter to his wife, written from the Treasury Department's newly constructed headquarters, Oliver Wolcott offers his candid opinion of the new capital.

"In the Company of Crazy People"

To Mrs. Wolcott.
Washington, July 4th, 1800.

I write this letter in the building erected for the use of the Treasury Department in the City of Washington, and this being a day of leisure, I shall be able to give you some idea of this famous place, the permanent seat of American government.

The City of Washington, or at least some part of it, is about forty miles from Baltimore. The situation is pleasant, and indeed beautiful; the prospects are equal to those which are called good, on the Connecticut River; the soil here is called good, but I call it bad. It is an exceedingly stiff, reddish clay, which becomes dust in dry, and mortar in rainy weather.

The Capitol and the President's House are built of a soft white stone, which is, however, said to be sufficiently durable, and are by far the most magnificent buildings I have ever seen. But one wing of the Capitol is finished; yet the solid contents of this wing are, I should suppose, four times greater than the Bank of the United States. There are several large square rooms, which are finished in a neat and elegant manner. The Senate room is magnificent in height and decorated in a grand style. The galleries are spacious, and in front of them is a colonnade of sixteen pillars, supported on arches. That part of the room which is appropriated for the use of the Senate is, however, less than the room which was occupied by that body in Philadelphia. The room designed for the temporary use of the House of Representatives is inelegant. The galleries for the sovereign people are spacious; but the Members will have less room than in Philadelphia, and many of their seats will be placed under the galleries. The external appearance of the House, except on the south side, which is intended to be joined to the center building, is magnificent. It is worth seeing and was built to be seen; but I can say but little in its favor, as a building calculated for convenience.

The President's House, or Palace, is about as large as the wing of the Capitol above described, except that it is not so high. It is highly decorated, and makes a good appearance, but is in a very unfinished state. I cannot but consider our presidents as very unfortunate men if they must live in this dwelling. It must be cold and damp in winter and cannot be kept in tolerable order without a regiment of servants. It was built to be looked at by visitors and strangers and will render its occupant an object of ridicule with some, and of pity with others.

The Capitol is situated on an eminence, which I should suppose was near the center of the immense country here called the city. It is a mile and a half from the President's House, and three miles on a straight line from Georgetown. There is one good tavern about forty rods from the Capitol, and several other houses are built and erecting; but I do not perceive how the Members of Congress can possibly secure lodgings, unless they will consent to live like scholars in a college, or monks in a monastery, crowded ten or twenty in one house, and utterly secluded from society. The only resource for those who wish to live comfortably will, I think, be found in Georgetown, three miles distant, over as bad a road, in winter, as the clay grounds near Hartford.

I have made every exertion to secure good lodgings near the office but shall be compelled to take them at the distance of more than half a mile. There are, in fact, but few houses at any one place, and most of them small miserable huts, which present an awful contrast to the public buildings. The people are poor, and as far as I can judge, they live like fishes, by eating each other. All the ground for several miles around the city being, in the opinion of the people, too valuable to be cultivated, remains unfenced. There are but few enclosures, even for gardens, and those are in bad order. You may look in almost any direction, over an extent of ground nearly as large as the city of New York, without seeing a fence or any object except brick kilns and temporary huts for laborers. Mr. Law, and a few other gentlemen, live in great splendor; but most of the inhabitants are low people, whose appearance indicates vice and intemperance, or negroes.

All the lands which I have described are valued by the superficial foot, at fourteen to twenty-five cents. There appears to be a confident expectation that this place will soon exceed any city in the world. Mr. Thornton, one of the Commissioners, spoke of a population of 160,000 people, as a matter of course, in a few years. No stranger can be here a day and converse with the proprietors without conceiving himself in the company of crazy people. Their ignorance of the rest of the world, and their delusions with respect to their own prospects, are without parallel. Immense sums have been squandered in buildings which are but partly finished, in situations which are not and never will be the scenes of business, while the parts near the public buildings are almost wholly unimproved. Greenleaf's Point presents the appearance of a considerable town, which had been destroyed by some unusual calamity. There are fifty or sixty spacious houses, five or six of which are inhabited by negroes and vagrants, and a few more by decent looking people; but there are no fences, gardens, nor the least appearance of business. This place is about a mile and a half south of the Capitol.

On the whole, I must say that the situation is a good one, and I perceive no reason for suspecting it to be unhealthy; but I had no conception, till I came here, of the folly and infatuation of the people who have directed the settlements. Though five times as much money has been expended as was necessary, and though the private buildings are in number sufficient for all who will have occasion to reside here, yet there is nothing convenient, and nothing plenty but provisions; there is no industry, society, or business. With great trouble and expense, much mischief has been done which it will be almost impossible to remedy.

Georgetown is a compact town, tolerably well built, and inhabited by a considerable number of genteel families. It is, however, almost impossible to get from one house to another in bad weather, owing to the ditches which have been formed by the drains. The ground is the most unequal upon which I have ever seen houses erected.

Abigail Adams

Abigail Adams (1744-1818) was the first woman to take residence in the White House in her role as First Lady to America's second President, John Adams. She was also the mother of the sixth President John Quincy Adams. Although Abigail Adams received little formal education in her youth, she possessed a keen intellect, demonstrated in the numerous letters she exchanged with her husband and other correspondents during the American Revolution and in the decades that followed. Toward the end of 1800, the decade during which Philadelphia served as the temporary capital of the United States was drawing to a close and the deadline for the removal of the seat of government to Washington, D.C. was quickly approaching. In this letter to her daughter, Abigail Adams offers an account of life in an unfinished capital city, and of taking up residence in an unfinished dwelling.

"Keep All This to Yourself"

To Mrs. Smith.
Washington, 21 November, 1800.

My Dear Child,

I arrived here on Sunday last, and without meeting with any accident worth noticing, except losing ourselves when we left Baltimore, and going eight or nine miles on the Frederick Road, by which means we were obliged to go the other eight through woods, where we wandered two hours without finding a guide, or the path. Fortunately, a straggling black came up with us, and we engaged him as a guide, to extricate us out of our difficulty; but woods are all you see, from Baltimore until you reach the city, which is only so in name. Here and there is a small cot, without a glass window, interspersed amongst the forests, through which you travel miles without seeing any human being. In the city there are buildings enough, if they were compact and finished, to accommodate Congress and those attached to it; but as they are, and scattered as they are, I see no great comfort for them. The river, which runs up to Alexandria, is in full view of my window, and I see the vessels as they pass and repass. The [President's] House is upon a grand and superb scale, requiring about thirty servants to attend and keep the apartments in proper order, and perform the ordinary business of the House and stables; an establishment very well proportioned to the President's salary. The lighting [of] the apartments, from the kitchen to parlors and chambers, is a tax indeed, and the fires we are obliged to keep to secure us from daily agues is another very cheering comfort. To assist us in this great castle, and render less attendance necessary, bells are wholly wanting, not one single one being hung through the whole house, and promises are all you can obtain. This is so great an inconvenience that I know not what to do, or how to do. The ladies from Georgetown and in the city have many of them visited me. Yesterday I returned fifteen visits, but such a place as Georgetown appears . . . why, our Milton is beautiful. But no comparisons; if they will put me up some bells, and let me have wood enough to keep fires, I design to be pleased. I could content myself almost anywhere three months; but, surrounded with forests, can you believe that wood is not to be had, because people cannot be found to cut and cart it! Briesler entered into a contract with a man to supply him with wood. A small part, a few cords only, has he been able to get. Most of that was expended to dry the walls of the House before we came in, and yesterday the man told him it was impossible for him to procure it to be cut and carted. He has had recourse to coals; but we cannot get grates made and set. We have, indeed, come into a new country.

You must keep all this to yourself, and, when asked how I like it, say that I write you the situation is beautiful, which is true. The House is made habitable, but there is not a single apartment finished, and all withinside, except the plastering, has been done since Briesler came. We have not the least fence, yard, or other convenience, without, and the great unfinished audience-room I make a drying-room of, to hang up the clothes in. The principal stairs are not up and will not be this winter. Six chambers are made comfortable; two are occupied by the President and Mr. Shaw; two lower rooms, one for a common parlor, and one for a levee-room. Upstairs there is the oval room, which is designed for the drawing room, and has the crimson furniture in it. It is a very handsome room now; but when completed, it will be beautiful. If the twelve years in which this place has been considered as the future seat of government, had been improved, as they would have been if in New England, very many of the present inconveniences would have been removed. It is a beautiful spot, capable of every improvement, and the more I view it, the more I am delighted with it.

Since I sat down to write, I have been called down to a servant from Mount Vernon, with a billet from Major Custis, and a haunch of venison, and a kind, congratulatory letter from Mrs. Lewis, upon my arrival in the city, with Mrs. Washington's love, inviting me to Mount Vernon, where, health permitting, I will go, before I leave this place.

The Senate is much behind-hand. No Congress has yet been made. 'T is said — — is on his way, but travels with so many delicacies in his rear, that he cannot get on fast, lest some of them should suffer.

Thomas comes in and says a House is made; so tomorrow through Saturday the President will meet them. Adieu, my dear. Give my love to your brother and tell him he is ever present upon my mind.

Affectionately your mother,

A. Adams.

Thomas Moore

The prolific Irish poet and balladeer Thomas Moore (1779-1852) often referred to himself as Anacreon, after the Greek poet of the sixth century B.C. Like Anacreon, Moore was fond of drinking songs and wrote verse that often ventured toward the bawdy. Moore toured the United States and Canada in 1803-1804 and met President Thomas Jefferson during a visit to Washington, D.C. During his visit, Moore stayed with Anthony Merry, then Great Britain's Minister to the United States. Merry reportedly had little use for America. Moore's sentiments apparently followed suit. Moore wrote the following poem as a letter to his friend and contemporary, the Irish physician Thomas Hume.

"Obelisks in Trees"

Epistle VII
To Thomas Hume Esq. M.D.
From The City of Washington.

'Tis evening now; the heats and cares of day
In twilight dews are calmly wept away.
The lover now, beneath the western star,
Sighs through the medium of his sweet segar,
And fills the ears of some consenting she
With puffs and vows, with smoke and constancy!
The weary statesman for repose hath fled
From halls of council to his negro's shed,

Where blest he woos some black Aspasia's grace,
And dreams of freedom in his slave's embrace!

  In fancy now, beneath the twilight gloom,
Come, let me lead thee o'er this modern Rome,
Where tribunes rule, where dusky Davi bow,
And what was Goose-Creek once is Tiber now!
This fam'd metropolis, where Fancy sees
Squares in morasses, obelisks in trees;
Which travelling fools and gazetteers adorn
With shrines unbuilt and heroes yet unborn.
Though nought but wood and ********* they see,
Where streets should run and sages *ought* to be!

  And look, how soft in yonder radiant wave,
The dying sun prepares his golden grave!
Oh great Potowmac! oh yon banks of shade!
Yon mighty scenes, in nature's morning made,
While still, in rich magnificence of prime,
She pour'd her wonders, lavishly sublime,
Nor yet had learn'd to stoop, with humbler care,
From grand to soft, from wonderful to fair!

  Say, were your towering hills, your boundless floods,
Your rich savannas and majestic woods,
Where bards should meditate and heroes rove,
And woman charm and man deserve her love!
Oh! was a world so bright but born to grace
Its own half-organiz'd, half-minded race
Of weak barbarians, swarming o'er its breast,
Like vermin, gender'd on the lion's crest?
Were none but brutes to call that soil their home,
Where none but demi-gods should dare to roam?
Or worse, thou mighty world! oh! doubly worse,

Did heaven design thy lordly land to nurse
The motley dregs of every distant clime,
Each blast of anarchy and taint of crime,
Which Europe shakes from her perturbed sphere,
In full malignity to rankle here?

   But, hush! — observe that little mount of pines,
Where the breeze murmurs and the fire-fly shines,
There let thy fancy raise, in bold relief,
The sculptur'd image of that veteran chief,
Who lost the rebel's in the hero's name,
And stept o'er prostrate loyalty to fame;
Beneath whose sword Columbia's patriot train
Cast off their monarch, that their mob might reign!

   How shall we rank thee upon glory's page?
Thou more than soldier and just less than sage!
Too form'd for peace to act a conqueror's part,
Too train'd in camps to learn a statesman's art,
Nature design'd thee for a hero's mould,
But, ere she cast thee, let the stuff grow cold!

   While warmer souls command, nay make their fate,
Thy fate made thee and forc'd thee to be great.
Yet Fortune, who so oft, so blindly sheds
Her brightest halo round the weakest heads,
Found *thee* undazzled, tranquil as before.
Proud to be useful, scorning to be more;
Less prompt at glory's than at duty's claim,
Renown the meed, but self-applause the aim;
All thou hast been reflects less fame on thee,
Far less than all thou hast forborn to be!

Now turn thee, Hume, where faint the moon-light falls
On yonder dome — and in those princely halls.
If thou canst hate, as oh! that soul must hate,
Which loves the virtuous and reveres the great,
If thou canst loath and execrate with me
That Gallic garbage of philosophy,
That nauseous slaver of these frantic times,
With which false liberty dilutes her crimes!
If thou hast got, within thy free-born breast,
One pulse, that beats more proudly than the rest,
With honest scorn for that inglorious soul,
Which creeps and winds beneath a mob's controul,
Which courts the rabble's smile, the rabble's nod,
And makes, like Egypt, every beast its god!
There, in those walls — but, burning tongue, forbear!
Rank must be reverenc'd, even the rank that's there:
So here I pause — and now, my Hume! we part;
But oh! full oft, in magic dreams of heart.
Thus let us meet, and mingle converse dear
By Thames at home, or by Potowmac here!
O'er lake and marsh, through fevers and through fogs,
Midst bears and yankees, democrats and frogs.
Thy foot shall follow me, thy heart and eyes
With me shall wonder, and with me despise!
While I, as oft, in witching thought shall rove
To thee, to friendship, and that land I love,
Where, like the air that fans her fields of green,
Her freedom spreads, unfever'd and serene;
Where sovereign man can condescend to see
The throne and laws more sovereign still than he!
Once more, adieu! — my weary eye-lid winks,
The moon grows clouded and my taper sinks.

John Melish

Scottish geographer and mapmaker John Melish (1771-1822) was apprenticed as a youth to a textile manufacturer in his native Glasgow. After distinguishing himself at the University of Glasgow, his subsequent career in the textile business brought him to the United States, where he traveled extensively along the east coast and throughout the western territories. Melish eventually chose to emigrate with his family from Scotland to America. He initially considered agricultural pursuits but chose instead to settle in Philadelphia and launch what became a highly successful business as a mapmaker. He is considered by the late cartographic historian Walter Ristow to be "one of the founders of American commercial map publishing."

In the following selection from his *Travels in the United States of America*, Melish recounts a meeting at the White House with President Thomas Jefferson on October 5th, 1806 and their conversations on a variety of subjects, including manufactures, ports, roads, and the scourge of yellow fever.

"Drain the Swamp"

In pursuance of the recommendation of my friends, I set out, this morning, at 8 o'clock, for the purpose of waiting on Mr. Jefferson. On my arrival at the President's House, I delivered my address to a servant, who in a few minutes returned with an answer, that Mr. Jefferson would be with me presently, and showed me into an elegant apartment.

Mr. Jefferson soon entered by an inner door, and requesting me to be seated, sat down himself; and immediately, and very frankly, entered into conversation, by asking where I had landed, and how long I had been in the country. Having informed him, he remarked that I would probably be travelling to the northward; I replied that I had been to the north and was now travelling to the southward. "And how do you like New York?" "Very much," said I; "it is one of the finest seaports I have seen and I presume will always continue to be the first commercial city in the United States." He observed that he found that idea generally entertained by strangers; that New York was a very fine situation and would unquestionably continue always to be a great commercial city; but it appeared to him that *Norfolk* would probably, in process of time, be the greatest seaport in the United States, New Orleans perhaps excepted. He pointed out the circumstance of the vast confluence of waters, that constituted the outlet of the Chesapeake Bay, on which Norfolk is situated, and remarked that these rivers were as yet but partially settled; but they were rapidly settling up, and, when the population was full, the quantity of surplus produce would be immense, and Norfolk would probably become the greatest depot in the United States, except New Orleans.

The conversation next turned upon the climate and season; on which the President remarked, that the country had this summer been remarkably healthy; that no case of epidemical sickness had come to his knowledge, some few of *bilious fever* and *fever and ague* excepted, at the foot of the mountains on James River, not far from where he lived; and which country was never known to experience any cases of the kind before. As this appeared singular, I inquired whether there was any way of accounting for it. He replied that the way he accounted for it was this:

"In ordinary seasons, there is a sufficiency of water to keep the rivers in a state of circulation, and no more; but this season there has been a long and very severe drought, which, in many places, has dried them up. The water has stagnated in pools, and sends out a putrid effluvia to some distance; which, being lighter than the atmosphere, ascends even some little way up the mountains, and reaches the abodes of those who thought themselves heretofore free from attack."

I was struck with the force of this remark and applied it to a circumstance that had come under my observation at Washington. The Capitol hill is elevated above the river upwards of 70 feet. Between this and the river there is a low meadow, about a mile broad, abounding with swamps and small shrubbery. In the autumn these swamps send out an effluvia which often affects the health of those who live on the hill. I noticed this circumstance and the President remarked that it was a case exactly in point. He said he had frequently observed from his windows, in the morning, the vapor to rise, and it seemed to have sufficient buoyancy to carry it to the top of the hill, and no further; there it settled, and the inhabitants, coming out of their warm rooms, breathed this cold contaminated vapor, which brought on agues and other complaints. He said he had frequently pointed out this to the people, and urged them to drain the swamp, but it was still neglected, although they had, besides suffering in their health, probably expended more in doctor's bills than it would have cost. "But, indeed," he continued, "mankind are exceedingly slow in adopting resolutions to prevent disease, and it is very difficult to convince them where they originate; particularly when the reasoning applied is the result of philosophical deduction."

The transition from this subject to that of the yellow fever was natural, and I introduced it by noticing Paine's essay on the subject. The President observed that it was one of the most sensible performances on that disease that had come under his observation. The remarks were quite philosophical, and not being calculated to excite any party-feeling, they might have a very useful tendency.

He then made a few remarks on the nature of the yellow fever itself. He observed that it evidently arose from breathing impure air, and impure air may be either generated in the country or imported. A case had come under his observation where it was imported. A vessel arrived at Norfolk, and the air in her hold was so pestilential, that every person who went into it was affected, and some of them died; but, on the discovery being made, the vessel was purified, and the fever did not spread. This was a local circumstance, he observed, and there may be many others, which are pernicious as far as they go, and care should be taken to prevent them. But a ship can never import a sufficient quantity of impure air to pollute a whole city, if that city be otherwise healthy, and, therefore, the origin of the yellow fever, *on an extended scale*, must be sought for in an impure air, generated from filth collected in and about great cities; and it was very expedient that this view of the subject should be enforced, in order to induce mankind to attend to one of the most important concerns in life: cleanliness.

I took notice of the bad state of the road between Baltimore and Washington, and expressed my surprise that it should remain in this state, so near the capital of the United States. The President observed, that the removal of the seat of government was a recent measure, and the country was so extensive, that it would necessarily be a considerable time before good roads could be made in all directions, but as it was a most important subject, it would be attended to as fast as circumstances would permit; and the road to Baltimore, being the great thoroughfare to the northern states, would probably be one of the first that would undergo a thorough repair. He then informed me, that both this subject and that of internal navigation by canals, were under consideration at the present time, upon a very extended scale, and probably a report would soon be published relative to them; and he had little doubt, but that in less than 20 years, turnpike roads would be general throughout the country; and a chain of canals would probably be cut, which would complete an inland navigation from Massachusetts to Georgia; and another to connect the eastern with the western waters.

I remarked that these would be most important improvements and would greatly facilitate internal intercourse; and as to manufactures, I presumed it would long continue to be the policy of the country to import them. He replied that this, like other branches, would of course find its level, and would depend upon the genius of the people; but it was astonishing, the progress that had been made in manufactures of late years. It would hardly be believed, he said, by strangers, but he had it on the best authority, that the manufactures of Philadelphia were greater in value annually, than were those of Birmingham 20 years ago; and he had no doubt but that manufactures, of articles of the first necessity, would increase until they became quite general through the country.

As the Non-Importation Act [1806] was then in dependence, I was naturally anxious to ascertain whether matters were likely to be adjusted with Britain, and, as modestly as possible, endeavored to turn the conversation that way. I was urged to this by two considerations. I was not sure but that part of our fall importation would come under the operation of the Non-Importation Act, if it took place; and being fully satisfied of the friendly disposition of the Whig party in Britain towards America, I would gladly have availed myself of an opportunity of expressing that opinion to the President. But on this subject Mr. Jefferson was, of course, reserved; though, from the few observations he made, I concluded that matters would ultimately be amicably adjusted. I was highly gratified by the expression of his opinion, on the character of my great favorite statesman Mr. Fox. Accounts had that morning reached Washington that Mr. Fox was in the last stage of his illness. I noticed the circumstance. "Poor man," said Mr. Jefferson, "I fear by this time he is no more, and his loss will be severely felt by his country; he is a man of the most liberal and enlightened policy, a friend to his country, and to the human race."

A gentleman then called upon him, I believe General Eaton, and I took my leave, highly pleased with the affability, intelligence, and good sense, of the President of America.

Paul Jennings

Paul Jennings (1799-1874) was enslaved at birth by future President James Madison at Montpelier, the Madison plantation in Orange County, Virginia. Jennings spent his youth at Montpelier as Madison's personal servant. When James Madison became President of the United States, he brought Paul Jennings with him to the White House.

Jennings was scarcely fifteen years old when, in August 1814, the British arrived in Washington, D.C. and set the capital city ablaze. During these tumultuous events, Jennings assisted the Madison family in their escape from the British advance and helped salvage some of the most sacred objects in the White House collection. Jennings' *Reminiscences*, considered by some to be the first White House memoir, offers an account of the siege of Washington.

"Beloved by Everybody in Washington"

After the war had been going on for a couple of years, the people of Washington began to be alarmed for the safety of the city, as the British held Chesapeake Bay with a powerful fleet and army. Everything seemed to be left to General Armstrong, then Secretary of War, who ridiculed the idea that there was any danger. But in August 1814, the enemy had got so near, there could be no doubt of their intentions. Great alarm existed, and some feeble preparations for defense were made. Commodore Barney's flotilla was stripped of men, who were placed in battery at Bladensburg, where they fought splendidly. A large part of his men were tall, strapping negroes, mixed with white sailors and marines. Mr. Madison reviewed them just before the fight, and asked Commodore Barney if his "negroes would not run on the approach of the British?" "No sir," said Barney, "they don't know how to run; they will die by their guns first." They fought till a large part of them were killed or wounded; and Barney himself wounded and taken prisoner. One or two of these negroes are still living here.

Well, on the 24th of August, sure enough, the British reached Bladensburg, and the fight began between 11 and 12. Even that very morning General Armstrong assured Mrs. Madison there was no danger. The President, with General Armstrong, General Winder, Colonel Monroe, Richard Rush, Mr. Graham, Tench Ringgold, and Mr. Duvall, rode out on horseback to Bladensburg to see how things looked. Mrs. Madison ordered dinner to be ready at 3, as usual; I set the table myself, and brought up the ale, cider, and wine, and placed them in the coolers, as all the Cabinet and several military gentlemen and strangers were expected. While waiting, at just about 3, as Sukey, the house-servant, was lolling out of a chamber window, James Smith, a free colored man who had accompanied Mr. Madison to Bladensburg, galloped up to the house, waving his hat, and cried out, "Clear out, clear out! General Armstrong has ordered a retreat!" All then was confusion. Mrs. Madison ordered her carriage, and passing through the dining room, caught up what silver she could crowd into her old-fashioned reticule, and then jumped into the chariot with her servant girl Sukey, and Daniel Carroll, who took charge of them. Joseph Bolin drove them over to Georgetown Heights. The British were expected in a few minutes. Mr. Cutts, her brother-in-law, sent me to a stable on 14th Street, for his carriage. People were running in every direction. John Freeman (the colored butler) drove off in the coachee with his wife, child, and servant; also a feather bed lashed on behind the coachee, which was all the furniture saved, except part of the silver and the portrait of Washington (of which I will tell you by-and-by).

I will here mention that although the British were expected every minute, they did not arrive for some hours; in the meantime, a rabble, taking advantage of the confusion, ran all over the White House, and stole lots of silver and whatever they could lay their hands on.

About sundown I walked over to the Georgetown ferry and found the President and all hands (the gentlemen named before, who acted as a sort of bodyguard for him) waiting for the boat. It soon returned, and we all crossed over, and passed up the road about a mile; they then left us servants to wander about. In a short time, several wagons from Bladensburg, drawn by Barney's artillery horses, passed up the road, having crossed the Long Bridge before it was set on fire. As we were cutting up some planks a white wagoner ordered us away and told his boy Tommy to reach out his gun, and he would shoot us. I told him "he had better have used it at Bladensburg." Just then we came up with Mr. Madison and his friends, who had been wandering about for some hours, consulting what to do. I walked on to a Methodist minister's, and in the evening, while he was at prayer, I heard a tremendous explosion, and, rushing out, saw that the public buildings, navy yard, ropewalks, &c., were on fire.

Mrs. Madison slept that night at Mrs. Love's, two or three miles over the river. After leaving that place, she called in at a house, and went upstairs. The lady of the house learning who she was, became furious, and went to the stairs and screamed out, "Miss Madison! If that's you, come down and go out! Your husband has got mine out fighting, and d—— you, you shan't stay in my house; so get out!" Mrs. Madison complied, and went to Mrs. Minor's, a few miles further, where she stayed a day or two, and then returned to Washington, where she found Mr. Madison at her brother-in-law's, Richard Cutts, on F Street. All the facts about Mrs. M. I learned from her servant Sukey. We moved into the house of Colonel John B. Taylor, corner of 18th Street and New York Avenue, where we lived till the news of peace arrived.

In two or three weeks after we returned, Congress met in extra session, at Blodgett's old shell of a house on 7th Street (where the General Post Office now stands). It was three stories high, and had been used for a theatre, a tavern, an Irish boarding house, &c.; but both Houses of Congress managed to get along in it very well, notwithstanding it had to accommodate the Patent Office, City and General Post Office, committee-rooms, and what was left of the Congressional Library, at the same time. Things are very different now.

The next summer, Mr. John Law, a large property-holder about the Capitol, fearing it would not be rebuilt, got up a subscription and built a large brick building (now called the Old Capitol, where the secesh prisoners are confined), and offered it to Congress for their use, till the Capitol could be rebuilt. This coaxed them back, though strong efforts were made to remove the seat of government north; but the southern members kept it here.

It has often been stated in print that when Mrs. Madison escaped from the White House, she cut out from the frame the large portrait of Washington (now in one of the parlors there) and carried it off. This is totally false. She had no time for doing it. It would have required a ladder to get it down. All she carried off was the silver in her reticule, as the British were thought to be but a few squares off and were expected every moment. John Susé (a Frenchman, then doorkeeper, and still living) and Magraw, the President's gardener, took it down and sent it off on a wagon, with some large silver urns and such other valuables as could be hastily got hold of. When the British did arrive, they ate up the very dinner, and drank the wines, &c., that I had prepared for the President's party.

When the news of peace arrived, we were crazy with joy. Miss Sally Coles, a cousin of Mrs. Madison, and afterwards wife of Andrew Stevenson, since Minister to England, came to the head of the stairs, crying out, "Peace! peace!" and told John Freeman (the butler) to serve out wine liberally to the servants and others. I played the President's March on the violin, John Susé and some others were drunk for two days, and such another joyful time was never seen in Washington. Mr. Madison and all his Cabinet were as pleased as any but did not show their joy in this manner.

Mrs. Madison was a remarkably fine woman. She was beloved by everybody in Washington, white and colored. Whenever soldiers marched by, during the war, she always sent out and invited them in to take wine and refreshments, giving them liberally of the best in the House. Madeira wine was better in those days than now, and more freely drank. In the last days of her life, before Congress purchased her husband's papers, she was in a state of absolute poverty, and I think sometimes suffered for the necessaries of life. While I was a servant to Mr. Webster, he often sent me to her with a market-basket full of provisions and told me whenever I saw anything in the house that I thought she was in need of, to take it to her. I often did this, and occasionally gave her small sums from my own pocket, though I had years before bought my freedom of her.

George Robert Gleig

As a young soldier in the British Army, George Robert Gleig (1796-1888) participated in several battles on American soil during the War of 1812, including the Battle of Bladensburg in the Maryland suburbs of Washington, D.C. This action is also known as the Bladensburg Races, a pejorative phrase coined at the Americans' expense which describes their hasty retreat in the face of advancing British troops.

Gleig accompanied the army in late August, 1814 as it set its sights on Washington, D.C., but his participation in burning the city was by his account more as an observer. He also confesses that his recounting of a certain episode in the culinary history of the White House is a second-hand retelling. Nevertheless, Gleig's *Narrative* demonstrates the author's flair for rousing detail, a talent he would demonstrate in numerous biographies and military histories during a prolific writing career.

"An Elegant Dinner"

The hour of noon was approaching, when a heavy cloud of dust, apparently not more than two or three miles distant, attracted our attention. From whence it originated there was little difficulty in guessing, nor did many minutes expire before surmise was changed into certainty; for on turning a sudden angle in the road, and passing a small plantation, which obstructed the vision towards the left, the British and American armies became visible to one another. The position occupied by the latter was one of great strength and commanding attitude. They were drawn up in three lines upon the brow of a hill, having their front and left flank covered by a branch of the Potomac, and their right resting upon a thick wood and a deep ravine. This river, which may be about the breadth of the Isis at Oxford, flowed between the heights occupied by the American forces, and the little town of Bladensburg. Across it was thrown a narrow bridge, extending from the chief street in that town to the continuation of the road, which passed through the very center of their position; and its right bank (the bank above which they were drawn up) was covered with a narrow stripe of willows and larch trees, whilst the left was altogether bare, low, and exposed. Such was the general aspect of their position as at the first glance it presented itself; of which I must endeavor to give a more detailed account, that my description of the battle may be in some degree intelligible.

I have said that the right bank of the Potomac was covered with a narrow stripe of willow and larch trees. Here the Americans had stationed strong bodies of riflemen, who, in skirmishing order, covered the whole front of their army. Behind this narrow plantation, again, the fields were open and clear, intersected, at certain distances, by rows of high and strong palings. About the middle of the ascent, and in the rear of one of these rows, stood the first line, composed entirely of infantry; at a proper interval from this, and in a similar situation, stood the second line; while the third, or reserve, was posted within the skirts of a wood, which crowned the heights. The artillery, again, of which they had twenty pieces in the field, was thus arranged: on the high road, and commanding the bridge, stood two heavy guns; and four more, two on each side of the road, swept partly in the same direction, and partly down the whole of the slope into the streets of Bladensburg. The rest were scattered, with no great judgment, along the second line of infantry, occupying different spaces between the right of one regiment, and the left of another; while the cavalry showed itself in one mass, within a stubble field, near the extreme left of the position. Such was the nature of the ground which they occupied, and the formidable posture in which they waited our approach; amounting, by their own account, to nine thousand men, a number exactly doubling that of the force which was to attack them.

In the meantime, our column continued to advance in the same order which it had hitherto preserved. The road conducted us for about two miles in a direction parallel with the river, and of consequence with the enemy's line; when it suddenly turned and led directly towards the town of Bladensburg. Being of course ignorant whether this town might not be filled with American troops, the main body paused here, till the advanced guard should reconnoiter. The result proved that no opposition was intended in that quarter, and that the whole of the enemy's army had been withdrawn to the opposite side of the stream, whereupon the army was again put in motion, and in a short time arrived in the streets of Bladensburg, and within range of the American artillery. Immediately on our reaching this point, several of their guns opened upon us, and kept up a quick and well directed cannonade, from which, as we were again commanded to halt, the men were directed to shelter themselves as much as possible behind the houses. The object of this halt, it was conjectured, was to give the General an opportunity of examining the American line, and of trying the depth of the river; because at present there appeared to be but one practicable mode of attack, by crossing the bridge, and taking the enemy directly in front. To do so, however, exposed as the bridge was, must be attended with bloody consequences, nor could the delay of a few minutes produce any mischief which the discovery of a ford would not amply compensate.

But in this conjecture we were altogether mistaken; for without allowing time to the column to close its ranks or to be formed by some of the many stragglers, who were now hurrying, as fast as weariness would permit, to regain their places, the order to halt was countermanded, and the word given to attack; and we immediately pushed on at double quick time, towards the head of the bridge. While we were moving along the street, a continued fire was kept up, with some execution, from those guns which stood to the left of the road; but it was not till the bridge was covered with our people that the two-gun battery upon the road itself began to play. Then, indeed, it also opened, and with tremendous effect; for at the first discharge almost an entire company was swept down; but whether it was that the guns had been previously laid with measured exactness, or that the nerves of the gunners became afterwards unsteady, the succeeding discharges were much less fatal. The riflemen likewise now galled us from the wooded bank, with a running fire of musketry; and it was not without trampling upon many of their dead and dying comrades, that the fight brigade established itself on the opposite side of the stream.

When once there, however, everything else appeared easy. Wheeling off to the right and left of the road, they dashed into the thicket, and quickly cleared it of the American skirmishers, who falling back with precipitation upon the first line, threw it into disorder before it had fired a shot. The consequence was that our troops had scarcely shown themselves when the whole of that line gave way, and fled in the greatest confusion, leaving the two guns upon the road in possession of the victors.

But here it must be confessed that the light brigade was guilty of imprudence. Instead of pausing till the rest of the army came up, they lightened themselves by throwing away their knapsacks and haversacks; and extending their ranks so as to show an equal front with the enemy, pushed on to the attack of the second line. The Americans, however, saw their weakness, and stood firm, and having the whole of their artillery, with the exception of those captured on the road, and the greater part of their infantry in this line, they first checked the ardor of the assailants by a heavy fire, and then, in their turn, advanced to recover the ground which was lost. Against this charge, the extended order of the British troops would not permit them to offer an effectual resistance, and they were accordingly borne back to the very thicket upon the river's brink, where they maintained themselves with determined obstinacy, repelling all attempts to drive them through it; and frequently following, to within a short distance of the cannon's mouth, such parts of the enemy's line as gave way.

In this state the action continued till the second brigade had likewise crossed and formed upon the right bank of the river; when the

44th Regiment moving to the right, and driving in the skirmishers, debouched upon the left flank of the Americans, and completely turned it. In that quarter, therefore, the battle was won; because the raw militiamen, who were stationed there as being the least assailable point, when once broken could not be rallied. But on their right, the enemy still kept their ground with much resolution; nor was it till the arrival of the 4th Regiment, and the advance of the British forces in firm array, to the charge, that they began to waver. Then, indeed, seeing their left in full flight, and the 44th getting in their rear, they lost all order, and dispersed, leaving clouds of riflemen to cover their retreat; and hastened to conceal themselves in the woods, where it would have been vain to follow them. The rout was now general throughout the whole line. The reserve, which ought to have supported the main body, fled as soon as those in its front began to give way; and the cavalry, instead of charging the British troops, now scattered in pursuit, turned their horses' heads and galloped off, leaving them in undisputed possession of the field, and of ten out of the twenty pieces of artillery.

This battle, by which the fate of the American capital was decided, began about one o'clock in the afternoon, and lasted till four. The loss on the part of the English was severe, since, out of two-thirds of the army, which were engaged, upwards of five hundred men were killed and wounded; and what rendered it doubly severe was, that among these were numbered several officers of rank and distinction. Colonel Thornton who commanded the light brigade; Lieutenant Colonel Wood commanding the 85th Regiment, and Major Brown who had led the advanced guard, were all severely wounded; and General Ross himself had a horse shot under him. On the side of the Americans the slaughter was not so great. Being in possession of a strong position, they were of course less exposed in defending than the others in storming it; and had they conducted themselves with coolness, and resolution, it is not conceivable how the day could have been won. But the fact is that with the exception of a party of sailors from the gun boats, under the command of Commodore Barney, no troops could behave worse than they did. The skirmishers were driven in as soon as attacked, the first line gave way without offering the slightest resistance, and the left of the main body was broken within half an hour after it was seriously engaged. Of the sailors, however, it would be injustice not to speak in the terms which their conduct merits. They were employed as gunners, and not only did they serve their guns with a quickness and precision which astonished their assailants, but they stood till some of them were actually bayonetted with fuses in their hands; nor was it till their leader was wounded and taken, and they saw themselves deserted on all sides by the soldiers, that they quitted the field. With respect to the British army, again, no line of distinction can be drawn. All did their duty, and none more gallantly than the rest; and though the brunt of the affair fell upon the light brigade, this was owing chiefly to the circumstance of its being at the head of the column, and perhaps, also, in some degree, to its own rash impetuosity. The artillery, indeed, could do little; being unable to show itself in the presence of a force so superior; but the six-pounder was nevertheless brought into action, and a corps of rockets proved of striking utility.

Our troops being worn down from fatigue, and of course as ignorant of the country as the Americans were the reverse, the pursuit could not be continued to any distance. Neither was it attended with much slaughter. Diving into the recesses of the forests, and covering themselves with riflemen, the enemy was quickly beyond our reach; and having no cavalry to scour even the high road, ten of the lightest of their guns were carried off in the flight. The defeat, however, was absolute, and the army, which had been collected for the defense of Washington, was scattered beyond the possibility of, at least, an immediate reunion; and as the distance from Bladensburg to that city does not exceed four miles, there appeared to be no farther obstacle in the way, to prevent its immediate capture.

An opportunity so favorable was not endangered by any needless delay. While the two brigades which had been engaged, remained upon the field to recover their order, the third, which had formed the reserve, and was consequently unbroken, took the lead, and pushed forward at a rapid rate towards Washington.

As it was not the intention of the British government to attempt permanent conquests in this part of America; and as the General was well aware that with a handful of men, he could not pretend to establish himself for any length of time in an enemy's capital, he determined to lay it under contribution, and to return quietly to the shipping. Nor was there anything unworthy of the character of a British officer, in this determination. By all the customs of war, whatever public property may chance to be in a captured town, becomes, confessedly, the just spoil of the conqueror; and in thus proposing to accept a certain sum of money in lieu of that property, he was showing mercy, rather than severity, to the vanquished. It is true that if they chose to reject his terms, he and his army would be deprived of their booty, because, without some more convenient mode of transporting it than we possessed, even the portable part of the property itself could not be removed. But, on the other hand, there was no difficulty in destroying it; and thus, though we should gain nothing, the American government would lose probably to a much greater amount than if they had agreed to purchase its preservation by the money demanded.

Such being the intention of General Ross, he did not march the troops immediately into the city but halted them upon a plain in its immediate vicinity, whilst a flag of truce was sent in with terms. But whatever his proposal might have been, it was not so much as heard; for scarcely had the party bearing the flag entered the street than they were fired upon from the windows of one of the houses, and the horse of the General himself, who accompanied them, killed. You will easily believe that conduct so unjustifiable, so direct a breach of the law of nations, roused the indignation of every individual from the General himself down to the private soldier. All thoughts of accommodation were instantly laid aside; the troops advanced forthwith into the town, and having first put to the sword all who were found in the house from which the shots were fired, and reduced it to ashes, they proceeded, without a moment's delay, to burn and destroy everything in the most distant degree connected with Government. In this general devastation were included the Senate House, the President's Palace, an extensive dockyard and arsenal, barracks for two or three thousand men, several large storehouses filled with naval and military stores, some hundreds of cannon of different descriptions, and nearly twenty thousand stand of small arms. There were also two or three public ropeworks which shared the same fate, a fine frigate pierced for sixty guns, and just ready to be launched, several gun-brigs and armed schooners, with a variety of gunboats and small craft. The powder magazines were of course set on fire and exploded with a tremendous crash, throwing down many houses in their vicinity, partly by pieces of the walls striking them, and partly by the concussion of the air; whilst quantities of shot, shell, and hand grenades, which could not otherwise be rendered useless, were thrown into the river. In destroying the cannon, a method was adopted which I had never before witnessed, and which, as it was both effectual and expeditious, I cannot avoid relating. One gun of rather a small caliber, was pitched upon as the executioner of the rest; and being loaded with ball, and turned to the muzzles of the others, it was fired, and thus beat out their breechings. Many, however, not being mounted, could not be thus dealt with; these were spiked, and having their trunnions knocked off, were afterwards cast into the bed of the river.

All this was as it should be and had the arm of vengeance been extended no farther, there would not have been room given for so much as a whisper of disapprobation. But unfortunately, it did not stop here; a noble library, several printing offices, and all the national archives were likewise committed to the flames, which, though no doubt the property of Government, might better have been spared. It is not, however, my intention to join the outcry, which will probably be raised against what they will term a line of conduct at once barbarous and unprofitable. Far from it; on the contrary, I cannot help admiring the forbearance and humanity of the British troops, since, irritated as they had every right to be, they spared as far as was possible, all private property, not a single house in the place being plundered or destroyed, except that from which the General's horse had been killed;

and those which were accidentally thrown down by the explosion of the magazines.

While the third brigade was thus employed, the rest of the army, having recalled its stragglers, and removed the wounded into Bladensburg, began its march towards Washington. Though the battle was ended by four o'clock, the sun had set before the different regiments were in a condition to move, consequently this short journey was performed in the dark. The work of destruction had also begun in the city, before they quitted their ground; and the blazing of houses, ships, and stores, the report of exploding magazines, and the crash of falling roofs, informed them, as they proceeded, of what was going forward. You can conceive nothing finer than the sight which met them as they drew near to the town. The sky was brilliantly illumined by the different conflagrations; and a dark red light was thrown upon the road, sufficient to permit each man to view distinctly his comrade's face. Except the burning of St. Sebastian's, I do not recollect to have witnessed, at any period of my life, a scene more striking or more sublime.

Having advanced as far as the plain, where the reserve had previously paused, the first and second brigades halted; and, forming into close column, passed the night in bivouac. At first, this was agreeable enough, because the air was mild, and weariness made up for what was wanting in comfort. But towards morning, a violent storm of rain accompanied with thunder and lightning came on, which disturbed the rest of all those who were exposed to it. Yet in spite of the disagreeableness of getting wet, I cannot say that I felt disposed to grumble at the interruption, for it appeared that what I had before considered as superlatively sublime, still wanted this to render it complete. The flashes of lightning seemed to vie in brilliancy, with the flames which burst from the roofs of burning houses, while the thunder drowned the noise of crumbling walls, and was only interrupted by the occasional roar of cannon, and of large depots of gunpowder, as they one by one exploded.

I need scarcely observe that the consternation of the inhabitants was complete, and that to them this was a night of terror. So confident had they been of the success of their troops, that few of them had dreamt of quitting their houses or abandoning the city; nor was it till the fugitives from the battle began to rush in, filling every place as they came with dismay, that the President himself thought of providing for his safety. That gentleman, as I was credibly informed, had gone forth in the morning with the army, and had continued among his troops till the British forces began to make their appearance. Whether the sight of his enemies cooled his courage or not, I cannot say, but, according to my informer, no sooner was the glittering of our arms discernible, than he began to discover that his presence was more wanted in the Senate than with the army; and having ridden through the ranks, and exhorted every man to do his duty, he hurried back to his own house, that he might prepare a feast for the entertainment of his officers, when they; should return victorious. For the truth of these details, I will not be answerable; but this much I know, that the feast was actually prepared; though instead of being devoured by American officers, it went to satisfy the less delicate appetites of a party of English soldiers. When the detachment, sent out to destroy Mr. Madison's house, entered his dining parlor, they found a dinner table spread, and covers laid for forty guests. Several kinds of wine, in handsome cut glass decanters, were cooling on the sideboard; plate holders stood by the fireplace, filled with dishes and plates; knives, forks and spoons, were arranged for immediate use; in short, everything was ready for the entertainment of a ceremonious party. Such were the arrangements in the dining room, whilst in the kitchen were others answerable to them in every respect. Spits, loaded with joints of various sorts, turned before the fire; pots, saucepans, and other culinary utensils, stood upon the grate; and all the other requisites for an elegant and substantial repast, were exactly in a state which indicated that they had been lately and precipitately abandoned.

You will readily imagine that these preparations were beheld by a party of hungry soldiers with no indifferent eye. An elegant dinner, even though considerably overdressed, was a luxury to which few of them, at least for some time back, had been accustomed; and which, after the dangers and fatigues of the day, appeared peculiarly inviting. They sat down to it, therefore, not indeed in the most orderly manner, but with countenances which would not have disgraced a party of aldermen at a civic feast; and having satisfied their appetites with fewer complaints than would have probably escaped their rival *gourmands*, and partaken pretty freely of the wines, they finished by setting fire to the house which had so liberally entertained them.

Francis Hall

Francis Hall (d. 1833) departed Liverpool on January 20th, 1816, bound for New York, sailing on an America vessel he described as "excellently built and commanded." After spending most of the year traveling throughout New York and Canada, he began the southern leg of his journey, traveling down the eastern seaboard, making numerous stops in Pennsylvania and Maryland, and finally reaching Washington, D.C. toward the end of the year.

Hall found Washington, D.C. both under construction and under renovation. Scarcely two years after the burning of the capital by the British, the Congress was meeting in a temporary building, not the Capitol, and the President was living in a temporary residence, not the White House. Hall reflected upon his visit in his *Travels in Canada and the United States*.

"Splitting Hairs"

The traveler, having passed through Bladensburg, on the east branch of the Patuxent, where the action was fought, which the Americans have nicknamed the "Bladensburg Races," crosses a sandy tract, interspersed with oak barrens and pine woods, until suddenly mounting a little rise, close to a poor cottage with its Indian corn patch, he finds himself opposite to the Capitol of the Federal City. It stands on an ancient bank of the Potomac, about eighty feet above the present level of the river; the course of which it commands, as well as the adjacent country, as far as the Alleghany Ridges. The edifice consists of two wings, intended to be connected by a center, surmounted by a dome or cupola. The design is pure and elegant, but the whole building wants grandeur. Each wing would not be a large private mansion: the interior has consequently a contracted appearance, a kind of economy of space disagreeably contrasting with the gigantic scale of nature without, as well as with our ideas of the growing magnitude of the American nation. The staircase, which is a kind of vestibule to the impression to be produced by the whole building, is scarcely wide enough for three persons to pass conveniently. The chambers of the Senate and Representatives are of very moderate dimensions, and the judgment hall, with its low-browed roof, and short columns, seems modeled after the prison of Constance in Marmion. Some of the decorations, too, are of very dubious taste. Mr. Latrobe has modeled a set of figures for the Chamber of Representatives, to personify the several states of the Union; but as it is not easy to discover an attribute, to say nothing of a poetical characteristic, by which Connecticut may be distinguished from Massachusetts, North Carolina from South Carolina, or Kentucky from Ohio, recourse must be had to the ungraceful expedient of a superscription to point out his own tutelary saint to each representative. Mr. Latrobe has, indeed, hit upon one device for Massachusetts; she is leading by the hand an ugly cub of a boy, representing Maine, which boy becomes a girl when Maine assumes her proper state; a puerile conceit. One cannot help regretting the Americans should have neglected to give their new Capitol a character of grandeur worthy of their territory and ambition. Private edifices rise, decay, and are replaced by others of superior magnificence, as the taste or growing opulence of the nation require; but public buildings should have a character answerable to their purpose; they bear upon them the seal of the genius of the age, and sometimes prophetically reveal the political destinies of the nations by which they are raised. The Romans communicated to their erections the durability of their empire. The Americans, in "their aspirations to be great," seem sometimes to look towards Roman models, but the imitation must be of things, not names; or instead of a noble parallel, they are in danger of producing a ludicrous contrast.

From the foot of the Capitol Hill there runs a straight road (intended to be a street) planted with poplars, for about two miles, to the President's House, a handsome stone mansion, forming a conspicuous object from the Capitol Hill. Near it are the public offices, and some streets nearly filled up. About half a mile further is a pleasant row of houses, in one of which the President at present resides. There are a few tolerable houses still further on the road to Georgetown, and this is nearly the sum total of the City for 1816. It used to be a joke against Washington that next door neighbors must go through a wood to make their visits; but the jest and forest have vanished together. There is now scarcely a tree betwixt Georgetown and the Navy Yard, two miles beyond the Capitol, except the poplars I have mentioned, which may be considered as the *locum tenentes* of future houses. I doubt the policy of such thorough clearing; clumps of trees are preferable objects to vacant spaces, and the city in its present state, being commenced from the extremities instead of the center, has a disjointed and naked appearance. The fiery ordeal has, however, fixed its destiny. Land and houses are rising in value, new buildings are erecting, and with the aid of the intended university, there is little doubt that Washington will attain as great an extent as can be expected for a city possessed of no commercial advantages, and created, not by the natural course of events, but by a political speculation. The plan, indeed, supposes an immense growth, but even if this were attainable, it seems doubtful how far an overgrown luxurious capital would be the fittest seat for learning, or even legislation. Perhaps the true interest of the Union would rather hold Washington sacred to science, philosophy, and the arts: a spot in some degree kept holy from commercial avarice, to which the Members of different states may repair to breathe an atmosphere untainted by local prejudices and find golden leisure for pursuits and speculations of public utility. Such fancies would be daydreams elsewhere and are so perhaps here; but America is young in the career of political life; she has the light of former ages, and the sufferings of the present to guide her; she has not crushed the spirits of the many, to build up the tyranny of the few, and, therefore, the prophetic eye of imagination may dwell upon her smilingly.

    I fell into very pleasant society at Washington. Strangers who intend staying some days in a town, usually take lodgings at a boarding house, in preference to a tavern. In this way, they obtain the best society the place affords; for there are always gentlemen, and frequently ladies, either visitors or temporary residents, who live in this manner to avoid the trouble of housekeeping. At Washington, during the sittings of Congress, the boarding houses are divided into messes, according to the political principles of the inmates; nor is a stranger admitted without some introduction, and the consent of the whole company. I chanced to join a Democratic mess, and name a few of its members with gratitude, for the pleasure their society gave me: Commodore Decatur and his lady, the Abbé Correa, the great botanist and plenipotentiary of Portugal, the Secretary of the Navy, the Secretary of the Navy Board, known as the author of a humorous publication, entitled "John Bull, and Brother Jonathan," with eight or ten Members of Congress, principally from the Western states, which are generally considered as most decidedly hostile to England, but whom I did not on this account find less good-humored and courteous. It is from thus living in daily intercourse with the leading characters of the country, that one is enabled to judge with some degree of certainty of the practices of its government; for to know the paper theory is nothing, unless it be compared with the instruments employed to carry it into effect. A political constitution may be nothing but a cabalistic form to extract money and power from the people; but then the jugglers must be in the dark, and "no admittance behind the curtain." This way of living affords too the best insight into the best part of society; for if in a free nation the depositaries of the public confidence be ignorant, or vulgar, it is a very fruitless search to look for the opposite qualities in those they represent; whereas, if these be well informed in mind and manners, it proves at the least an inclination towards knowledge and refinement, in the general mass of citizens, by whom they are selected.

My own experience obliges me to a favorable verdict in this particular. I found the little circle into which I had happily fallen, full of good sense and good humor, and never quitted it without feeling myself a gainer on the score, either of useful information or of social enjoyment.

The President, or rather his lady, holds a drawing-room weekly, during the sitting of Congress. He takes by the hand those who are presented to him; shaking hands being discovered in America to be more rational and manly than kissing them. For the rest, it is much as such things are everywhere, chatting, and tea, compliments and ices, a little music, (some scandal, I suppose, among the ladies,) and to bed. Nothing in these assemblies more attracted my notice, than the extraordinary stature of most of the western members; the room seemed filled with giants, among whom moderately sized men crept like pigmies. I know not well to what the difference may be attributed, but the surprising growth of the inhabitants of the Western states is a matter of astonishment to those of the eastern, and of the coastline generally. This phenomenon, which is certainly a considerable stumbling block to the Abbé Raynal's theory, may probably be resolved into the operation of three positive causes, and one negative, namely, plentiful but simple food, a healthy climate, constant exercise in the open air, and the absence of mental irritation. In a more advanced stage of society, luxurious and sedentary habits produce in the rich that enfeeblement of vitality, which scanty food, and laborious or unwholesome occupations bring upon the poor. The only persons to be compared with these Goliaths of the West, were six Indian chiefs from Georgia, Choctaws or Chickasaws, who, having come to Washington on public business, were presented at Mrs. Madison's drawing-room. They had a still greater appearance of muscular power than the Americans; and while looking on them, I comprehended the prowess of those ancient knights whose single might held an army in check, "and made all Troy retire."

The sittings of Congress are held in a temporary building during the repair of the Capitol. I attended them frequently and was fortunate enough to be present at one interesting debate on a change in the mode of Presidential elections. Most of the principal speakers took a part in it: Messrs. Gaston, Calhoun, and Webster in support of it; Randolph and Grosvenor against it. The merits of the question were not immediately to be comprehended by a stranger, but their style of speaking was, in the highest degree, correct and logical, particularly that of Mr. Webster of New Hampshire, whose argumentative acuteness extorted a compliment from Mr. Randolph himself, "albeit unused to the complimenting mood." Mr. Grosvenor, both in action and language, might be considered a finished orator, as far as our present notions of practical oratory extend. Mr. Randolph, whose political talents, or rather political success, is said to be marred by an eccentric turn of thought, which chimes in with no party, seems rather a brilliant than a convincing speaker; his elocution is distinct and clear to shrillness, his command of language and illustration seems unlimited; but he gave me the idea of a man dealing huge blows against a shadow, and wasting his dexterity in splitting hairs. His political sentiments are singular: he considers the government of the United States as an elective monarchy. "Torture the constitution as you will," said he, in the course of the debate, "the President will elect his successor, and that will be his son whenever he has one old enough to succeed him." No expressions are used, either of approbation or the contrary; whatever may be the opinion of the House, the most perfect attention is given to each Member; nor, however long he may speak, is he ever interrupted by those indications of impatience so common in our House of Commons. This may reasonably be accounted for by supposing, that their average speeches are, in themselves better; or more agreeably, by conjecturing, that the American idea of excellence is put at a lower standard than our own. Both the talents, however, and behavior of the Members, seem worthy of the government, and of what America is, and may be. Their forms of business and debate nearly resemble those of our parliament; always excepting wigs and gowns, a piece of grave absurdity well omitted: for it is surely an odd conceit, to fancy the dignity of the first officers of States attached to, or supported by, large conglomerations of artificial hair.

Henry Bradshaw Fearon

Henry Bradshaw Fearon (1793-1842) provides perhaps the best description of the purpose of his visit to the United States in the subtitle of his *Sketches of America*, further delineating the work as: *A Narrative of a Journey of Five Thousand Miles through the Eastern and Western States of America; Contained in Eight Reports Addressed to the Thirty-nine English Families by Whom the Author was Deputed, in June 1817, to Ascertain Whether Any, and What Part of the United States Would be Suitable for their Residence.* Fearon was clearly up to the task. As was the case with many foreign travelers to the city, his complimentary remarks on Washington, D.C. are few, and his criticisms are blunt.

"Human Beings are Sold in the Streets"

It has been so fashionable with natives, as well as foreigners, to ridicule the Federal City, that I had anticipated the reality of Moore's description of...

"This famed metropolis, where fancy sees
Squares in morasses, obelisks in trees"

But in this I was pleasingly disappointed.
The River Potomac, at this place, is only navigable for small craft near its banks. Besides the Potomac, the River "Tiber" runs through the city; its stream is about the width of the Paddington Canal. The

ridiculous though characteristic vanity displayed in altering it from the original name of "Goose Creek" to that of the Tiber has been happily exposed by Moore.

The President's Palace, and the Capitol, situated on opposite hills, are the chief public buildings, both of which were nearly destroyed by the buccaneering incursions of our countrymen, who acted, perhaps, agreeably to their orders, but certainly in opposition to the feelings, judgment, and character of the British people. These buildings are now rapidly rising into increased splendor. The Capitol, in which are both houses of the legislature, and several public offices, stands on a bank of the Potomac, seventy feet above the level of that river. It as yet consists of but two wings, intended to be connected by a center, surmounted by a dome. The architect is Mr. Latrobe. In the internal construction of this building, he has not evinced even a common knowledge of what contributes to convenience, and still less to elegance of appearance. The apartments are small, crowded, and without unity of design. The exterior, when completed, will, however, produce a really grand effect. Some of the pillars are of a native marble, of a peculiarly novel and beautiful description, bearing some resemblance to the finest specimens of mosaic. The Americans, however, are not content with the productions of their own country. They have made large imports from Italy of its most expensive marble; and so anxious is even the President himself for "foreign ornament," that he has imported chairs at one hundred dollars each, though the cabinetmakers of Baltimore would have equaled, and I believe surpassed them in every particular, at the price of sixty dollars!

The President's House is at the opposite end of "Pennsylvania Avenue," commanding a most beautiful prospect. On each side of it stands a large brick building; one of which is the Treasury, the other the War and Navy offices. These are to be connected with the Palace, which, when completed, would form an ornament even to St. Petersburg itself. Upon a second visit to the Capitol, I explored nearly all its recesses. Marks of the late conflagration are still very apparent, while the walls bear evidence of public opinion in relation to that transaction, which seems to have had the singular fate of casting disgrace upon both the Americans and British. Some of the pencil drawings exhibit the military commander hanging upon a tree; others represent the President running off without his hat or wig; some, Admiral Cockburn robbing hen-roosts, to which are added such inscriptions as, "The capital of the Union lost by cowardice;" "Curse cowards;" "A ----- sold the city for 5,000 dollars;" "James Madison is a rascal, a coward, and a fool;" "Ask no questions," &c.

The Post Office is a large brick building, situated at about equal distances from the President's House and the Capitol. Under the same roof is the Patent Office, and also the National Library, for the use of Members of Congress. In the first of these departments, I witnessed upwards of nine hundred specimens of native mechanical genius. This would appear to afford decisive proof that Americans are not deficient in inventive talent, though it cannot be extensively, or with profit, called into action, until your little island ceases to be the universal workshop. The Library is small, consisting of but 3,000 volumes; but it is select and well chosen, and includes various classes of literature, having been the property of Mr. Jefferson, for which he obtained from the United States 20,000 dollars. The former Library, containing from 7 to 8,000, was destroyed by our *enlightened* countrymen. So great has been, at some periods, the depreciation of property in this city, that in 1802, what had originally cost 200,000 dollars, was sold for 25,000. This decay continued to go on, until the visit of General Ross, and the subsequent signature of peace. Since that time, it seems to have risen, like the phoenix from the flames, and is once more partially increasing in prosperity. There are now a number of two- and three-story brick buildings, none of which are uninhabited; and also some small wooden houses, though, according to the original [L'Enfant] Plan, none were to be built less than three stories high, and all to have marble steps. But the childish folly of this scheme was soon subverted by the natural course of events; and though the existence of *"lower orders,"* even in the capital of the Republic, may not accord with the vanity of its legislators, they ought to be told, that neither prosperity nor population can be possessed by any nation, without a due admixture of the *natural classes* of society.

The population of Washington City is about 9,000; of Georgetown, 6,000; of Alexandria, 8,000; and of all other parts of the District of Columbia, 7,000; making a total of 30,000. *Alexandria*, which is seven miles from the city, may be considered the seaport. *Georgetown* is the residence of shopkeepers, and *Washington* the depot for officeholders, place-hunters, and boardinghouse keepers; none of whom would appear to be in possession of too much of this world's goods. Between these three divisions of this District there exists considerable jealousy.

Rents are as high as elsewhere. Mechanics are fully employed, and well paid. Shopkeepers are too numerous, and none of them remarkably successful. British goods abound, as in every other part of America. When I had been here a few hours, I went to a store to purchase a pair of worsted gloves. They were of the commonest kind, such as are sold in London at 8s, 6d. per dozen. The price was half a dollar per pair. I presented a Philadelphia one dollar note; it would not be taken without a discount of 2½ per cent. I then tendered a Baltimore note of the same amount. This being one hundred miles nearer was accepted. The storekeeper had no silver change; to remedy which, he took a pair of scissors and divided the note between us. I enquired if the half would pass, and being answered in the affirmative, took it without hesitation, knowing the want of specie throughout the country, and being previously familiarized with Spanish dollars cut into every variety of size. I now find that demi-notes are a common circulating medium. Capital is generally wanted, though my enquiries do not lead me to believe that it can be employed here with anything more than ordinary advantage. The increase of the Federal City cannot be rapid. Here is fine natural scenery, but no decidedly great natural advantages; little external commerce, a barren soil, a scanty population, enfeebled too by the deadly weight of absolute slavery, and no direct means of communication with the Western country. For the apparently injudicious selection of such a spot upon which to raise the capital of a great nation, several reasons are given. Some have even gone so far as to attribute to General Washington the influence of pecuniary interest, his property being in the neighborhood. But the most common argument adduced in support of the choice is that it is central, or rather that it *was* so; for the recent addition of new States has removed the center very far west, so much so indeed, that the inhabitants of Lexington affirm, that *their* town must on that ground soon become the capital; and even the people of St. Louis, in the Missouri, put in their claim, that city being said to be geographically the exact center of the Union. But assuming that Washington were central, I do not see much validity in the argument, at least if we are to be influenced in our judgment by any country in the old world. Where is the important nation, whose capital is placed exactly in the center of its dominions? Spain is perhaps the only country which can be adduced, and no very favorable conclusion can be drawn from such an instance, though unquestionably if rivers and soil, if roads and canals, all united to recommend that situation, it would be in some other respects extremely convenient; but this not being the case, the knowledge of Euclid must be dispensed with for something of more practical, though perhaps more vulgar utility.

There may be other objections to this capital. Among them I would venture to suggest, that the legislators, and rulers of a nation, ought to reside in that city which has the most direct communication with all parts of their country, and of the world at large they ought to see with their own eyes, and hear with their own ears, without which, though possessed of the best intentions, they must often be in error. Newspaper communications, letters, and agents, are but substitutes, and sometimes very poor ones; besides which, I conceive that mere expedients should not be admitted in national legislation. Unless this city increases with a rapidity unsanctioned by the most sanguine anticipation, the American lawmakers will be half a century behind what they would become by a residence in New York or Philadelphia. Another objection to Washington may suggest itself to some minds, in its neighborhood to Virginia. The "Virginian Dynasty," as it has been called, is a subject of general, and I think very just, complaint throughout other parts of America. This State has supplied four of the five Presidents, and also a liberal number of occupants of every other government office. The Virginians very modestly assert that this monopoly does not proceed from corrupt influence but is a consequence of the buoyancy and vigor of their natural talent. Without entering into the controversy, whether or not seventeen States can supply a degree of ability equal to that of Virginia single-handed, I must express my want of respect for a State in which every man is either a slaveholder, or a defender of slavery, a State in which landed property is not attach able for debt, a State in which human beings are sold in the streets by the public auctioneer, are flogged without trial at the mercy of their owner or his agents, and are killed almost without punishment. Yet these men dare to call themselves democrats, and friends of liberty! From such democrats, and such friends of liberty, good Lord deliver us!

The customs of society at this season differ, I presume, in some degree, from those portions of the year when Congress is not sitting. Tea parties, and private balls, are now very frequent. Mr. Bagot, the English Ambassador, and his lady, are particularly assiduous in their attentions to all classes, and maintain a strict conformity with the habits of the place. Their cards of invitation are left at my boardinghouse for different gentlemen every day. The Speaker (Mr. Clay) gives public periodical dinners. A drawing room is held weekly at the President's House: it is generally crowded. There is little or no difficulty in getting introduced on these occasions. Mr. Monroe is a very plain, practical man of business. The custom is shaking, and not the degrading one of kissing, hands. Conversation, tea, ice, music, chewing tobacco, and excessive spitting, afford employment for the evening. The dress of the ladies is very elegant, though that of the gentlemen is too frequently rather ungentlemanly.

The theatre is a miserable building. I have attended several representations in it by the same company which I saw when in Pittsburgh.

Incledon has been here; the Washington critics think him too vulgar, and also an indifferent singer!

In this city I witnessed also the exhibitions of *Sema Sama*, the Indian juggler, from London. My chief attention was directed to the audience; their disbelief of the possibility of performing the numerous feats advertised, and their inconceivable astonishment at witnessing the actual achievement, appeared extreme, approaching almost to childish wonder and astonishment.

The few private families to which I have had introductions, do not evince a more accurate knowledge of that English word *comfort* than I have remarked elsewhere; indeed, I would class them a century inferior to Boston and half a century behind New York. The boardinghouses and inns partake of the same characteristics. I first applied at the chief, which is Davis's Indian Queen tavern. Most of the door handles are broken; the floor of the coffee room is strewed with bricks and mortar, caused by the crumbling of the walls and ceiling, and the character of the accommodations is in unison with this unorganized state of things. The charges are as high as at the very first London hotel.

George Watterston

A resident of Washington, D.C. for most of his life, George Watterston (1783-1854) enjoyed a versatile career in law and letters. He practiced law in Maryland and in the District, edited various local publications, and served as the third Librarian of Congress. As Librarian, Watterston oversaw the rebuilding of the library's collection after the British burned the Capitol in 1814. As an author, Watterston wrote fictional works under pseudonyms and guidebooks under his own name. The following is excerpted from an early work in the form of an epistolary novel, entitled *Letters from Washington*, written by a "Foreigner," and addressed to his imaginary correspondent "*Lord B.*"

"Considerably Above Mediocrity"

LETTER III.
Washington, 1818.

Lord B.:

I had yesterday the honor of an introduction to Mr. Monroe, the present Chief Magistrate of the United States. "It is seldom," says Dr. Johnson, "that we find men or places such as we expect to find them," and I must confess that in the present instance, the truth of this observation has been realized. I found Mr. Monroe a little different from what my fancy had pictured him, but neither a Lilliputian nor a

Patagonian. He appears to be between fifty and sixty years of age, with a form above the middle size, compact, muscular, and indicating a constitution of considerable hardiness and vigor; his countenance exhibits lineaments of great severity, and seems as if it had been seldom irradiated by the rays of joy, or softened by the touch of sensibility; he does smile, however, but not like Shakespeare's Cassius,

" . . . in such a sort
As if he mocked himself and scorned his spirit
That could be moved to smile at anything."

At these moments, there is a benignity and suavity in him, that invite confidence and repel suspicion. He is rather awkward in his address for a man who has mingled so much in polite society, and his manners and habiliments are more those of a plain country gentleman, than an accomplished statesman or a profound politician. Awkwardness of manners, however, seems to be more common among the Americans than I had conceived. Their most eminent men are, I think, deficient in that ease, elegance, and grace, which distinguish the prominent political characters of France and England. The nature of their government has a tendency to beget this, by preventing those sacrifices to the graces, which are made in the more refined and polished nations of Europe. The importance and magnitude of their pursuits, and their general association with what we call the lower ranks of society, preclude the acquisition of those exterior embellishments so industriously cultivated by our countrymen. A disciple of Chesterfield, with all his refinement and fascination, would be regarded in this country as a mere *petite maitre*, calculated only to charm the eye and to fascinate the heart of female ignorance. But I have wandered from my subject. Mr. Monroe is attached to what was once denominated the Republican Party; for at present all party distinctions seem to be lost, and the parties themselves wholly amalgamated. In his political career, he has manifested the most unimpeachable and unbending integrity, and though long before the public, has seldom failed to meet the expectations and to gratify the wishes of the people.

That he possesses ambition will not be denied; but his ambition is limited to the attainment of excellence and distinction within the bounds of patriotism and honor. If he has not the unbending sternness of Cato, he has the more pleasing and benignant integrity of Fabricius. Mr. Monroe entered early into public life and has performed the various and complicated duties of a soldier, a politician, and a statesman. His mind has been accustomed to dwell on the nature of governments and the revolutions of empire; subjects so vast produce a correspondent enlargement of intellect and sweep of comprehension. The mind which is occupied in trifles will not be apt to amaze by its greatness, or astonish by its magnificence; it may glitter, but will never blaze.

The peculiar character and magnitude of Mr. Monroe's pursuits have withheld his attention from the minor and less important subjects of literature, and he is very far from what we should call a man of reading or general science. The know ledge he possesses has been acquired more by personal observation, laborious reflection, and frequent conversation, than by the repeated perusals of books, to which his important occupations would not permit him to devote his time, but he has examined and reexamined that knowledge till it has in fact become his own, recreated by combination, established by practice, and tested by experience. It is said, his mind is neither rich nor brilliant, but capable of the most laborious analysis, and the most patient research, not hasty in its decisions, and not easily changed when its decisions are formed. Judgment appears to be his prominent intellectual feature, and in the examination of any object, he seldom suffers it to be darkened by prejudice, or warped by passion. This brief sketch, my lord, will satisfy you I presume, that no man could be chosen, better calculated to fill the dignified station he holds under this government, and that no man could be more cordially and sincerely disposed to further the interests and to promote the prosperity and happiness of his country.

Mrs. Monroe, to whom I was also introduced, is a lady of retired and domestic habits, not ungraceful and apparently very amiable.

Having resided in Europe with her husband, she has acquired some of its manners and a good deal of its polish. She receives company but returns no visits; she seems more attached to the silence and peace of obscurity than the bustle, confusion and glare of public assemblies, but to preserve the custom established by her predecessor, a lady, it is said, of great elegance of manners and much dignity of deportment, she gives what we call *conservationi,* but what is here termed *drawing rooms,* for the purpose of gratifying the wishes and curiosity of such strangers as may please to visit her and the President. These *conservationi* are conducted on principles of republican simplicity and are widely different from the magnificence and splendor of the English levees. They appeared to me, however, very unpleasant. The rooms are so crowded, the hum of voices so loud, and the motion of the company so incessant, that the possibility of continuing a conversation on any subject, is wholly precluded, and you are obliged to move with the multitude, by whom you are jostled every instant, without the power of enjoying the "feast of reason," or even the pleasures of sense.

Mr. Monroe has never been blessed with male issue, and what is remarkable, out of the five presidents who have served since the organization of this government, but one has had sons. I mention this merely as a curious circumstance. Mr. J. Q. Adams, the present Secretary of State, is the son of the second President of the United States, and a man of great talent, information, and industry. Mr. Monroe, since his elevation to the presidential chair, is said to have discovered much sagacity in the selection of his cabinet counsel or executive officers. These are the secretaries of State, War, Treasury, Navy, and Attorney General, all of whom, with one exception, possess the rare gifts of nature in no ordinary degree; and who have already rendered themselves conspicuous in the walks of literature, the fields of eloquence, and on the theatre of politics. You will understand that I do not mean to include in these remarks the Secretary of the Navy, (the exception I have mentioned) with whom I have no acquaintance, and with whom, from what cause I am unable to say, the American public seem to be a little dissatisfied.

Mr. Adams has distinguished himself in the paths of literature and politics. The early part of his life seems to have been devoted to the acquisition of general knowledge which has been subsequently augmented by travel observation and reflection. He was once attached to the Party by whom his father was chosen President, but very soon after the Republican administration came into power, he was induced to change his opinions, and to abandon what might have been the prejudices of education, for principles which I have no doubt, he conceived to be more consonant to his feelings, and more consistent with his ideas of liberty and independence. Whatever may be said as to the motive which produced the change, I have no hesitation in thinking it originated entirely from principle, and that his feelings and sentiments were more in harmony and unison with the Party he joined than the one he had forsaken. The conduct he has since pursued has evinced the integrity of his motives, and the sincerity of his attachment to his Party and his country; and the confidence which that country has reposed in him is evidence that she also has been influenced by a similar opinion.

Mr. Adams is in person short, thick, and fat, resembling a little in his face the portrait of his father which you have seen; and neither very agreeable nor very repulsive. He is between forty-five and fifty years of age and seems to be vigorous and healthy. He is regular in his habits, and moral and temperate in his life. To great talent, he unites unceasing industry and perseverance, and an uncommon facility in the execution of business. Though he has read much, and drank "deep of the Pierian Spring," he seems not to solicit the character which literature bestows, and what will seem extraordinary to you, chooses rather to be ranked among men of business than among men of science.

Mr. Adams is extremely plain and simple, both in his manners and habiliments; and labors to avoid alike the foolery and splendor of "fantastic fashion," and the mean and inelegant costume of affected eccentricity. He is evidently well skilled in the rhetorical art on which he has lectured, and in which he displays considerable research and ability; but whether he succeeded in reducing his principles to practice, while a member of the Senate, I am not able to say. I should infer, however, that his speeches were more correct and polished, if they were not more eloquent, than those of his coadjutors in legislation. Yet after all, my Lord, there is something more required to complete an orator than the mere knowledge and practice of those principles which rhetoricians have established as the groundwork of this art. If there be an absence of that peculiar kind of talent, or want of that peculiar enthusiasm, which propels the mind to embrace with ardor and delight the profession of an orator, the most intimate and accurate knowledge, or the most perfect dexterity in the use of the "rhetorician's tools" will be inadequate to produce excellence. And however skillfully a man may round his periods and balance his sentences, select his phrases, or direct their harmony; without that ethereal and incomprehensible power which gives animation to matter, sweeps through nature like the lightning of Heaven, and creates and embodies and unfolds; he will still be cold and tame and spiritless, correct indeed but frigid, regular but insensible. From what I can learn, Mr. Adams, with all his knowledge and talent, did not attain the first rank among American orators. He wanted enthusiasm and fire; he wanted that nameless charm, which in oratory as well as poetry, delights and fascinates, and leads the soul captive, without the desire of resistance, or the consciousness of error.

In the higher grades of eloquence, where the passions are excited and acted on, and the whole mind wrought up to a kind of frenzy by weakening the dominion of reason, Mr. Adams did not excel; but in close argumentation, in logical analysis, in amplification and regular disposition, he is said to have been inferior to none. With great knowledge of art, he was however defective in the *ars celare artem*, an essential ingredient in the composition of an orator. His personal appearance too, which is not very prepossessing or agreeable, must have operated against him and rendered his eloquence less effective and resistless. Notwithstanding these defects, he was considerably above mediocrity, and maintained a character as an orator, inferior to but few in this country.

Mr. Adams's prominent inclination, however, appears to be political. To be eminent as a statesman is his predominant ambition; and I doubt not he will attain this character from the nature of his mind and the tenor of his studies. Much indeed is required to form a statesman. He must have a mind that will enable him, in some degree, to remove the veil of futurity; to compare the present with the past; to yield to the government of reason and be uninfluenced by the attractions of passion. "He must comprehend," says Mirabeau, "all the defects of our social existence, discern the degree of improvement of which we are susceptible, calculate the advantages that result from the possession of liberty, estimate the danger of confusion and tumult, study the art of preparing men for felicity and conduct them towards perfection, by the plainest and most obvious paths. His survey must extend beyond ordinary limits; he must examine climates, deliberate on circumstances, and yield to events without suffering them to master him."

To extensive research and general knowledge, Mr. Adams adds great powers of observation. His residence as Minister at the Courts of St. James and St. Petersburg; has enlarged his stack of facts and rendered his information more correct and practical. He is not one of those statesmen who theorize when experience can afford its aid, and avoids the application of abstract principles, when plainer and more obvious ones are calculated to subserve the object in view. He is sedate, circumspect, and cautious; reserved, but not distant; grave, but not repulsive. He receives, but seldom communicates, and discerns with great quickness, motives however latent, and intentions however concealed by the contortions of cunning, or the drapery of hypocrisy. This penetration seems to be intuitive and natural, and not the result of a mere acquaintance with men, or a long and intimate association with the different classes of society. It is the operation of native judgment and not the exercise of acquired cunning. This excellence is common to the people of the east, but whether it originates from education or from any peculiar organization of the physical powers, I am not sufficiently master of the theory of Helvetius and Godwin to determine. Mr. Adams has more capacity than genius; he can comprehend better than he can invent; and execute nearly as rapidly as he can design.

Though as a public minister, he had no great opportunity to display his powers, yet, from the little he exhibited, a judgment may be formed of his ability in that character. He has all the penetration, shrewdness, and perseverance necessary to constitute an able diplomatist, united with the capacity to perceive, and the eloquence to enforce, what would conduce to the welfare and interests of his country.

Mr. Adams is a good writer. A State paper of his which I have lately seen, is composed with great ability, and though not sufficiently condensed, evinces much skill and dexterity in the art of composition, with which he is evidently well acquainted. In short, my Lord, there is no public character in the United States, that has more intellectual power, the moral inclination to be more useful, or that will labor with greater assiduity to discharge the important duties he owes to himself and to his country.

Auguste Levasseur

Auguste Levasseur (1795-1878) served as private secretary to Gilbert du Mortier, Marquis de Lafayette (1757-1834) during his farewell tour of the United States. Levasseur recounted the historic event in *Lafayette in America in 1824 and 1825*. John D. Godham (1794-1830) rendered an English translation of Levasseur's original work for Carey and Lea of Philadelphia in 1829.

Lafayette was a hero of the American Revolution. Wounded during the Battle of Brandywine, he continued to command American troops and advocated for the American cause in his native France until the British were defeated at Yorktown. During subsequent revolutionary periods in France, Lafayette found himself variously arrested, exiled, or imprisoned until he withdrew from public life in his later years. Approaching seventy, Lafayette embarked upon a farewell tour of the United States. He was given a hero's welcome in every state he visited, but nowhere was his reception as emotionally received as in Washington, D.C.

"The Name of Lafayette"

After resting two days at Baltimore, we set out for Washington City. General Lafayette wished to depart privately, and the citizens, always solicitous to satisfy his desires, contented themselves with calling in the evening employed several hours, and left in our hearts impressions of profound melancholy. We commenced our journey on the 1st of August, accompanied by two members of the Baltimore committee. A few miles from Washington we were met by an elegant carriage, which drew up near us, from which a young gentlemen alighted and inquired for General Lafayette. This was the eldest son of the new President Mr. [John Quincy] Adams, who was sent by his father to the nation's guest, to inform him that he had solicited and obtained from the citizens of the metropolis, permission to offer him the use of the President's House. The general accepted the invitation for himself and travelling companions, entered Mr. Adams's carriage, and we continued on our route. Our two members of the Baltimore committee had not anticipated such an occurrence, which threw them into considerable embarrassment. They had been zealous "Jackson men," and had declared themselves strongly against Mr. Adams during the election; of this Mr. Adams was not ignorant, and on this occasion, it appeared difficult to them to present themselves under the auspices of General Lafayette, without exposing themselves to the chance of being thought willing to make the *amende honorable*. They determined to separate from our party, on entering the city, and took lodgings in a hotel.

During the canvass of the presidential election, I had frequently heard the adversaries of Mr. Adams accuse him of aristocratic habits, contracted, as they said, in the foreign courts at which he had passed many years. This accusation appeared to me much opposed to what I had seen and have related of his conduct in the steamboat going from Frenchtown to Baltimore; but, at length, in consequence of hearing the charge frequently repeated, I began to fear, that, with the exercise of power, he might fall into what we call in Europe the manners of a prince; my surprise was therefore the more agreeable, to find, on reaching Washington, that the President was not changed. It is true, we found Mr. Adams in the place of Mr. Monroe; but the public man was still the same. The plainness of the domestics, and facility of access to the House, appeared not to have undergone the least alteration, and in Mr. Adams's reception of us we experienced all the cordiality of his predecessor. He soon ascertained why our companions had not remained with us, and hastened to send them an invitation to dinner, which they accepted without embarrassment or hesitation, as men who understood the politeness intended them, but who did not consider themselves as being in any way pledged by accepting it.

The lodgings prepared for us in his own house by the President were plain, but commodious and in good taste. Anxious to enable General Lafayette to enjoy the repose he thought him to need after so many and such long voyages, and after numerous and profound emotions, he secluded himself with us in entire privacy. Aided by Mrs. Adams, her two sons, and two nieces, he made us taste, if I may so express myself, the sweets of domestic life. During the early portion of our stay, there rarely set down to table or around the hearth more than two or three persons at once, and usually these were some public officers who, after being occupied all day with the President in business, were detained by him to dinner and the familiar conversation of the evening. It was during this period which glided away so swiftly that I could appreciate the character of Mr. Adams, whom I had previously known only by the eulogies of his friends or the attacks of opponents. I discovered that the first had but done him justice, and the last been misled by party spirit. It is difficult to find a more upright and better cultivated intellect than is possessed by the successor of Mr. Monroe. The beautiful reliefs of the Capitol, to which he is not a stranger; his treatise on weights and measures, and the numerous diplomatic missions he has discharged with distinction, bear witness to his good taste in the arts, the correctness of his scientific judgment, and his skill in politics. As to the accusation of aristocracy, which some have preferred against him, it is sufficiently refuted by his manners, which remain unaltered by his elevation to the chief magistracy of the Republic.

On the 6th of September, the anniversary of Lafayette's birth, the President gave a grand dinner, to which all the public officers, and numerous distinguished persons then in Washington, were invited. The company had already assembled and were about to sit down to table, when the arrival of a deputation from the city of New York was announced, which came to present to General Lafayette, on behalf of the City Council, a book containing an account of all the transactions and events occurring during his stay in that city. This magnificent volume, removed from its case, and exhibited to the company, excited general admiration. It is in fact a masterpiece that may be compared with the most beautiful and rich of those manuscripts which formed the glory and reputation of libraries before the discovery of printing: It contained fifty pages, each ornamented with vignettes designed and painted with the greatest skill; views and portraits perfectly executed, completed this work, of which the writing was done by Mr. Bragg, and the paintings by Messrs. Burton, Inman, and Cummings. The view of the Capitol at Washington, of the City Hall of New York, and the portraits of Washington, Lafayette, and Hamilton, left nothing to be desired; and in order that this beautiful work should be altogether national, it was upon American paper, and bound by Mr. Foster of New York with admirable richness and elegance.

General Lafayette gratefully accepted this fine present, to which the President and his Cabinet gave additional value by placing their signatures in it. Although a large company partook of this dinner, and it was intended to celebrate Lafayette's birthday, it was very serious, I may say, almost sad. We were all too much preoccupied by the approaching journey to be joyous: we already felt, by anticipation, the sorrowfulness of separation. Towards the conclusion of the repast, the President, contrary to diplomatic custom, which forbids toasts at his table, arose and proposed the following: "To the 22nd of February and 6th of September, birthdays of Washington and Lafayette." Profoundly affected to find his name thus associated with Washington, the General expressed his thanks to the President, and gave this toast, "To the Fourth of July, the birthday of liberty in both hemispheres."

At last, the day which we ardently wished for, and whose approach, however, filled us with profound sadness, the day which would begin to convey us towards our country, but must, at the same time, separate us from a nation which had so many claims to our admiration and affection, the day of our departure, the 7th of September, dawned radiantly.

The workshops were deserted, the stores were left unopened, and the people crowded around the President's Mansion, while the militia were drawn up in a line on the road the nation's guest was to move to the shore. The municipality collected about the General to offer him the last homage and regrets of their fellow citizens.

At eleven o'clock he left his apartment, slowly passed through the crowd which silently pressed after him, and entered the principal vestibule of the presidential dwelling, where the President, surrounded by his cabinet, various public officers, and principal citizens, had waited for him a few minutes. He took his place in the center of the circle which was formed on his approach; the doors were open, in order that the people who were assembled without might observe what took place, and the slight murmur of regrets which were heard at first among the crowd, was succeeded by a solemn and profound silence; the President, then visibly agitated by emotion, addressed him as follows, in the name of the American nation and government:

"General Lafayette: It has been the good fortune of many of my distinguished fellow citizens, during the course of the year now elapsed, upon your arrival at their respective places of abode, to greet you with the welcome of the nation. The less pleasing task now devolves upon me, on bidding you, in the name of the nation, adieu.

"It were no longer seasonable, and would be superfluous, to recapitulate the remarkable incidents of your early life, incidents which associated your name, fortunes and reputation, in imperishable connection with the independence and history of the North American Union.

"The part which you performed at that important juncture was marked with characters so peculiar, that, realizing the fairest fable of antiquity, its parallel could scarcely be found in the *authentic* records of human history.

"You deliberately and perseveringly preferred toil, danger, the endurance of every hardship, and the privation of every comfort, in defense of a holy cause, to inglorious ease, and the allurements of rank, affluence, and unrestrained youth, at the most splendid and fascinating court of Europe.

"That this choice was not less wise than magnanimous, the sanction of half a century, and the gratulations of unnumbered voices, all unable to express the gratitude of the heart with which your visit to this hemisphere has been welcomed, afford ample demonstration.

"When the contest of freedom, to which you had repaired as a voluntary champion, had closed, by the complete triumph of her cause in this country of your adoption, you returned to fulfil the duties of the philanthropist and patriot in the land of your nativity. There, in a consistent and undeviating career of forty years, you have maintained, through every vicissitude of alternate success and disappointment, the same glorious cause to which the first years of your active life had been devoted, the improvement of the moral and political condition of man.

"Throughout that long succession of time, the people of the United States, for whom, and with whom you had fought the battles of liberty, have been living in the full possession of its fruits; one of the happiest among the family of nations. Spreading in population; enlarging in territory; acting and suffering according to the condition of their nature; and laying the foundations of the greatest, and, we humbly hope, the most beneficent power that ever regulated the concerns of man upon earth.

"In that lapse of forty years, the generation of men with whom you cooperated in the conflict of arms, has nearly passed away. Of the general officers of the American army in that war, you alone survive. Of the sages who guided our councils; of the warriors who met the foe in the field or upon the wave, with the exception of a few, to whom unusual length of days has been allotted by heaven, all now sleep with their fathers. A succeeding, and even a third generation, have arisen to take their places; and their children's children, while rising up to call them blessed, have been taught by them, as well as admonished by their own constant enjoyment of freedom, to include in every benison upon their fathers, the name of him who came from afar, with them and in their cause to conquer or to fall.

"The universal prevalence of these sentiments was signally manifested by a resolution of Congress, representing the whole people, and all the States of this Union, requesting the President of the United States to communicate to you the assurances of grateful and affectionate attachment of this government and people, and desiring that a national ship might be employed, at your convenience, for your passage to the borders of your country.

"The invitation was transmitted to you by my venerable predecessor; himself bound to you by the strongest ties of personal friendship, himself one of those whom the highest honors of his country had rewarded for blood early shed in her cause, and for a long life of devotion to her welfare. By him the services of a national ship were placed at your disposal. Your delicacy preferred a more private conveyance, and a full year has elapsed since you landed upon our shores. It were scarcely an exaggeration to say that it has been, to the people of the Union, a year of uninterrupted festivity and enjoyment, inspired by your presence. You have traversed the twenty-four states of this great confederacy: You have been received with rapture by the survivors of your earliest companions in arms: You have been hailed as a long absent parent by their children, the men and women of the present age: And a rising generation, the hope of future time, in numbers surpassing the whole population of that day when you fought at the head and by the side of their forefathers, have vied with the scanty remnants of that hour of trial, in acclamations of joy at beholding the face of him whom they feel to be the common benefactor of all. You have heard the mingled voices of the past, the present, and the future age, joining in one universal chorus of delight at your approach; and the shouts of unbidden thousands, which greeted your landing on the soil of freedom, have followed every step of your way, and still resound, like the rushing of many waters, from every corner of our land.

"You are now about to return to the country of your birth, of your ancestors, of your posterity. The Executive Government of the Union, stimulated by the same feeling which had prompted the Congress to the designation of a national ship for your accommodation in coming hither, has destined the first service of a frigate, recently launched at this metropolis, to the less welcome, but equally distinguished trust, of conveying you home. The name of the ship has added one more memorial to distant regions and to future ages, of a stream already memorable, at once in the story of your sufferings and of our independence.

"The ship is now prepared for your reception and equipped for sea. From the moment of her departure, the prayers of millions will ascend to heaven that her passage may be prosperous, and your return to the bosom of your family as propitious to your happiness, as your visit to this scene of your youthful glory has been to that of the American people.

"Go, then, our beloved friend; return to the land of brilliant genius, of generous sentiment, of heroic valor; to that beautiful France, the nursing mother of the twelfth Louis, and the fourth Henry; to the native soil of Bayard and Coligni, of Turenne and Catinat, of Fenelon and d'Aguesseau. In that illustrious catalogue of names which she claims as of her children, and with honest pride holds up to the admiration of other nations, the name of Lafayette has already for centuries been enrolled. And it shall henceforth burnish into brighter fame; for if, in after days, a Frenchman shall be called to indicate the character of his nation by that of one individual, during the age in which we live, the blood of lofty patriotism shall mantle in his cheek, the fire of conscious virtue shall sparkle in his eye, and he shall pronounce the name of Lafayette. Yet we, too, and our children, in life and after death, shall claim you for our own. You are ours by that more than patriotic self-devotion with which you flew to the aid of our fathers at the crisis of their fate. Ours by that long series of years in which you have cherished us in your regard. Ours by that unshaken sentiment of gratitude for your services which is a precious portion of our inheritance. Ours by that tie of love, stronger than death, which has linked your name, for the endless ages of time, with the name of Washington.

"At the painful moment of parting from you, we take comfort in the thought, that wherever you may be, to the last pulsation of your heart, our country will be ever present to your affections; and a cheering consolation assures us, that we are not called to sorrow most of all, that we shall see your face no more. We shall indulge the pleasing anticipation of beholding our friend again. In the meantime, speaking in the name of the whole people of the United States, and at a loss only for language to give utterance to that feeling of attachment with which the heart of the nation beats, as the heart of one man, I bid you a reluctant and affectionate farewell."

An approving murmur drowned the last words of Mr. Adams and proved how deeply the auditors sympathized with the noble sentiments he had expressed in favor of France, and her children whose whole life and recent triumph would add still more to his glory and exaltation. General Lafayette, deeply affected with what he heard, was obliged to pause a few moments before he was able to reply. At last, however, after having made an effort to regain his voice, he thus expressed himself:

"Amidst all my obligations to the general government, and particularly to you, sir, its respected chief magistrate, I have most thankfully to acknowledge the opportunity given me, at this solemn and painful moment, to present the people of the United States with a parting tribute of profound, inexpressible gratitude.

"To have been, in the infant and critical days of these states, adopted by them as a favorite son, to have participated in the toils and perils of our unspotted struggle for independence, freedom and equal rights, and in the foundation of the American era of a new social order, which has already pervaded this, and must, for the dignity and happiness of mankind, successively pervade every part of the other hemisphere, to have received at every stage of the revolution, and during forty years after that period, from the people of the United States, and their representatives at home and abroad, continual marks of their confidence and kindness, has been the pride, the encouragement, the support of a long and eventful life.

"But how could I find words to acknowledge that series of welcomes, those unbounded and universal displays of public affection, which have marked each step, each hour, of a twelve months' progress through the twenty-four states, and which, while they overwhelm my heart with grateful delight, have most satisfactorily evinced the concurrence of the people in the kind testimonies, in the immense favors bestowed on me by the several branches of their representatives, in every part and at the central seat of the confederacy?

"Yet, gratifications still higher await me; in the wonders of creation and improvement that have met my enchanted eye, in the unparalleled and self-felt happiness of the people, in their rapid prosperity and insured security, public and private, in a practice of good order, the appendage of true freedom, and a national good sense, the final arbiter of all difficulties, I have had proudly to recognize a result of the republican principles for which we have fought, and a glorious demonstration to the most timid and prejudiced minds, of the superiority, over degrading aristocracy or despotism, of popular institutions founded on the plain rights of man, and where the local rights of every section are preserved under a constitutional bond of union. The cherishing of that union between the States, as it has been the fare well entreaty of our great paternal Washington, and will ever have the dying prayer of every American patriot, so it has become the sacred pledge of the emancipation of the world, an object in which I am happy to observe that the American people, while they give the animating example of successful free institutions, in return for an evil entailed upon them by Europe, and of which a liberal and enlightened sense is everywhere more and more generally felt, show themselves every day more anxiously interested.

"And now, sir, how can I do justice to my deep and lively feelings for the assurances, most peculiarly valued, of your esteem and friendship, for your so very kind references to old times, to my beloved associates, to the vicissitudes of my life, for your affecting picture of the blessings poured by the several generations of the American people on the remaining days of a delighted veteran, for your affectionate remarks on this sad hour of separation, on the country of my birth, full, I can say, of American sympathies, on the hope so necessary to me of my seeing again the country that has designed, near a half century ago, to call me hers? I shall content myself, refraining from superfluous repetitions, at once, before you, sir, and this respected circle, to proclaim my cordial confirmation of every one of the sentiments which I have had daily opportunities publicly to utter, from the time when your venerable predecessor, my old brother in arms and friend, transmitted to me the honorable invitation of Congress, to this day, when you, my dear sir, whose friendly connection with me dates from your earliest youth, are going to consign me to the protection, across the Atlantic, of the heroic national flag, on board the splendid ship, the name of which has been not the least flattering and kind among the numberless favors conferred upon me.

"God bless you, sir, and all who surround us. God bless the American people, each of their States, and the Federal Government. Accept this patriotic farewell of an overflowing heart; such will be its last throb when it ceases to beat."

In pronouncing these last words, General Lafayette felt his emotion to be rapidly increasing, and threw himself into the arms of the President, who mingled his tears with those of the national guest, in repeating those heartrending words, Adieu! Adieu! The spectators, overcome by the same feelings, also shed tears and surrounded their friend, once more to take him by the hand. To abridge this scene, which could not be suffered much longer, the General retired for a short time into his own apartment, where Mrs. Adams, surrounded by her daughters and nieces came to express their wishes and regrets. On the evening before, this lady, whose cultivated mind and amenity of character had greatly contributed to the pleasure of our visit to the President's House, had presented him with a fine bust of her husband, and had added to this present a copy of verses in French, whose charm and elegance proved that this was not the first occasion in which her muse had spoken in our language.

Detained as if by a magic spell, General Lafayette could not make up his mind to leave his friends; a thousand pretexts seemed to retard the definitive moment of separation, but at last the first of the twenty-four guns, which announced his departure, having been heard, he again threw himself into Mr. Adams's arms, expressed to him his last good wishes for the American nation, and retired to his carriage. The President repeated the signal of adieu from the top of the steps, and at this sign the colors of the troops which were drawn up before the President's House were bowed to the earth.

Captain Basil Hall

Captain Basil Hall (1788-1844) joined the Royal Navy at thirteen years of age. He was promoted to Lieutenant at nineteen and made Captain before he turned thirty, by which time he had seen the world. His early work entitled *Extracts from a Journal Written on the Coasts of Chili, Peru, and Mexico* proved successful and was published in several editions. Shortly thereafter he left the navy, married, and went on to enjoy a prolific writing career.

Hall's *Travels in North America*, published in three volumes, went through as many editions, and proved quite popular at home. However, the work was resoundingly criticized in some circles in the United States, owing to the author's stark depiction of slavery in America.

"Do You Mean to Buy the Lad, Sir?"

Although the debates in the National Legislature formed the chief object of interest at Washington, many other incidental matters arose, from time to time, to vary the picture. The following advertisement caught my eye, in one of the newspapers:

Marshal's Sale. By authority of a writ of fieri facias, issued from the Clerk's Office of the Circuit Court, in this District, for the County of Washington, to me directed, I shall expose to sale, for cash, on Tuesday, the 15th instant, Negro George, a slave for life, and about sixteen years old. Seized and taken in execution of, as the goods and chattels of Zachariah Hazle, and will be sold to satisfy a debt due by him to William Smith. Sale to be at the County Courthouse Door, and to commence at 12 o'clock, M.

Tench Ringgold,
Marshal District of Columbia.
Jan 10 — dts

I had often, in the course of my life, in the British West India possessions, and elsewhere, seen slavery in full operation; but as I had never happened to be actually present at the sale of a negro, I resolved to witness it for once, and in a place where, at first sight, such an incident might least of all have been looked for.

I repaired to the County Courthouse, accordingly, at noon, on the 15th of January 1827, and having found my way along an empty passage, I reached a door, from which people were departing and others entering, like bees crowding in and out of a hive. This was the Court of Justice. But the matters under discussion were either so completely technical, or my head was so full of the black boy, that I could not follow what was going on.

I came again into the passage, and walked along to the front door, which nearly faces the Capitol, distant about one-third of a mile. The flags were just hoisted on the top of the building, which intimate that the Senate and the House of Representatives had assembled to discuss the affairs of this free nation, slavery amongst the rest.

The only man I could see in the passage, was a great heavy-looking black fellow, who appeared so much downcast and miserable, that I settled within myself that this must needs be no other than Negro George, placed there for inspection. But the Deputy Marshal, who entered at this moment, holding in one hand the advertisement copied above, and in the other the writ of fieri facias alluded to therein, undeceived me, by saying that the man I pointed to was a slave indeed, though not for sale, but that I should see the other immediately.

It was soon buzzed about, I suspect, amongst the purchasers, that a suspicious-looking stranger was making enquiries respecting the boy; for a tall man, wrapped in a cloak, whom I had observed for some time cutting large junks of tobacco from a lump which he drew from his waistcoat pocket, and thrusting them into his mouth, evidently in a fidget, now came up to me, and said, with an air of affected carelessness, "Do you mean to buy the lad, sir?"

"I? Oh, no!" I exclaimed.

The tall man drew a satisfied breath on hearing this, and said, in a more natural tone, "I am glad of it, sir, for I do, and am very anxious to succeed, because I know the chap well, and have become interested in him, and he himself . . . ah!, there he stands . . . wishes to become my property."

"How is that?"

"Why," said he, "you must know that his owner was indebted to me fifty dollars, and would not or could not pay me, so I had a lien upon this boy, and the Court allowed me to have him latterly, pending the litigations. There have been three or four lawsuits about him, and he has been knocking about from hand to hand ever since March 1822, five years, and he is now to be sold to satisfy this debt."

"What says the boy to all this?" I asked.

"Come here, George," he called, and the lad joined us. "Don't be scared, my boy," said the gentleman, "there is no one going to hurt you."

"Oh, I am not scared," answered the boy, though he trembled all the while. He looked very ill at ease, I thought, and I soon found out the cause, in his apprehension of being purchased by a person of whom, I suppose, he had some previous knowledge, and whose looks certainly were as little inviting as anything could well be. He was a short, lean man, with a face deeply wrinkled, not so much with age or care, as with the deep seams of intemperance. His two little eyes were placed so far back in his head, that you could not see them in profile, and when viewed in front through a pair of enormous spectacles sparkled in a very ominous manner; while his straight, scanty, and disordered hair, formed an appropriate skyline to the picture. I began to take considerable interest in the little fellow's fate, and whispered to my tall companion, that I hoped he would get the boy.

After various delays, the slave was put up to auction, at the end of the passage, near which four or five persons had by this time collected. There was a good deal of laughing and talking amongst the buyers, and several jests were sported on the occasion, of which their little victim took no more notice, than if he had been a horse or a dog. In fact, he was not a chubby shining little negro, with a flat nose, thick lips, and woolly hair, but a slender, delicate-looking youth, more yellow than black, with an expression every way suitable, I thought, with the forlorn situation in which he was placed, for both his parents, and all his brothers and sisters, he told me, had been long ago sold into slavery, and sent to the Southern States, Florida or Alabama, he knew not where!

"Well, gentlemen," cried the Deputy Marshal, "will you give us a bid? Look at him, as smart a fellow as ever you saw, works like a tiger!"

One of the spectators called out, "Come, I'll say 25 dollars;" another said 35, another said 40, and at last 100 dollars were bid for him.

From the spot where I was standing, in the corner, behind the rest of the party, I could see all that was passing. I felt my pulse accelerating at each successive offer, and my cheek getting flushed, for the scene was so very new that I almost fancied I was dreaming.

The interest, after a time, took a different character, to which, however, I by no means wished to give utterance, or in any shape to betray; but at this moment, the Deputy Marshal, finding the price to hang at 100 dollars, looked over to me, and said, "Do give us a bid, sir, won't you?"

My indignation was just beginning to boil over at this juncture, and I cried out, in answer to this appeal, with more asperity than good sense or good breeding, "No! no! I thank God we don't do such things in my country!"

"And I wish, with all my heart," said the auctioneer, in a tone that made me sorry for having spoken so hastily, "I wish we did not do such things here."

"Amen!" said several voices.

The sale went on.

"We can't help it, however," observed the Marshal; "we must do our duty. 100 dollars are bid, gentlemen! One hundred dollars!"

The ominous personage with the deep-set eyes now called out, to my horror, and that of the poor boy, "120!"

Just at this moment a farmer, who had come from the country, and seemed pleased with the looks of the youth, nodded to the auctioneer, and said, "130."

My tall friend now said, "140," which was echoed by the newcomer with, "142!"

Upon which these two bidders, having exchanged looks, walked apart for a couple of minutes, whispering something which I did not hear. I observed the farmer nod several times, as if assenting to some compromise. They now returned, and the tall gentleman said, "I will give 143 dollars for him," while the other, though more than once appealed to by the auctioneer, spoke no more.

"143 dollars are bid for this lad! One hundred and forty-three dollars. Once! Twice! Are you all done, gentlemen? Thrice! The lad is yours, sir, a slave for life!"

I patted the boy on the head, wished his new master, my tall friend, all joy of his bargain, and ran off as fast as I could down one of the avenues, hoping, by change of place, to get rid of the entanglement of many unpleasant thoughts which crowded upon me during the sale; and perhaps willing, by a good scamper over the ground, to satisfy myself of the identity of my own freedom.

I asked a gentleman afterwards whether such things were common in that part of the country. Instead of answering my question, he picked up a newspaper at random, and pointed out the following advertisement:

Marshal's Sale. By authority of a writ of fieri facias, issued from the Clerk's Office of the Circuit Court of this District, for the County of Washington, to me directed, I shall expose to public sale, for cash, on

Monday, 31st instant, the following slaves, viz.: Charity, Fanny, Sandy, Jerry, Nace, Harry, Jem, Bill, Anne, Lucy; Nancy and her five children, George, Penn, Mary, Francis, and Henry; Flora and her seven children, Robert, Joseph, Fanny, Mary, Jane, Patty, and Betsy; Harry; and also four mules, four carts, one carriage and harness. Seized and taken in execution, as the goods and chattels of John Threlkeld, and will be sold to satisfy a debt due by him to the Bank of the United States, use of the United States, and the Bank of the United States. Sale to be at the dwelling of Alexander Burrows, and commence at 11 o'clock a. m.

Tench Ringgold,
Marshal of the District of Columbia.
Dec 24 — dts

I should be doing the inhabitants of the District of Columbia great injustice, and also leave a needless degree of pain on the minds of others, were I not to mention the sincere desire which is felt, and perhaps, as far as possible, acted upon, in that quarter, to remedy, if not altogether to remove, an evil apparently so inconsistent with the principles applied to everything else in America.

James Fenimore Cooper

In 1824, the novelist James Fenimore Cooper (1789-1851) was among those New Yorkers who welcomed Lafayette as he embarked upon his farewell tour of the United States. When Cooper spent several years in Europe and lived as an American in Paris, Lafayette returned the courtesy. Cooper's *Notions of the Americans* was written, according to some sources, in response to a suggestion from Lafayette. Furnish Europeans with a more positive outlook on the United States; more positive, say, than some British observers had offered to date. In his *Notions*, authored by "a Travelling Bachelor" and dedicated to his alterego "John Cadwallader, of Cadwallader, in the State of New York," Cooper composed a series of letters written to a private club of imaginary gentlemen from different European countries. In this excerpt of a letter addressed to Count Jules de Béthizy, Cooper describes what an evening or *drawing-room* at the White House *might* have been like during the recent administration of President James Monroe.

"The Manners of the Country"

We reached the White House at nine. The court (or rather the grounds) was filled with carriages, and the company was arriving in great numbers. On this occasion two or three additional drawing-rooms were opened, though the frugality of Congress has prevented them from finishing the principal reception-room of the building.

The people furnish the entire house. It is the practice to make a moderate appropriation for that purpose, at the accession of each new President.

I will acknowledge the same sort of surprise that I felt at the Castle Garden féte, at finding the assemblage so respectable, in air, dress, and deportment. Determined to know exactly in what view to consider this ceremony, I gave my companion no peace until everything was explained.

The "evening" at the White House, or the drawing-room, as it is sometimes pleasantly called, is in fact a collection of all classes of people who choose to go to the trouble and expense of appearing in dresses suited to an ordinary evening party. I am not sure that even dress is much regarded; for I certainly saw a good many men there in boots. The females were all neatly and properly attired, though few were ornamented with jewelry. Of course, the poorer and laboring classes of the community would find little or no pleasure in such a scene. They consequently stay away. The infamous, if known, would not be admitted: for it is a peculiar consequence of the high tone of morals in this country, that grave and notorious offenders rarely presume to violate the public feeling by invading society. Perhaps if Washington were a large town, the "evenings" could not exist; but as it is, no inconvenience is experienced.

Squeezing through the crowd, we achieved a passage to a part of the room where Mrs. Monroe was standing, surrounded by a bevy of female friends. After making our bows here, we sought the President. The latter had posted himself at the top of the room, where he remained most of the evening, shaking hands with all who approached.

It is a mistaken opinion, however, that shaking hands is a custom not to be dispensed with in America. Most people practice it certainly, for it is thought to be a frank, manly, and, if you will, a republican usage. But in a certain class, it is not considered a mark of breeding to be too free with the hand, in casual introductions. Two gentlemen meeting would be apt to touch their hats (unless intimates) just as in Europe, though either of them would offer his hand to anyone who he thought expected it. When a European, therefore, offers to shake hands with an American of breeding, unless on familiar terms, he mistakes the manners of the country. The natural feeling of gentlemanly reserve is the guide there, as it is with us.

Near him stood all the Secretaries, and a great number of the most distinguished men of the nation. Cadwallader pointed out the different judges, and several Members of both Houses of Congress, whose reputations were quite familiar to me. Individuals of importance from all parts of the Union were also here and were employed in the manner usual to such scenes. Thus far the "evening" would have been like any other excessively crowded assembly; but while my eyes were roving over the different faces, they accidentally fell on one they knew. It was the master of an inn, in one of the larger towns. My friend and myself had passed a fortnight in his house. I pointed him out to Cadwallader, and I am afraid there was something like a European sneer in my manner as I did so.

"Yes, I have just shaken hands with him," returned my friend, coolly. "He keeps an excellent tavern, you must allow; and what is more, had not that circumstance been the means of your making his acquaintance, you might have mistaken him for one of the magnates of the land. I understand your look, *Count de* . . . , better than you understand the subject at which you are smiling. Fancy, for a moment, that this assembly were confined to a hundred or two, like those eminent men you see collected in that corner, and to these beautiful and remarkably delicate women you see standing near us; in what, except name, would it be inferior to the best collections of your side of the ocean? You need not apologize, for we understand one another perfectly. I know Europe rather better than you know America, for the simple reason, that one part of Europe is so much like another, that it is by no means an abstruse study, So far as mere manners are concerned; whereas, in America, there exists a state of things that is entirely new. We will make the comparison, not in the way you are at this moment employed in doing, but in the way common sense dictates."

"It is very true that you meet here a great variety of people of very many conditions of life. This person you see on my left is a shopkeeper from New York: no, not the one in black, but the genteel-looking man in blue. I dare say you took him for an attaché of one of the legations. And this lovely creature, who demeans herself with so much elegance and propriety, is the daughter of a mechanic of Baltimore. In this manner we might dissect half the company, perhaps; some being of better, and some of worse, exteriors. But what does it all prove? Not that the President of the United States is obliged to throw open his doors to the rabble, as you might be tempted to call it, for he is under no sort of obligation to open his doors to anybody. But he chooses to see the world, and he must do one of two things. He must make invidious and difficult selections, which, in a public man, would excite just remarks in a government like ours, or he must run the hazard of remaining three or four hours in a room filled with a promiscuous assembly. He has wisely chosen the latter."

"What is the consequence? Your ears are not offended by improper discourse. Your individuality is not wounded by impertinence, nor even your taste annoyed by any very striking coarseness of manner. Now it appears to me, that every American should exult in this very exhibition. Not for the vulgar reason that it is proof of the equality of our rights, for it is a mistake to think that society is a necessary dependent of government. In this respect the 'evenings' are some such deception as that ceremony one hears of in Europe, in which sovereigns wash the feet of beggars. But he should exult that the house of his first magistrate can be thrown open to the world, and an assembly so well-behaved, so decent, so reasonable, so free alike from sheepishness and presumption, in short so completely creditable, in every point of view, is collected by the liberty. Open the doors of one of your palaces in this manner and let us see what would be the character of the company."

"There is a good sense in our community, which removes all dangers of unpleasant consequences from too much familiarity. It imposes the necessity on him who would be thought a gentleman, of being circumspect and reasonable, but it leaves him sufficiently the master of all his movements and associations. The seeming scarcity of high-bred men in this country, compared with the number one sees in Europe, is much less owing to our form of government, than the fact that they are so widely scattered. Quite half, too, of what is called fastidious breeding, is purely conventional, and, to make conventions, men must meet."

"I have known a cartman leave his horse in the street and go into a reception-room to shake hands with the President. He offended the good sense of all present, because it was not thought decent that a laborer should come in a dirty dress on such an occasion; but while he made a trifling mistake in this particular, he proved how well he understood the difference between government and society. He knew the levee was a sort of homage paid to political equality in the person of the First Magistrate, but he would not have presumed to enter the house of the same person as a private individual without being invited, or without a reasonable excuse in the way of business."

"There are, no doubt, individuals who mistake the character of these assemblies, but the great majority do not. They are simply a periodical acknowledgment that there is no legal barrier to the advancement of anyone to the first association in the Union. You perceive there are no masters of ceremonies, no ushers, no announcing, nor indeed any let or hindrance to the ingress of all who please to come; and yet how few, in comparison to the whole number who might enter, do actually appear. If there is any man, in Washington, so dull as to suppose equality means a right to thrust himself into any company he pleases, it is probable he satisfies his vanity by boasting that he can go to the White House once a fortnight as well as a governor or anybody else. You will confess his pride is appeased at a cheap rate. Any prince can collect a well-dressed and well-behaved crowd by calling his nobles around him; but I fancy the President of the United States is the only head of a nation who need feel no apprehension of throwing open his doors to everybody. Until you can show an assembly composed of similar materials, which shall equal this, not only in decency but in ease and in general manners, you ought in reason to be content to confess your inferiority."

You will perceive the utter impossibility of having an opinion of your own, dear Jules, when a man is obstinately bent on considering things always in reference to common sense, instead of consulting the reverend usages which have been established by the world, whether founded on prejudice or not. So far as mere appearance goes, 1 must confess, however, my friend was not very wrong, since the company at the White House, on this occasion, was certainly as well-behaved, all things considered, as could be wished.

Benjamin Perley Poore

Benjamin Perley Poore (1820-1887) was a 19th century newspaperman whose career coincided with the rise in government printing and publishing in the Nation's Capital. His memoir, *Perley's Reminiscences,* provides eyewitness accounts of many significant events in the history of Washington, D.C. Journalists today remember him as one of the founders of the Gridiron Club, the city's oldest private organization dedicated to the profession. In this excerpt from his *Reminiscences,* "Perley" recounts scenes from the first inauguration of the 7th President of the United States, Andrew Jackson.

"A Noisy Mob"

The weather on the 4th of March 1829 was serene and mild, and at an early hour Pennsylvania Avenue, then unpaved, with a double row of poplar trees along its center, was filled with crowds of people, many of whom had journeyed immense distances on foot. The officials at Washington, who were friends of Mr. Adams, had agreed not to participate in the inaugural ceremonies, and the only uniformed company of light infantry, commanded by Colonel Seaton, of the *National Intelligencer*, had declined to offer its services as an escort. A number of old Revolutionary officers, however, had hastily organized themselves, and waited on General Jackson to solicit the honor of forming his escort to the Capitol, an offer which was cordially accepted. The General rode in an open carriage which had been placed at his disposal and was surrounded by these gallant veterans. The assembled thousands cheered lustily as their favorite passed along, every face radiant with defiant joy, and every voice shouting "Hurrah for Jackson!"

After the installation of John C. Calhoun as Vice-President in the Senate Chamber, the assembled dignitaries moved in procession through the rotunda to the east front of the Capitol. As the tall figure of the President-elect came out upon the portico and ascended the platform, uplifted hats and handkerchiefs waved a welcome, and shouts of "Hurrah for Jackson!" rent the air. Looking around for a moment into ten thousand upturned and exultant human faces, the President-elect removed his hat, took the manuscript of his address from his pocket, and read it with great dignity. When he had finished, Chief Justice Marshall administered the oath, and as the President, bending over the sacred Book, touched it with his lips, there arose such a shout as was never before heard in Washington, followed by the thunder of cannons, from two light batteries nearby, echoed by the cannon at the Navy Yard and at the Arsenal. The crowd surged toward the platform, and had it not been that a ship's cable had been stretched across the portico steps would have captured their beloved leader. As it was, he shook hands with hundreds, and it was with some difficulty that he could be escorted back to his carriage and along Pennsylvania Avenue to the White House. Meanwhile Mr. Adams, who had refused to participate in the pageant, was taking his usual constitutional horseback exercise when the thunder of the cannon reached his ears and notified him that he was again a private citizen.

The broad sidewalks of Pennsylvania Avenue were again packed as the procession returned from the Capitol. "I never saw such a crowd," wrote Daniel Webster to a friend. "Persons have come five hundred miles to see General Jackson, and they really seem to think that the country is rescued from some dreadful danger." Hunters of Kentucky and Indian fighters of Tennessee, with sturdy frontiersmen from the Northwest, were mingled in the throng with the more cultured dwellers on the Atlantic slope.

On their arrival at the White House, the motley crowd clamored for refreshments and soon drained the barrels of punch, which had been prepared, in drinking to the health of the new Chief Magistrate. A great deal of china and glassware was broken, and the East Room was filled with a noisy mob. At one time General Jackson, who had retreated until he stood with his back against the wall, was protected by a number of his friends, who formed a living barrier about him. Such a scene had never before been witnessed at the White House, and the aristocratic old Federalists saw, to their disgust, men whose boots were covered with the red mud of the unpaved streets standing on the damask satin-covered chairs to get a sight at the President of their choice.

Late in the afternoon President Jackson sat down to dinner with Vice-President Calhoun and a party of his personal friends, the central dish on the table being a sirloin from a prize ox, sent to him by John Merkle, a butcher of Franklin Market, New York. Before retiring that night, the President wrote to the donor: "Permit me, sir, to assure you of the gratification which I felt in being enabled to place on my table so fine a specimen from your market, and to offer you my sincere thanks for so acceptable a token of your regard for my character."

This was naturally the commencement of a series of presents which poured in on President Jackson during the eight years of his administration. So palpable a bid for other tokens of regard for the President's character could hardly fail to evoke responses. From the days of Solomon, it has been true that "a man's gift maketh room for him," and though many of Jackson's gift-senders failed to find the room made, yet it was true nevertheless that room was seldom made where the gifts were not forthcoming, so come the gifts did in abundance.

The Democratic journalists from all parts of the country were also well represented at the inauguration, attracted, doubtless, by this luring, semi-official declaration in the *Telegraph*: "We know not what line of policy General Jackson will adopt. We take it for granted, however, that he will reward his friends and punish his enemies."

Thomas Hamilton

Scottish author and traveler Thomas Hamilton (1789-1842) visited the United States in 1830 and toured several of its major cities, including Boston, New York, Philadelphia, and Washington, D.C. During his visit to the Nation's Capital, Hamilton observed the administration of justice by the Supreme Court of the United States. In this excerpt from Hamilton's *Men and Manners in America*, the author reflects upon the Court's chambers, its jurisdiction, its power to enforce judicial decisions, and the demeanor of its justices.

"A Wise Institution"

In the basement story of one of the wings of the Capitol is the hall of the Supreme Court of the United States. It is by no means a large or handsome apartment; and the lowness of the ceiling, and the circumstance of its being underground, give it a certain cellar-like aspect, which is not pleasant. This is perhaps unfortunate, because it tends to create in the spectator the impression of justice being done in a corner; and, that while the business of legislation is carried on with all the pride, pomp, and circumstance of glorious debate, in halls adorned with all the skill of the architect, the administration of men's rights is considered an affair of secondary importance.

Though the American law courts are no longer contaminated by wigs, yet the partiality for robes would appear not yet to be wholly extinct. The judges of the Supreme Court wear black Geneva gowns; and the proceedings of this tribunal are conducted with a degree of propriety, both judicial and forensic, which leaves nothing to be desired. I certainly witnessed none of those violations of public decency, which in the State Courts are matters of ordinary occurrence. There was no lounging either at the bar or on the bench; nor was it, apparently, considered necessary to sink the gentleman in the lawyer, and assume a deportment in the discharge of professional duty which would not be tolerated in private society.

The Supreme Court consists of seven judges, removable only by impeachment, and possesses Federal jurisdiction over the whole Union. It sits annually in Washington for about two months and is alone competent to decide on questions connected with the Constitution or laws of the United States. Though possessing original jurisdiction in a few cases, its chief duties consist in the exercise of an appellate jurisdiction from the Circuit Courts, which are held twice a year in the different States.

It would be tedious to enumerate the various cases in which the Federal Courts, in their three gradations of Supreme, Circuit, and District, exercise an exclusive or concurrent jurisdiction. It is enough that it should be generally understood that the Supreme Court is the sole expounder of the written Constitution; and when we consider how open this important instrument has been proved to diversity of interpretation, what opposite meanings have been put upon its simplest clauses, and, in short, that the Constitution is precisely whatever four judges of this court may choose to make it, it will be seen how vitally important is the power with which it has been entrusted, and how difficult must be its exercise.

But the difficulties of the Supreme Court do not end here. Its jurisdiction extends not over a homogeneous population, but a variety of distinct communities, born under different laws, and adopting different forms in their administration.

Causes before the State Courts, in which the laws of the United States are even collaterally involved, are removable by writ of error to the Supreme Federal Court, and the decision of the State Court may be affirmed or reversed. In the latter case, a mandate is issued directing the

State Court to conform its judgment to that of the Supreme Court. But the State tribunal is at perfect liberty to disregard the mandate, should it think proper; for the principle is established, that no one court can command another, but in virtue of an authority resting on express stipulation, and it is the duty of each judicature to decide how far this authority has been constitutionally exercised.

Then the legislatures of different States have found it occasionally convenient to pass laws for the purpose of defrauding their foreign creditors, while, in the case of Great Britain at least, the Federal Government is bound by express treaty that no lawful impediment shall be interposed to the recovery of the debts due by American citizens to British subjects. Under such circumstances, the Federal Court, backed by the whole honest portion of the people, certainly succeeded in putting a stop to the organized system of State swindling adopted by Kentucky after the late war; but awkward circumstances occurred, and the question may yet be considered practically undecided, whether the State legislatures possess a controlling power over the execution of a judgment of the Supreme Court.

Should a case occur, as is far from improbable, in which the Federal Legislature and Judiciary are at variance, it would, no doubt, be the duty of the latter to declare every unconstitutional act of the former null and void. But under any circumstances, the Court has no power to enforce its decrees. For instance, let us take the Indian question, and suppose, that in defiance of treaties, Georgia should persist in declaring the Creek and Cherokee Indians subject to the State laws, in order to force them to migrate beyond the Mississippi. The Indians appeal to the Supreme Court, and demand protection from unprincipled violence. The Court recognizes their rights, and issues its mandate, which is just so much wastepaper, unless the Government chooses to send a military force along with it, which neither the present Congress nor Executive would be inclined to do.

With all its sources of weakness, however, the United States Court is a wise institution. It is truly the sheet-anchor of the Union; and the degree of respect in which its decrees are held, may be considered as an exact index of the moral strength of the compact by which the discordant elements of the Federal Commonwealth are held together.

The most distinguished lawyers of the Union practice in the Supreme Court, and I had there an opportunity of hearing many of the more eminent Members of Congress. During my stay there was no jury trial, and the proceedings of the Court consisted chiefly in delivering judgments, and in listening to legal arguments from the bar. The tone of the speeches was certainly very different from anything I had heard in Congress. The lawyers seemed to keep their declamation for the House of Representatives, and in the Supreme Court spoke clearly, logically, and to the point. Indeed, I was more than once astonished to hear men whose speeches in Congress were rambling and desultory, in an extreme degree, display, in their forensic addresses, great legal acuteness, and resources of argument and illustration of the first order. In addressing the bench, they seemed to cast the slough of their vicious peculiarities, and spoke, not like schoolboys contending for a prize, but like men of high intellectual powers, solicitous not to dazzle but to convince.

District of Columbia

In 1830, the Washington-based publisher Jonathan Elliot (also styled *Elliott*) brought out one of the most useful references to the city that had been published to date. Elliot's *Historical Sketches of the Ten Miles Square Forming the District of Columbia* offered up a veritable smorgasbord of facts and figures about the Nation's Capital, including details of its founding, its near destruction during the War of 1812, information on public buildings, and a digest of the city's "Corporation Laws," i.e. Washington, D.C. laws that were currently on the books. The following excerpts from Elliot's *Ten Miles Square* summarize the city's "Black Codes" of the period.

"Thirty-Nine Lashes"

Negroes, Mulattoes, &c. All free negroes or mulattoes must have their names registered within ten days from the time of their coming to live within the limits of the corporation: males above 16 and females above 14 years. The city registrar who registers the same, is required to furnish a permit to the head of each family, or to every single person, if not married, for which he is to charge 25 cents. Those neglecting to obtain such certificate to be fined six dollars, or to be imprisoned for each neglect for a time not exceeding ten days.

Slaves, or free blacks or mulattoes, must not assemble in the street, or any in other place in a tumultuous manner: for each offense, slaves not to receive more than twenty lashes, and free blacks or mulattoes to be fined in a sum not more than twenty dollars, or in case of inability to pay, to be imprisoned for a time not exceeding ninety days.

No slave, nor free black or mulatto, can play at any game or chance, under a penalty of ten dollars for each offense: in case of inability to pay, imprisonment 30 days; or if a slave, to receive fifteen lashes on the bare back.

All vagrants, &c. who in any way disturb the public peace, to be apprehended, and made to give security for good behavior for one year, or be subject to a fine of twenty dollars, or imprisonment for a time not exceeding ninety days. Public prostitutes are subject to fine or imprisonment.

Any free black or mulatto allowing of a dance at his or her house, without first obtaining the license from a justice of the peace, or the Mayor, to be fined twenty dollars; or in case of inability or refusal to pay, to be imprisoned for a time exceeding ninety days; or if a slave, to receive ten lashes.

Any slave, or free black or mulatto found at large in the streets, after ten o'clock at night, from the first of April to the 1st of October; or after 9 o'clock from the 1st of October to the 1st of April, shall be apprehended, unless such slaves have a pass, or if a free colored person, a pass from a justice of the peace. A slave so offending to receive thirty-nine lashes; and a free black fined in a sum not exceeding twenty dollars; or on refusal to pay, imprisonment for ninety days. The master of slaves to pay the fines or require the slave to be whipped; in case of whipping, fifty cents to be paid by the owner to the constable.

Any person entertaining a slave after 10 o'clock at night shall be fined five dollars, except the slave shall have been sent on business.

When any colored persons are apprehended, on any of the above charges, they are to be confined in the lock-up house of each ward. Constables neglecting their duty in executing this law to be fined five dollars.

Penalty on non-residents for hiring, (tax unpaid), twenty dollars; penalty on resident, twenty dollars, and five dollars per month after; slaves to be recorded within twenty days.

Francis Trollope

When Frances Milton Trollope (1779-1863) first set sail for America in November 1827, her family was in difficult financial circumstances, and she was in search of a solution. Over the course of her three-year visit, Mrs. Trollope dabbled in various speculations, but returned to England with even greater challenges ahead. Now in the throes of middle age but determined to resolve her difficulties and care for her children, she took to writing. Her first work, *Domestic Manners of the Americans*, proved highly successful in England and launched her prolific and successful writing career.

Mrs. Trollope's *Domestic Manners of the Americans* often painted an unflattering portrait of the United States and Mrs. Trollope was criticized for her well-sharpened quill. Nevertheless, it remains one of the most familiar social commentaries on 19th century America.

"One Hand Hoisting the Cap of Liberty"

By far the shortest route to Washington, both as to distance and time, is by land; but I much wished to see the celebrated Chesapeake Bay, and it was therefore decided that we should take our passage in the steamboat. It is indeed a beautiful little voyage, and well worth the time it costs; but as to the beauty of the Bay, it must, I think, be felt only by sailors. It is, I doubt not, a fine shelter for ships, from the storms of the Atlantic, but its very vastness prevents it striking the eye as beautiful: it is, in fact, only a fine sea view. But the entrance from it into the Potomac River is very noble and is one of the points at which one feels conscious of the gigantic proportions of the country, without having recourse to a graduated pencil case.

The passage up this river to Washington is interesting, from many objects that it passes, but beyond all else, by the view it affords of Mount Vernon, the seat of General Washington. It is there that this truly great man passed the last years of his virtuous life, and it is there that he lies buried: it was easy to distinguish, as we passed, the cypress that waves over his grave.

The latter part of the voyage shows some fine river scenery; but I did not discover this till some months afterwards, for we now arrived late at night.

Our first object the next morning was to get a sight of the Capitol, and our impatience sent us forth before breakfast. The mists of morning still hung around this magnificent building when first it broke upon our view, and I am not sure that the effect produced was not the greater for this circumstance. At all events, we were struck with admiration and surprise. None of us, I believe, expected to see so imposing a structure on that side of the Atlantic. I am ill at describing buildings. but the beauty and majesty of the American Capitol might defy an abler pen than mine to do it justice. It stands so finely too, high, and alone.

The magnificent western facade is approached from the city by terraces and steps of bolder proportions than I ever before saw. The elegant eastern front, to which many persons give the preference, is on a level with a newly planted but exceedingly handsome enclosure, which, in a few years, will offer the shade of all the most splendid trees which flourish in the Union, to cool the brows and refresh the spirits of the Members. The view from the Capitol commands the city and many miles around, and it is itself an object of imposing beauty to the whole country adjoining.

We were again fortunate enough to find a very agreeable family to board with; and soon after breakfast left our comfortless hotel near the water, for very pleasant apartments in F Street.

I was delighted with the whole aspect of Washington; light, cheerful, and airy, it reminded me of our fashionable watering-places. It has been laughed at by foreigners, and even by natives, because the original Plan of the city was upon an enormous scale, and but a very small part of it has been as yet executed. But I confess I see nothing in the least degree ridiculous about it; the original design, which was as beautiful as it was extensive, has been in no way departed from, and all that has been done has been done well. From the base of the hill on which the Capitol stands extends a street of most magnificent width, planted on each side with trees, and ornamented by many splendid shops. This street, which is called Pennsylvania Avenue, is above a mile in length, and at the end of it is the handsome mansion of the President; conveniently near to his residence are the various public offices, all handsome, simple, and commodious; ample areas are left round each, where grass and shrubs refresh the eye. In another of the principal streets is the General Post Office, and not far from it a very noble Town Hall. Towards the quarter of the President's House are several handsome dwellings, which are chiefly occupied by the foreign ministers. The houses in the other parts of the city are scattered, but without ever losing sight of the regularity of the original Plan; and to a person who has been travelling much through the country, and marked the immense quantity of new manufactories, new canals, new railroads, new towns, and new cities, which are springing, as it were, from the earth in every part of it, the appearance of the metropolis rising gradually into life and splendor is a spectacle of high historic interest. Commerce had already produced large and handsome cities in America before she had attained to an individual political existence, and Washington may be scorned as a metropolis, where such cities as Philadelphia and New York exist; but I considered it as the growing metropolis of the growing population of the Union, and it already possesses features noble enough to sustain its dignity as such.

The residence of the foreign legations and their families gives a tone to the society of this city which distinguishes it greatly from all others. It is also, for a great part of the year, the residence of the Senators and

Representatives, who must be presumed to be the elite of the entire body of citizens, both in respect to talent and education. This cannot fail to make Washington a more agreeable abode than any other city in the Union. The total absence of all sights, sounds, or smells of commerce adds greatly to the charm. Instead of drays you see handsome carriages; and instead of the busy bustling hustle of men, shuffling on to a sale of "dry goods" or "prime broad stuffs," you see very well-dressed personages lounging leisurely up and down Pennsylvania Avenue.

Mr. Pishey Thompson, the English bookseller, with his pretty collection of all sorts of pretty literature, fresh from London, and Mr. Somebody, the jeweler, with his brilliant shop full of trinkets, are the principal points of attraction and business. What a contrast to all other American cities! The Members, who pass several months every year in this lounging easy way, with no labor but a little talking, and with the *douceur* of eight dollars a day to pay them for it, must feel the change sadly when their term of public service is over.

There is another circumstance which renders the evening parties at Washington extremely unlike those of other places in the Union; this is the great majority of gentlemen. The expense, the trouble, or the necessity of a ruling eye at home, one or all of these reasons, prevents the Members' ladies from accompanying them to Washington; at least, I heard of very few who had their wives with them. The female society is chiefly to be found among the families of the foreign ministers, those of the Officers of State, and of the few Members, the wealthiest and most aristocratic of the land, who bring their families with them. Some few independent persons reside in or near the city, but this is a class so thinly scattered that they can hardly be accounted a part of the population.

But, strange to say, even here a theatre cannot be supported for more than a few weeks at a time. I was told that gambling is the favorite recreation of the gentlemen, and that it is carried to a very considerable extent; but here, as elsewhere within the country, it is kept extremely well out of sight. I do not think I was present with a pack of cards a dozen times during more than three years that I remained in the country. Billiards are much played, though in most places the amusement is illegal. It often appeared to me that the old women of a state made the laws, and the young men broke them.

Notwithstanding the diminutive size of the city, we found much to see, and to amuse us. The Patent Office is a curious record of the fertility of the mind of man when left to its own resources; but it gives ample proof also that it is not under such circumstances it is most usefully employed. This Patent Office contains models of all the mechanical inventions that have been produced in the Union, and the number is enormous. I asked the man who showed these, what proportion of them had been brought into use. He said about one in a thousand. He told me also, that they chiefly proceeded from mechanics and agriculturists settled in remote parts of the country, who had begun by endeavoring to hit upon some contrivance to enable them to get along without sending some thousand and odd miles for the thing they wanted. If the contrivance succeeded, they generally became so fond of this offspring of their ingenuity that they brought it to Washington for a patent.

At the Secretary of State's office, we were shown autographs of all the potentates with whom the Union were in alliance; which, I believe, pretty well includes all. To the parchments bearing these royal signs manually were appended, of course, the Official Seals of each, enclosed in gold or silver boxes of handsome workmanship. I was amused by the manner in which one of their own, just prepared for the Court of Russia, was displayed to us, and the superiority of their decorations pointed out. They were superior, and in much better taste than the rest; and I only wish that the feeling that induced this display would spread to every corner of the Union and mix itself with every act and with every sentiment. Let America give a fair portion of her attention to the arts and the graces that embellish life, and I will make her another visit, and write another book as unlike this as possible.

Among the royal signatures, the only ones which much interested me were two from the hand of Napoleon. The earliest of these, when he was First Consul, was a most illegible scrawl, and, as the tradition went, was written on horseback; but his writing improved greatly after he became an Emperor, the subsequent signature being firmly and clearly written. I longed to steal both.

The purity of the American character, formed and founded on the purity of the American government, was made evident to our senses by the display of all the offerings of esteem and regard which had been presented by various sovereigns to the different American Ministers who had been sent to their courts. The object of the law which exacted this deposit from every individual so honored, was, they told us, to prevent the possibility of bribery being used to corrupt any envoy of the Republic. I should think it would be a better way to select for the office such men as they felt could not be seduced by a sword or a snuffbox. But they, doubtless, know their own business best.

The Bureau for Indian Affairs contains a room of great interest: the walls are entirely covered with original portraits of all the Chiefs who, from time to time, have come to negotiate with their Great Father, as they call the President. These portraits are by Mr. King, and, it cannot be doubted, are excellent likenesses, as are all the portraits I have ever seen from the hands of that gentleman. The countenances are full of expression, but the expression in most of them is extremely similar; or rather, I should say that they have but two sorts of expression; the one is that of very noble and warlike daring, the other of a gentle and naive simplicity, that has no mixture of folly in it, but which is inexpressibly engaging, and the more touching, perhaps, because at the moment we were looking at them, those very hearts which lent the eyes such meek and friendly softness, were wrung by a base, cruel, and most oppressive act of their Great Father.

We were at Washington at the time that the measure for chasing the last of several tribes of Indians from their forest homes was canvassed in Congress, and finally decided upon by the fiat of the President. If the American character may be judged by their conduct in this matter, they are most lamentably deficient in every feeling of honor and integrity. It is among themselves, and from themselves, that I have heard the statements which represent them as treacherous and false almost beyond belief in their intercourse with the unhappy Indians. Had I, during my residence in the United States, observed any single feature in their national character that could justify their eternal boast of liberality and the love of freedom, I might have respected them, however much my taste might have been offended by what was peculiar in their manners and customs. But it is impossible for any mind of common honesty not to be revolted by the contradictions in their principles and practice. They inveigh against the governments of Europe, because, as they say, they favor the powerful and oppress the weak. You may hear this declaimed upon in Congress, roared out in taverns, discussed in every drawing room, satirized upon the stage, nay, even anathematized from the pulpit: listen to it, and then look at them at home; you will see them with one hand hoisting the cap of liberty, and with the other flogging their slaves. You will see them one hour lecturing their mob on the indefeasible rights of man, and the next driving from their homes the children of the soil, whom they have bound themselves to protect by the most solemn treaties.

In justice to those who approve not this treacherous policy, I will quote a paragraph from a New York paper, which shows that there are some among them who look with detestation on the bold bad measure decided upon at Washington in the year 1830.

"We know of no subject, at the present moment, of more importance to the character of our country for justice and integrity than that which relates to the Indian tribes in Georgia and Alabama, and particularly the Cherokees in the former state. The Act passed by Congress, just at the end of the session, cooperating with the tyrannical and iniquitous statute of Georgia, strikes a formidable blow at the reputation of the United States, in respect to their faith, pledged in almost innumerable instances, in the most solemn treaties and compacts."

There were many objects of much interest shown us at this Indian Bureau; but, from the peculiar circumstances of this most unhappy and ill-used people, it was a very painful interest.

The dresses worn by the Chiefs when their portraits were taken are many of them splendid, from the embroidery of beads and other ornaments; and the room contains many specimens of their ingenuity, and even of their taste. There is a glass case in the room, wherein are arranged specimens of worked muslin, and other needlework, some very excellent handwriting, and many other little productions of male and female Indians, all proving clearly that they are perfectly capable of civilization. Indeed, the circumstance which renders their expulsion from their own, their native lands, so peculiarly lamentable, is that they were yielding rapidly to the force of example; their lives were no longer those of wandering hunters, but they were becoming agriculturists, and the tyrannical arm of brutal power has not now driven them, as formerly, only from their hunting grounds, their favorite springs, and the sacred bones of their fathers, but it has chased them from the dwellings their advancing knowledge had taught them to make comfortable; from the newly-ploughed fields of their pride; and from the crops their sweat had watered. And for what? To add some thousand acres of territory to the half-peopled wilderness which borders them.

The Potomac, on arriving at Washington, makes a beautiful sweep, which forms a sort of bay, round which the city is built. Just where it makes the turn, a wooden bridge is thrown across, connecting the shores of Maryland and Virginia. This bridge is a mile and a quarter in length and is ugly enough. The Navy Yard, and Arsenal, are just above it, on the Maryland side, and make a handsome appearance on the edge of the river, following the sweep above mentioned. Near the Arsenal (much too near) is the penitentiary, which, as it was just finished, and not inhabited, we examined in every part. It is built for the purpose of solitary confinement for life. A gallows is a much less nerve-shaking spectacle than one of these awful cells, and assuredly, when imprisonment therein for life is substituted for death, it is no mercy to the criminal; but if it be a greater terror to the citizen, it may answer the purpose better. I do not conceive, that out of a hundred human beings who had been thus confined for a year, one would be found at the end of it who would continue to linger on there, *certain it was forever*, if the alternative of being hanged were offered to them. I had written a description of these horrible cells, but Captain Hall's picture of a similar building is so accurate, and so clear, that it is needless to insert it.

Still following the sweep of the river, at the distance of two miles from Washington, is Georgetown, formerly a place of considerable commercial importance, and likely, I think, to become so again, when the Ohio and Chesapeake Canals, which there mouths into the Potomac, shall be in full action. It is a very pretty town, commanding a lovely view, of which the noble Potomac and the almost nobler Capitol are the great features. The country rises into a beautiful line of hills behind Washington, which form a sort of undulating terrace on to Georgetown; this terrace is almost entirely occupied by a succession of gentlemen's seats. At Georgetown the Potomac suddenly contracts itself, and begins to assume that rapid, rocky, and irregular character which marks it afterwards, and renders its course, till it meets the Shenandoah at Harper's Ferry, a series of the most wild and romantic views that are to be found in America.

Attending the debates in Congress was, of course, one of our great objects; and, as an English woman, I was perhaps the more eager to avail myself of the privilege allowed. It was repeatedly observed to me that, at least in this instance, I must acknowledge the superior gallantry of the Americans, and that they herein give a decided proof of surpassing the English in a wish to honor the ladies, as they have a gallery in the House of Representatives erected expressly for them, while in England they are rigorously excluded from every part of the House of Commons.

But the inference I draw from this is precisely the reverse of that suggested. It is well known that the reason why the House of Commons was closed against ladies was, that their presence was found too attractive, and that so many Members were tempted to neglect the business before the House, that they might enjoy the pleasure of conversing with the fair critics in the galleries, that it became a matter of national importance to banish them, and they were banished. It will be long ere the American legislature will find it necessary to pass the same law for the same reason. A lady of Washington, however, told me an anecdote which went far to show that a more intellectual turn in the women, would produce a change in the manners of the men. She told me that when the Miss Wrights were in Washington with General Lafayette, they very frequently attended the debates, and that the most distinguished Members were always crowding round them. For this unwonted gallantry they apologized to their beautiful countrywomen by saying, that if they took equal interest in the debates, the galleries would be always thronged by the Members.

The privilege of attending these debates would be more valuable could the speakers be better heard from the gallery; but, with the most earnest attention, I could only follow one or two of the orators, whose voices were peculiarly loud and clear. This made it really a labor to listen; but the extreme beauty of the chamber was of itself a reason for going again and again. It was, however, really mortifying to see this splendid hall, fitted up in so stately and sumptuous a manner, filled with men sitting in the most unseemly attitudes, a large majority with their hats on, and nearly all spitting to an excess that decency forbids me to describe.

Among the crowd, who must be included in this description, a few were distinguished by not wearing their hats, and by sitting on their chairs like other human beings, without throwing their legs above their heads. Whenever I enquired the name of one of these exceptions, I was told that it was Mr. This, or Mr. That, *of Virginia.*

One day we were fortunate enough to get placed on the sofas between the pillars, on the floor of the House; the galleries being shut up, for the purpose of making some alterations, which it was hoped might improve the hearing in that part of the House occupied by the Members, and which is universally complained of, as being very defective. But in our places on the sofas we found we heard very much better than upstairs, and well enough to be extremely amused by the rude eloquence of a thorough horse and alligator orator from Kentucky, who entreated the House repeatedly to "go the whole hog."

If I mistake not, every debate I listened to in the American Congress was upon one and the same subject, namely, the entire independence of each individual State, with regard to the Federal Government. The jealousy on this point appeared to me to be the very strangest political feeling that ever got possession of the mind of man. I do not pretend to judge the merits of this question. I speak solely of the very singular effect of seeing man after man start eagerly to his feet, to declare that the greatest injury, the basest injustice, the most obnoxious tyranny that could be practiced against the State of which he was a Member, would be a vote of a few million dollars for the purpose of making their roads or canals; or for drainage; or, in short, for any purpose of improvement whatsoever.

During the month we were at Washington, I heard a great deal of conversation respecting a recent exclusion from Congress of a gentleman, who, by every account, was one of the most esteemed men in the House, and, I think, the father of it. The crime for which this gentleman was outvoted by his own particular friends and admirers was that he had given his vote for a grant of public money for the purpose of draining a most lamentable and unhealthy district, called *"the Dismal Swamp."*

One great boast of the country is that they have no national debt, or that they shall have none in two years. This seems not very wonderful, considering their productive tariff, and that the income paid to their President is £6,000 *per annum*; other government salaries being in proportion, and all internal improvements, at the expense of the government treasury, being voted unconstitutional.

The Senate Chamber is, like the Hall of Congress, a semicircle, but of very much smaller dimensions. It is most elegantly fitted up, and what is better still, the Senators, generally speaking, look like gentlemen. They do not wear their hats, and the activity of youth being happily past, they do not toss their heels above their heads. I would I could add they do not spit; but, alas! "I have an oath in heaven," and may not write an untruth.

A very handsome room, opening on a noble stone balcony is fitted up as a library for the Members. The collection, as far as a very cursory view could enable me to judge, was very like that of a private English gentleman, but with less Latin, Greek, and Italian. This room also is elegantly furnished; rich Brussels carpet; library tables, with portfolios of engravings; abundance of sofas, and so on. The view from it is glorious, and it looks like the abode of luxury and taste.

I can by no means attempt to describe all the apartments of this immense building, but the magnificent rotunda in the center must not be left unnoticed. It is, indeed, a noble hall, a hundred feet in diameter, and of an imposing loftiness, lighted by an ample dome.

Almost any pictures (excepting the cartoons) would look paltry in this room, from the immense height of the walls; but the subjects of the four pictures which are placed there are of such high historic interest that they should certainly have a place somewhere, as national records. One represents the signing of the Declaration of Independence; another, the resignation of the presidency by the great Washington; another the celebrated victory of General Gates at Saratoga; and the fourth . . . I do not well remember, but I think it is some other martial scene, commemorating a victory; I rather think that of Yorktown.

One other object in the Capitol must be mentioned, though it occurs in so obscure a part of the building, that one or two Members to whom I mentioned it, were not aware of its existence. The lower part of the edifice, a story below the rotunda, &c., has a variety of committee rooms, courts, and other places of business. In a hall leading to some of these rooms, the ceiling is supported by pillars, the capitals of which struck me as peculiarly beautiful. They are composed of the ears and leaves of the Indian corn, beautifully arranged, and forming as graceful an outline as the acanthus itself. This was the only instance I saw, in which America has ventured to attempt national originality; the success is perfect. A sense of fitness always enhances the effect of beauty. I will not attempt a long essay on the subject, but if America, in her vastness, her immense natural resources, and her remote grandeur, would be less imitative, she would be infinitely more picturesque and interesting.

The President has regular evening parties, every other Wednesday, which are called his levees; the last syllable is pronounced by everyone as long as possible, being exactly the reverse of the French and English manner of pronouncing the same word. The effect of this, from the very frequent repetition of the word in all companies, is very droll, and for a long time I thought people were quizzing these public days. The reception rooms are handsome, particularly the grand saloon, which is elegantly, nay, splendidly furnished; this has been done since the visit of Captain Hall, whose remarks upon the former state of this room may have hastened its decoration; but there are a few anomalies in some parts of the entertainment, which are not very courtly. The company are about as select as that of an Easter Day ball at the Mansion House.

The churches at Washington are not superb; but the Episcopalian and Catholic were filled with elegantly dressed women. I observed a greater proportion of gentlemen at church at Washington than anywhere else.

The Presbyterian ladies go to church three times in the day, but the general appearance of Washington on a Sunday is much less puritanical than that of most other American towns; the people walk about, and there are no chains in the streets, as at Philadelphia, to prevent their riding or driving, if they like it.

The ladies dress well, but not so splendidly as at Baltimore. I remarked that it was not very unusual at Washington for a lady to take the arm of a gentleman, who was neither her husband, her father, nor her brother. This remarkable relaxation of American decorum has been probably introduced by the foreign legations.

At about a mile from the town, on the high terrace ground above described, is a very pretty place, to which the proprietor has given the name of Kalorama. It is not large, or in any way magnificent, but the view from it is charming; and it has a little wood behind, covering about two hundred acres of broken ground, that slopes down to a dark cold little river, so closely shut in by rocks and evergreens, that it might serve as a noonday bath for Diana and her nymphs. The whole of this wood is filled with wildflowers, but such as we cherish fondly in our gardens.

A ferry at Georgetown crosses the Potomac, and about two miles from it, on the Virginian side, is Arlington, the seat of Mr. Custis, who is the grandson of General Washington's wife. It is a noble looking place, having a portico of stately white columns, which, as the mansion stands high, with a background of dark woods, forms a beautiful object in the landscape. At Georgetown is a nunnery, where many young ladies are educated, and at a little distance from it, a college of Jesuits for the education of young men, where, as their advertisements state, "the humanities are taught."

We attended mass at the chapel of the nunnery, where the female voices that performed the chant were very pleasing. The shadowy form of the veiled abbess in her little sacred parlor, seen through a grating and a black curtain, but rendered clearly visible by the light of a Gothic window behind her, drew a good deal of our attention; every act of genuflection, even the telling her beads, was discernible, but so mistily that it gave her, indeed, the appearance of a being who had already quitted this life, and was hovering on the confines of the world of shadows.

The convent has a considerable enclosure attached to it, where I frequently saw from the heights above it, dark figures in awfully thick black veils, walking solemnly up and down.

The American lady, who was the subject of one of Prince Hohenlohe's celebrated miracles, was pointed out to us at Washington. All the world declare that her recovery was marvelous.

There appeared to be a great many foreigners at Washington, particularly French. In Paris I have often observed that it was a sort of fashion to speak of America as a new Utopia, especially among the young liberals, who, before the happy accession of Philip, fancied that a country without a king was the land of promise; but I sometimes thought that, like many other fine things, it lost part of its brilliance when examined too nearly....

The theatre was not open while we were in Washington, but we afterwards took advantage of our vicinity to the city, to visit it. The house is very small, and most astonishingly dirty and void of decoration, considering that it is the only place of public amusement that the city affords. I have before mentioned the want of decorum at the Cincinnati theatre, but certainly that of the capital at least rivalled it in the freedom of action and attitude; a freedom which seems to disdain the restraints of civilized manners. One man in the pit was seized with a violent fit of vomiting, which appeared not in the least to annoy or surprise his neighbors; and the happy coincidence of a physician being at that moment personated on the stage, was hailed by many of the audience as an excellent joke, of which the actor took advantage, and elicited shouts of applause by saying, "I expect my services are wanted elsewhere."

The spitting was incessant; and not one in ten of the male part of the illustrious legislative audience sat according to the usual custom of human beings; the legs were thrown sometimes over the front of the box, sometimes over the side of it; here and there a Senator stretched his entire length along a bench, and in many instances the front rail was preferred as a seat.

I remarked one young man, whose handsome person, and most elaborate toilet, led me to conclude he was a first-rate personage and so I doubt not he was. Nevertheless, I saw him take from the pocket of his silk waistcoat a lump of tobacco, and daintily deposit it within his cheek.

I am inclined to think this most vile and universal habit of chewing tobacco is the cause of a remarkable peculiarity in the male physiognomy of Americans; their lips are almost uniformly thin and compressed. At first I accounted for this upon Lavater's theory, and attributed it to the arid temperament of the people; but it is too universal to be so explained; whereas the habit above mentioned, which pervades all classes (excepting the literary) well accounts for it, as the act of expressing the juices of this loathsome herb, enforces exactly that position of the lips, which gives this remarkable peculiarity to the American countenance.

A Member of Congress died while we were at Washington, and I was surprised by the ceremony and dignity of his funeral. It seems that whenever a Senator or Member of Congress dies during the session, he is buried at the expense of the government, (this ceremony not coming under the head of internal improvement), and the arrangements for the funeral are not interfered with by his friends but become matters of State. I transcribed the order of the procession as being rather grand and stately.

>Chaplains of both Houses.
>Physicians who attended the deceased.
>Committee of arrangement.
>THE BODY,
>(Pall borne by six Members.)
>The Relations of the deceased,
>with the Senators and Representatives
>of the State to which he belonged, as Mourners.
>Sergeant at Arms of the House of Representatives.
>The House of Representatives,
>Their Speaker and Clerk preceding.
>The Senate of the United States.
>The Vice-President and Secretary preceding,
>The President.

The procession was of considerable extent, but not on foot, and the majority of the carriages were hired for the occasion. The body was interred in an open "graveyard" near the city. I did not see the monument erected on this occasion, but I presume it was in the same style as several others I had remarked in the same burying ground, inscribed to the memory of Members who had died at Washington. These were square blocks of masonry without any pretension to splendor.

Tyrone Power

The life of Irish actor Tyrone Power (1797-1841) was cut short when he and all other passengers and crew were lost at sea aboard the *SS President*, then bound from New York to Liverpool, in March 1841. Power was a successful actor and comedian in his native Ireland. While he often portrayed Irish characters in productions with Irish themes, Power avoided playing typical stock characters based on his countrymen, characters he considered clichéd. Like many 19th century actors, Power toured the United States in hopes of establishing himself among audiences there, a goal he was well on his way to accomplishing when he boarded the *SS President* on its fateful voyage. In his *Impressions of America*, Tyrone Power reflects upon his experiences in the theatre and among society in Washington, D.C.

"Stray Men Turned Loose"

Theatre, Washington

I made my *début* professionally in the capital upon the 12th of February [1834]. The theatre here was a most miserable-looking place, the worst I met with in the country, ill-situated, and difficult of access; but it was filled nightly by a very delightful audience; and nothing could be more pleasant than to witness the perfect *abandon* with which the gravest of the Senate laughed over the diplomacy of the "Irish Ambassador." They found allusions and adopted sayings applicable to a crisis when party feelings were carried to extremity. The elaborate display of eloquence with which Sir Patrick seeks to *bother* the Spanish envoy was quoted as the very model of a speech for a non-committal orator, and recommended for the study of several gentlemen who were considered as aiming at this convenient position, very much to their amusement.

The pieces were ill-mounted, and the company unworthy the capital, with the exception of two very pretty and very clever native actresses, Mesdames Willis and Chapman. The latter I had the satisfaction of seeing soon after transferred to New York, in which city she became a monstrous favorite, both in tragedy and comedy: a very great triumph for Mrs. Chapman, for she succeeded Miss [Fanny] Kemble in some of her best parts, and an excellent comic actress, a Mrs. Sharpe, acting on the same night Julia in "The Hunchback," and the Queen of Hearts in "High, Low, Jack, and Game," with a cleverness which rarely accompanies such versatility.

I have much pleasure in offering this just tribute to a very amiable person, who has, since my departure from the States, quitted the stage, on which, had she been fortunately situated, she would have had very few superiors.

I wonder there are not many more native actresses, since I am sure there is a great deal of latent talent in society here both for opera and the drama. The girls, too, are generally well educated; are pretty, have much expression, a naturally easy carriage, and great imitative powers. The latter talent is singularly common amongst them; and I have met, not one, but many young women, who would imitate the peculiarities of any actress or actor just then before the public with an accuracy and humor quite remarkable.

I acted here seven nights on this occasion, and visited the city again in May, when I passed three or four weeks most agreeably. I had the pleasure, too, during this last visit, of seeing the plans for a theatre worthy the audience, and which, I trust, has by this time been happily erected, as the greatest part of the fund needed was readily subscribed for; and the attempt can hardly fail amongst a people so decidedly theatrical, and who are, besides, really in absolute want of public amusements for the number of stray men turned loose here during the session, many of whom are without other home than the bar-room of an inn, or better means of keeping off *ennui* than gin-sling or the gaming-table.

Impressions of Washington Society, Public and Private

I attended several large assemblies at Washington, and must here, after a second visit, and so much experience as my opportunities afforded, enter my protest against the sweeping ridicule it has pleased some writers to cast upon these doings here; since I saw none of those outrageously unpresentable women, or coarsely habited and ungainly men, so amusingly arrayed by some of my more observant predecessors. I can only account for it by referring to the rapid changes ever taking place here, and to which I have alluded in my introduction to these "Impressions."

The ordinary observances of good society are, I should say, fully understood and fully practiced at these public gatherings, and not more of the ridiculous presented than might be observed at any similar assemblage in England, if half so much; since here I have commonly found that persons who have no other claims to advance save money or a seat in the legislature, very wisely avoid *reunions*, where they could neither look to receive nor bestow pleasure.

It is quite true that many of these members, all of whom are by rank eligible to society, maybe met with, who are more rusty of bearing than most of those within St. Stephen's; but I will answer for this latter assembly outfacing them in samples of rudeness, ill-breeding, and true vulgarity: for it is a striking characteristic of the American, that, if not conventionally polished perhaps, you will rarely find him either rude or discourteous; whilst amongst those who, in the nature of the government, are elevated from a comparatively obscure condition to place and power, although refinement cannot be inserted as an addendum to the official diploma, the aspirant usually adopts with his appointment a quiet formal strain of ceremony, which protects himself, and can never give offence to any.

In the absence of that ease and self-possession which can only be acquired by long habitual intercourse with well-bred persons, this surely is the wisest course that could be adopted, and a hundred degrees above that fidgety, jackdaw-like assumption of *nonchalance* with which the ill-bred amongst ourselves seek to cover their innate vulgarity.

At all these assemblies, as elsewhere, great real attention is paid to women; and I vow I have, in this respect, seen more ill-breeding, and selfish rudeness, at a fashionable rout in England, than could be met with, at any decent crush, from Natchitoches to Marblehead. Beyond these points within the States I speak not, since without them the land is strange to me.

No levee of the President's has occurred during my sojourn here; but I learn that in the true spirit of democracy, the doors on these occasions are open to every citizen without distinction of rank or costume; consequently, the assemblage at such times may be oddly compounded enough.

As for private society in Washington, although limited, it can in no place be conducted in a manner more agreeable or extended to the stranger with more unostentatious freedom. Once presented to a family, and the house is thenceforward open to you. From twelve o'clock until two, the inmates either visit or receive visitors: between these hours, the question, "Are the ladies at home?" being answered in the affirmative, you walk into the drawing-room without farther form; and, joining the circle, or enjoying a *tête-à-tête*, as it may happen, remain just so long as you receive or can impart amusement.

Again, after six, if you are so disposed, you sally forth to visit. If the family you seek beat home, you find its members forming a little group or groups, according to the number present, each after their age and inclination; and politics, dress, or scandal are discussed: or, if the night be serene; and what lovely nights have I witnessed here, even at this early season! (May). You make a little party to the covered stoup, or balcony, extended along the back-front of most houses; and here a song, a romp, a waltz, or a quiet still talk, while away hours of life, unheeded until passed, but never to be recalled without pleasure. About eleven the guests generally depart, and by midnight the great avenue of this city is hardly disturbed by a footfall; not a sound comes on the ear except the short, fierce wrangle of packs of vagrant curs crossing each other's hunting-ground, which they are as tenacious of as the Indians are of their prairies.

At this hour I used often, after returning from a party, such as is described above, to put on my morning-gown and slippers, and light my pipe, then sallying forth, have strolled from Fuller's to the Capitol; and climbing its bold hill, have looked down along the sleeping city, speculating upon its possible destinies until my fancies waxed threadbare, and then quietly returned, making a distance of nearly three miles, without encountering an individual or hearing the sound of a human voice.

At set balls even, the first hour of morning generally sees ample space on the till then crowded floor; and the most ardent pleasure-lovers rarely overleap the second by many minutes.

The consequence of this excellent plan is that, although the ladies are weak in numbers, they are always, to use an expressive sporting phrase, ready to come again; rising, the morning after a dance, unwearied and elastic in mind and body. I hope, for the sake of my American friends, it will be very long before these healthful hours are changed to those which custom has made fashionable in England; hours that soon fade the roses even on their most genial soil, the cheeks of the fair girls of Britain, blighting the healthful and the young, and withering the aged and the weak.

Much of the population of Washington is migratory; and, during a long session, samples may be found here of all classes, from every part of the Union, whether represented or not. There are, however, generally resident a few old Southern families, who, together with the foreign ministers and their suites, form the nucleus of a permanent society, where the polish of Europe is grafted upon the simple and frank courtesy of the best of America. Were it not in violation of a rule I have imposed upon myself as imperative, I could name families here whose simple yet refined manners would do honor to any community, and from an intercourse with whom the most fastidious conventionalist would return satisfied.

Theodore Dwight, Jr.

Connecticut native Theodore Dwight, Jr. (1796-1866) studied at Yale, where his uncle Timothy Dwight was President, and subsequently traveled in Europe before settling in New York, where began his career as a schoolmaster. Dwight's father Theodore Sr. was founder of the New York *Daily Advertiser* where the younger Dwight learned the newspaper trade. He would go on to edit his own publication, *Dwight's American Magazine*, write a history of Connecticut, and author several travel books. In his *Things as They Are,* Dwight shared his recollections of Washington, D.C.

"Such Things are Salutary"

I never visit Washington without being reminded of the miscalculations which were made by some of our wisest men, in relation to the growth of the city in population and importance. The magnificence of the Plan is evident to every eye, and so is the total want of power to complete it. Broad avenues, named after the states, stretch indeed from the center towards various points; but some of them are impassable, and others lead to nothing worth seeing. Unlike the great roads which met in the Roman forum in the days of Roman greatness, they are more like some of them at the present day, which conduct only to a deserted and sterile region in the vicinity. Still there is one gratification to be derived from the public disappointment in relation to the growth of the Federal City: the intrigues of a court are more exposed to view than they could be in a large metropolis; and the shades of a great population are not extended over them for their concealment. In European capitals, public men are much less exposed to public scrutiny; and great facilities are enjoyed for all sorts of intrigues. Besides, everything connected with the grandeur and brilliancy of power loses much of its importance in Washington, because so much of the interior of things is exposed to view. In this city visitors and inhabitants are alike impressed with what they see. Every year presents many new faces in the Houses of Congress, where new interests are maintained with the same ardor as before. When you call on a friend, you are perhaps introduced into the same chamber you were in the last winter, with the same two beds in the corners, the same display of gilt-edged paper, and sealing-wax upon the table, and the same symptoms around you of public business and partisan spirit, while you reflect that the former occupant of the room and of one of the beds, restored again to private life, is five hundred or a thousand miles off, divested of his feathers, and a fortunate man if not the worse for his campaign at the seat of government.

In the streets of Washington, no warning seems omitted from which a spectator might learn patriotism, and a statesman honesty. The stage-horses wheel as gracefully to receive the unsuccessful applicant for office as to bring the court favorite to his lodgings; and the minister's furniture shines as bright at the auctioneer's door on the day of his taking leave as it did on the evening of his first drawing room. Oh, the silent lessons I have read at the auctioneer's on ambition and her reward, the boasted purity of a popular government, the value and splendor of real virtue, and the contemptible character of her counterfeits! Indeed, so severe are some of the sarcasms thus practically presented, that I was once ready to exclaim against the punishment inflicted on a late favorite of fortune, then newly sunk in disgrace, as greater than he could bear.

The carpets on which his flatterers had stood, with smiles and compliments for him, were now cheapened on account of the dust of courtiers' feet, and the peculiar obsequiousness with which the surface had been scraped at audiences and levees. But, ah! The bowls and dishes, the cups, and glasses out of which so many simpering mouths had been so lately fed, and now scarcely dry from the unavailing banquets; what emblems were they of the hollowness and brittleness of the station they had recently embellished! The minion had before possessed my secret contempt and abhorrence; but I could now have saved him the pangs of such a show. And yet such things are salutary. If they are able to affect others as they affected me, a walk through Pennsylvania Avenue might cure the most ambitious and corrupt of statesmen and courtiers.

Some of the inhabitants of Washington have had intelligence and observation enough to afford much interesting information in relation to public men and national affairs. What we receive through the newspapers, or other channels little more correct, passes under their own eyes. And indeed, perhaps, no part of the country is left so much alone to form unbiased opinions. While speeches are made in Congress, written out, amended, and published by thousands to influence some county, state, or number of states, nobody tries to discolor things to the Washingtonians, knowing that it would be in vain. Everything is therefore left to be seen by them without disguise; and the consequence is, they often form correct opinions, and speak with becoming frankness. It is gratifying also to reflect that local interests and influences are not likely to engross and control the attention of the government in so great a degree as they have often done in large cities; and there is no mob to overawe or even to threaten their freedom.

To an American who has seen any of the capitals of Europe, the absence of military display is one of the most agreeable features in view, wherever he turns. There is not a soldier to guard gates or doors in Washington, with the single exception of those at the Navy Yard, a mile or more from the Capitol. The total want of every sign of military preparation is also very accordant with one's feelings. After the last war with England, a felon imprisoned for some crime confessed, as I recollect, that during his career of iniquity he had entered into a conspiracy to seize President Madison and deliver him to the British ships then lying in the Potomac, while he was a sentinel to guard the President's House. As there was not even a wall of sufficient height to prevent an approach to the doors, and no other obstacle, such a plan might have been easily accomplished, I suppose, under favorable circumstances, by mere surprise. Though danger was thus in one instance incurred by the neglect to take military precautions, how much better it is than to have the display of paid soldiers at every turn, and to become familiar with the music and the weapons of death! From some acquaintance with the feelings and habits of foreigners, I can say with great confidence, that probably a large proportion of the intelligent men of Europe would learn with surprise that there is not a soldier on guard in the capital of the United States, even during the sessions of Congress, although the familiar fact excites not a thought in our minds.

Harriet Martineau

By the time she visited the United States in 1835, Harriet Martineau (1802-1876) was already an established and successful author in her native England, writing on social issues including political economy, poor laws, and taxation. A two-year tour of the U.S. produced the popular but controversial *Society in America*, which was criticized there for its portrayals of slavery and for her observations on the "political nonexistence of women." Martineau's *Retrospect of Western Travel* appeared shortly thereafter and was conceived as a more popular work, yet it draws on the same experiences as *Society in America*. It was written, as Martineau states in her Preface, to offer to an English audience "what the Americans do not want; a picture of the aspect of the country, and of its men and manners." While she often succeeded in this regard, Ms. Martineau also appreciated the character of honorable men when she encountered them.

"The Great American Lawyer"

Our pleasantest evenings were some spent at home in a society of the highest order. Ladies, literary, fashionable, or domestic, would spend an hour with us on their way from a dinner to a ball. Members of Congress would repose themselves by our fireside. Mr. Clay, sitting upright on the sofa, with his snuffbox ever in his hand, would discourse for many an hour in his even, soft, deliberate tone, on any one of the great subjects of American policy which we might happen to start, always amazing us with the moderation of estimate and speech which so impetuous a nature has been able to attain. Mr. Webster, leaning back at his ease, telling stories, cracking jokes, shaking the sola with burst after burst of laughter, or smoothly discoursing to the perfect felicity of the logical part of one's constitution, would illuminate an evening now and then. Mr. Calhoun, the cast-iron man, who looks as if he had never been born and never could be extinguished, would come in sometimes to keep our understandings upon a painful stretch for a short while, and leave us to take to pieces his close, rapid, theoretical, illustrated talk, and see what we could make of it. We found it usually more worth retaining as a curiosity than as either very just or useful. His speech abounds in figures, truly illustrative, if that which they illustrate were but true also. But his theories of government (almost the only subject on which his thoughts are employed), the squarest and compactest that ever were made, are composed out of limited elements, and are not therefore likely to stand service very well. It is at first extremely interesting to hear Mr. Calhoun talk; and there is a never-failing evidence of power in all he says and does which commands intellectual reverence; but the admiration is too soon turned into regret, into absolute melancholy. It is impossible to resist the conviction that all this force can be at best but useless and is but too likely to be very mischievous. His mind has long lost all power of communicating with any other. I know of no man who lives in such utter intellectual solitude. He meets men and harangues the fireside as in the Senate; he is wrought like a piece of machinery, set a going vehemently by a weight, and stops while you answer. He either passes by what you say or twists it into a suitability with what is in his head and begins to lecture again. Of course, a mind like this can have little influence in the Senate, except by virtue, perpetually wearing out of what it did in its less eccentric days; but its influence at home is to be dreaded. There is no hope that an intellect so cast in narrow theories will accommodate itself to varying circumstances; and there is every danger that it will break up all that it can, in order to remold the materials in its own way. Mr. Calhoun is as full as ever of his nullification doctrines; and those who know the force that is in him, and his utter incapacity of modification by other minds (after having gone through as remarkable a revolution of political opinion as perhaps any man ever experienced), will no more expect repose and self-retention from him than from a volcano in full force. Relaxation is no longer in the power of his will. I never saw anyone who so completely gave me the idea of possession. Half an hour's conversation with him is enough to make a necessarian of anybody. Accordingly, he is more complained of than blamed by his enemies. His moments of softness in his family, and when recurring to old College days, are hailed by all as a relief to the vehement working of the intellectual machine; a relief equally to himself and others. Those moments are as touching to the observer as tears on the face of a soldier.

One incident befell during my stay which moved everybody. A representative from South Carolina was ill, a friend of Mr. Calhoun's; and Mr. Calhoun parted from us one day, on leaving the Capitol, to visit this sick gentleman. The physician told Mr. Calhoun on his entrance that his friend was dying and could not live more than a very few hours. A visitor, not knowing this, asked the sick man how he was. "To judge by own feelings," said he "much better; but by the countenances of my friends, not." And he begged to be told the truth. On hearing it, he instantly beckoned Mr. Calhoun to him, and said, "I hear they are giving you rough treatment in the Senate. Let a dying friend implore yow to guard your looks and words so as that no undue warmth may make you appear unworthy your principles." "This was friendship, strong friendship," said Mr. Calhoun to me and to many others; and it had its due effect upon him. A few days after, Colonel Benton, a fantastic Senator from Missouri, interrupted Mr. Calhoun in a speech, for the purpose of making an attack upon him which would have been insufferable if it had not been too absurdly worded to be easily made anything of. He was called to order; this was objected to; the Senate divided upon the point of order, being dissatisfied with the decision of the chair. In short Mr. Calhoun sat for full two hours hearing his veracity talked about before his speech could proceed. He sat in stern patience, scarcely moving a muscle the whole time; and, when it was all settled in his favor, merely observed that his friends need not fear his being disturbed by an attack of this nature from such a quarter and resumed his speech at the precise point where his argument had been broken off. It was great and would have satisfied the "strong friendship" of his departed comrade if he could have been there to see it.

Our active-minded genial friend Judge Story found time to visit us frequently, though he is one of the busiest men in the world; writing half a dozen great lawbooks every year; having his full share of the business of the Supreme Court upon his hands; his professorship to attend to; the District Courts at home in Massachusetts, and a correspondence which spreads half over the world. His talk would gush out for hours, and there was never too much of it for us; it is so heartfelt, so lively, so various; and his face all the while, notwithstanding his gray hair, showing all the mobility and ingenuousness of a child's. There is no tolerable portrait of Judge Story, and there never will be. I should like to bring him face to face with a person who entertains the common English idea of how an American looks and behaves. I should like to see what such a one would make of the quick smiles, the glistening eye, the gleeful tone, with passing touches of sentiment; the innocent self-complacency, the confiding, devoted affections of the great American lawyer; The preconception would be totally at fault.

With Judge Story sometimes came the man to whom he looked up with feelings little short of adoration: the aged Chief Justice Marshall. There was almost too much mutual respect in our first meeting; we knew something of his individual merits and services; and he maintained through life, and carried to his grave, a reverence for woman as rare in its kind as in its degree. It had all the theoretical fervor and magnificence of Uncle Toby's, with the advantage of being grounded upon an extensive knowledge of the sex. He was the father and the grandfather of women; and out of this experience he brought, not only the love and pity which their offices and position command, and the awe of purity which they excite in the minds of the pure, but a steady conviction of their intellectual equality with men; and with this, a deep sense of their social injuries. Throughout life he so invariably sustained their cause, that no indulgent libertine dared to flatter and humor; no skeptic, secure in the possession of power, dared to scoff at the claims of woman in the presence of Marshall, who, made clearsighted by his purity, knew the sex far better than either.

How delighted we were to see Judge Story bring in the tall majestic, bright-eyed old man! Old by chronology, by the lines on his composed face, and by his services to the Republic; but so dignified, so fresh, so present to the time, that no feeling of compassionate consideration for age dared to mix with the contemplation of him. The first evening he asked me much about English politics, and especially whether the people were not fast ripening for the abolition of our religious establishment; an institution which after a long study of it, he considered so monstrous in principle, and so injurious to true religion in practice, that he could not imagine that it could be upheld for anything but political purposes. There was no prejudice here on account of American modes being different; for he observed that the clergy were there, as elsewhere, far from being in the van of society, and lamented the existence of much fanaticism in the United States; but he saw the evils of an establishment the more clearly, not the less, from being aware of the faults in the administration of religion at home. The most animated moment of our conversation was when I told him I was going to visit Mr. Madison on leaving Washington. He instantly sat upright in his chair, and with beaming eyes began to praise Mr. Madison. Madison received the mention of Marshall's name in just the same manner; yet these men were strongly opposed in politics, and their magnanimous appreciation of each other underwent no slight or brief trial.

Captain Frederick Marryat

The prolific English author and veteran of Her Majesty's Royal Navy Captain Frederick Marryat (1792-1848), best known today as a writer of adventuresome sea tales, was basking in the recent success of his novel of the Napoleonic Wars *Mr. Midshipman Easy* when he visited the United States in 1837-1838. He was well-received, at first. However, ongoing tensions between upper and lower Canada spilled over into his visit. Marryat gave a speech in Toronto in which he praised a certain upper Canadian loyalist, Lieutenant Drew, for his role in "cutting out" (capturing at anchor or in harbor) the American ship *Caroline*, which *sans* crew the loyalists sent to her destruction over Niagara Falls. Afterward, Captain Marryat found himself and his books rather less welcome in the United States.

"Long-Winded Speeches About Nothing"

Washington. — Here are assembled from every State in the Union, what ought to be the collected talent, intelligence, and high principle of a free and enlightened nation. Of talent and intelligence there is a very fair supply, but principle is not so much in demand; and in everything, and everywhere, by the demand the supply is always regulated.

Everybody knows that Washington has a Capitol; but the misfortune is that the Capitol wants a city. There it stands, reminding you of a general without an army, only surrounded and followed by a parcel of ragged little dirty boys; for such is the appearance of the dirty, straggling, ill-built houses which lie at the foot of it.

Washington, notwithstanding, is an agreeable city, full of pleasant, clever people, who come there to amuse and be amused; and you observe in the company (although you occasionally meet some very queer importations from the Western settlements) much more *usage du monde* and continental ease than in any other parts of the State. A large portion of those who come up for the meeting of Congress, as well as of the residents, having travelled, and thereby gained more respect for other nations, are consequently not so conceited about their own country as are the majority of the Americans.

If anything were required to make Washington a more agreeable place than it is at all times, the arrival and subsequent conduct of Mr. Fox as British ambassador would be sufficient. His marked attention to all the Americans of respectability; his *empressement* in returning the calls of English gentlemen who may happen to arrive; his open house; his munificent allowance, dedicated wholly to the giving of fêtes and dinner parties as his Sovereign's representative; and, above all, his excessive urbanity, can never be forgotten by those who have ever visited the Capitol.

The Chamber of the House of Representatives is a fine room, and taking the average of the orations delivered there, it possesses this one great merit: *you cannot hear in it.* Were I to make a comparison between the Members of our House of Commons and those of the House of Representatives, I should say that the latter have certainly great advantages. In the first place, the Members of the American Senate and House of Representatives are paid, not only their travelling expenses to and fro but eight dollars a day during the sitting of Congress. Out of these allowances many save money, and those who do not, are at all events enabled to bring their families up to Washington for a little amusement. In the next place, they are so comfortably accommodated in the house, every man having his own well-stuffed armchair, and before him his desk, with his papers and notes! Then they are supplied with everything, even to penknives with their names engraved on them, each knife having two pen-blades, one whittling blade, and a fourth to clean their nails with, showing on the part of the government a paternal regard for their cleanliness as well as convenience. Moreover, they never work at night, and do very little during the day.

It is astonishing how little work they get through in a session at Washington. This is owing to every member thinking himself obliged to make two or three speeches, not for the good of the nation, but for the benefit of his constituents. These speeches are printed and sent to them, to prove that their member makes some noise in the House. The subject upon which he speaks is of little consequence, compared to the sentiments expressed.

It must be full of eagles, star-spangled banners, sovereign people, claptrap, flattery, and humbug. 1 have said that very little business is done in these Houses; but this is caused not only by their long-winded speeches about nothing, but by the fact that both Parties (in this respect laudably following the example of the old country) are chiefly occupied, the one with the paramount and vital consideration of keeping in, and the other with that of getting in, thus allowing the business of the nation, (which after all is not very important, unless such a trump as the Treasury Bill turns up), to become a very secondary consideration.

And yet there are principle and patriotism among the Members of the legislature, and the more to be appreciated from their rarity, Like the seeds of beautiful flowers, which, when cast upon a manure-heap, spring up in greater luxuriance and beauty, and yield a sweeter perfume from the rankness which surrounds them, so do these virtues show with more grace and attractiveness from the hotbed of corruption in which they have been engendered. But there has been a sad falling-off in America since the last war, which brought in the Democratic Party with General Jackson. America, if she would wish her present institutions to continue, must avoid war; the best security for her present form of government existing another half century, is a state of tranquility and peace; but of that hereafter. As for the Party at present in power, all I can say in its favor is, that there are three clever gentlemen in it:

Mr. Van Buren, Mr. Poinsett, and Mr. Forsyth. There may be more, but I know so little of them, that I must be excused if I do not name them, which otherwise I should have had great pleasure in doing.

Mr. Van Buren is a very gentleman-like, intelligent man; very proud of talking over his visit to England, and the English with whom he was acquainted. It is remarkable, that although at the head of the Democratic Party, Mr. Van Buren has taken a step striking at the very roots of their boasted equality, and one on which General Jackson did not venture, *i. e.* he has prevented the monocracy from intruding themselves at his levees. The police are now stationed at the door, to prevent the intrusion of any improper person. A few years ago, a fellow would drive his cart, or hackney coach, up to the door; walk into the saloon in all his dirt, and force his way to the president, that he might shake him by the one hand, whilst he flourished his whip in the other. The revolting scenes which took place when refreshments were handed round, the injury done to the furniture, and the disgust of the ladies, may be well imagined. Mr. Van Buren deserves great credit for this step, for it was a bold one; but I must not praise him too much, or he may lose his next election.

The best lounge at Washington is the Library of the Capitol, but the books are certainly not very well treated. I saw a copy of Audubon's *Ornithology*, and many other valuable works, in a very dilapidated state; but this must be the case when the library is open to all, and there are so many juvenile visitors. Still, it is much better than locking it up, for only the bindings to be looked at. It is not a library for show, but for use, and is a great comfort and amusement.

There are three things in great request amongst Americans of all classes: male, I mean. To wit: oysters, spirits, and tobacco. The first and third are not prohibited by Act of Congress, and may be sold in the Capitol, but spirituous liquors may not. I wondered how the Members could get on without them, but upon this point I was soon enlightened. Below the basement of the building is an oyster shop and refectory. The refectory has been permitted by Congress upon the express stipulation that no spirituous liquors should be sold there, but lawmakers are too often law breakers all over the world. You go there and ask for pale sherry, and they hand you gin; brown sherry, and it is brandy; madeira, whiskey; and thus do these potent, grave, and reverend signors evade their own laws, beneath the very hall wherein they were passed in solemn conclave.

It appears that tobacco is considered very properly as an article of fashion. At a store close to the hotel, the board outside informs you that among fashionable requisites to be found there are gentlemen's shirts, collars, gloves, silk handkerchiefs, and the best chewing tobacco. But not only at Washington, but at other large towns, I have seen at silk-mercers and hosiers this notice stuck up in the window: "*Dulcissimus* chewing tobacco." So prevalent is the habit of chewing, and so little, from long custom, do the ladies care about it, that I have been told that many young ladies in the south carry, in their work-boxes, &c., pig-tail, nicely ornamented with gold and colored papers; and when their swains are at fault, administer to their wants, thus meriting their affections by such endearing solicitude.

I was rather amused in the Senate at hearing the claims of parties who had suffered during the last war, and had hitherto not received any redress, discussed for adjudication. One man's claim, for instance, was for a cow: value thirty dollars, eaten up, of course, by the Britishers. It would naturally be supposed that such claims were unworthy the attention of such a body as the Senate, or when brought forward, would have been allowed without comment: but it was not so. The Member who saves the public money always finds favor in the eyes of the people, and therefore every Member tries to save as much as he can, except when he is himself a party concerned. And there was as much arguing and objecting, and discussion of the merits of this man's claim, as there would be in the English House of Commons at passing the Navy Estimates. Eventually he lost it. The claims of the Fulton family were also brought forward when I was present in the House of Representatives. Fulton was certainly the father of steam-navigation in America, and to his exertions and intelligence, America may consider herself in a great degree indebted for her present prosperity. It once required six or seven months to ascend the Mississippi, a passage which is now performed in fifteen days. Had it not been for Fulton's genius, the west would still have remained a wild desert, and the now flourishing cotton growing States would not yet have yielded the crops which are the staple of the Union. The claim of his surviving relatives was a mere nothing, in comparison with the debt of gratitude owing to that great man; yet Member after Member rose to oppose it with all the ingenuity of argument. One asserted that the merit of the invention did not belong to Fulton; another, that even if it did, his relatives certainly could found no claim upon it; a third rose and declared that ho would prove that, so far from the government owing money to Fulton, Fulton was in debt to the government. And thus did they go on, showing to their constituents how great was their consideration for the public money, and to the world (if another proof were required) how little gratitude is to be found in a democracy. The bill was thrown out, and the race of Fultons left to the chance of starving, for anything that the American nation seemed to care to the contrary. Whitney, the inventor of the gin for clearing the cotton of its seeds (perhaps the next greatest boon ever given to America), was treated in the same way. And yet, on talking over the question, there were few of the Members who did not individually acknowledge the justice of their claims, and the duly of the State to attend to them; but the *majority* would not have permitted it, and when they went back to their constituents to be re-elected, it would have been urged against them that they had voted away the public money, and they would have had the difficult task of proving that the interests of the *majority*, and of the majority alone, had regulated their conduct in Congress.

Philip Hone

Philip Hone (1780-1851) was a New York merchant, philanthropist, and politician who by age forty had amassed a respectable fortune. Hone traveled in Europe and purchased a fine home on Broadway, where he entertained New York's most socially and politically influential citizens. After serving one term as Mayor (1826-1827) he settled into a comfortable quasi-retirement. In subsequent years Philip Hone would become a prolific diarist.

Hone was a critic of President Andrew Jackson and his administration, as well as of Jackson's successor, the newly defeated one-termer Martin van Buren. In the following diary entries, the well-connected Philip Hone reflects upon a visit to Washington, D.C. during the change in administrations, and makes observations on various political factions.

"Loco Focos"

Washington, Feb. 18 [1841].

Left Baltimore in the nine o'clock train and arrived here about the opening of the Houses of Congress; got a tolerable room at Gadsby's, that caravansary of long, cold galleries, never-ceasing ringing of bells, negligent servants, small pillows, and scanty supply of water. I am better off, even in these particulars, than three-fourths of the people in the house; but, if a man wishes to appreciate the comforts of home, let him come to Washington. As for the eating part, I am fortunately situated. I am regularly entered of Mr. Granger's mess, with his daughter, and Meredith, which promises well, if I should have any chance to enjoy their society.

I found an invitation to dine with the Russian Minister, which he had politely sent in anticipation of my coming, and accordingly rode over to his residence at Georgetown, where I met a large party of distinguished gentlemen, embracing most of the leading Whigs. The dinner was a magnificent affair, a ponderous set-out; it was like dining in a gold mine; immense, lofty, and massy gilt candelabras on the table, in which I counted eighty wax candles burning, besides others in different parts of the room; rich ornaments of every description; a great variety of wines, some of which were good, but the cuisine not comparable with an everyday dinner at my own house. Servants below stairs with gilt-laced cocked hats, and surrounding the table with tarnished liveries, which, from their variety, would seem intended to represent all the provinces of Russia; but the host did the honors with great propriety, and treated me with marked attention. The number was about four and twenty, of which I remember the following: Monsieur [de] Bacourt, French Minister; Mr. Fox, British Minister; Mr. Stockel, Russian Secretary; Mr. Webster, Mr. Clay, Mr. Crittenden, Mr. Tallmadge, Mr. Rives, Mr. Merrick, Mr. Henderson, Mr. Bayard, Mr. Southard, Mr. Dawson, Mr. Cushing, Mr. Meredith, Mr. Reverdy Johnson, Mr. Austen of Massachusetts, Richard Peters, Mr. Mangum, Mr. Sargent, and Colonel Stuart. There was whist after dinner. I got at a table with Messrs. Bodisco, Fox, and Clay, and sat until we were the survivors of the large party.

February 19.

I called this morning upon President Van Buren. He received me alone in his study, in the kindest and most gracious manner; talked a little about the late political contest, professed an undiminished friendship for me, notwithstanding my opposition, which he said he had been gratified to learn had been unaccompanied by the use of any expression of personal disrespect. He is fat and jolly, with the same self-satisfied smile upon his countenance. A stranger would be greatly at a loss to discover anything to indicate that he was a defeated candidate for the high office which he is about to vacate.

The Supreme Court was for two hours the point of superior attraction. Mr. Webster was engaged in one of those great arguments on a constitutional question in which he stands unrivalled, the interest of which was enhanced from its being one of the last in which he will be engaged. He has resigned his seat in the Senate, of which he will take leave on Monday, and on the 4th of March he commences a new sphere of action as Secretary of State in General Harrison's Cabinet. The Supreme Court presented a sublime and beautiful spectacle during Mr. Webster's argument. The solemn temple of justice was filled with an admiring auditory, consisting of a large proportion of well-dressed ladies, who occupied the seats within the bar; the nine judges, in their magisterial robes, attentive and thoughtful; and all minds and bodies bent upon one great object, and that object a single man, of commanding presence and intellectual aspect, not remarkably correct in his costume nor graceful in his action, but commanding, by the force of his giant intellect, an irresistible control over the minds of all who heard him, and enchaining all their faculties to one point of observation and attention. It was, in truth, a noble illustration of the power of mind over the material faculties of humanity . . . .

February 22.

I have been all day in the Senate, and greatly interested. The principal business was an animated debate on a motion made by Mr. Crittenden to bring a bill, formerly presented by him, to prevent the interference of officeholders in elections. This motion was supported in an eloquent speech by the mover and the leading Whigs, and opposed by Messrs. Buchanan, Calhoun, Wright, etc., and defeated by a strict Party vote. They could not stand the implied odium which the passage of such an act would cast upon the Party going out of power, nor acknowledge the magnanimity of their successors in binding themselves in advance not to use the same means to secure a continuance of their own, which have heretofore been employed against them. Mr. Preston's speech in support of this measure gave rise to an incident of considerable excitement. He closed his speech with an eulogium upon Mr. Crittenden, on the occasion of his quitting the Senate to assume the office of Attorney-General in General Harrison's administration. Never did human voice utter anything more beautiful than this well-merited panegyric. It was warm and glowing, tender and touching, by turns. The Senate was full, and the galleries crowded to the utmost. I was seated on the floor, behind the eloquent Carolinian. The audience seemed to be rapt in mute attention until the close, when the effect was irresistible, and there was a pretty general applause in the galleries. This unwonted outbreak gave great offence to the Loco Focos. Several arose at once, and with loud screams and violent gesticulation demanded the clearing of the galleries. "Turn them out!" said Clay of Alabama, Sevier, Cuthbert, and even Calhoun. "Turn out the blackguards!" exclaimed the refined Mr. Benton, striking the desk with great vehemence; and the Vice-President, with evident reluctance, proceeded to give the harsh order. Mr. Clay, with his wonted suavity, interposed to save the ladies. He was "sure they could not have joined in the offence and ought not to be included in the punishment;" and the Vice-President, nothing loath, saved them and the men in their gallery from being turned away to gratify the spleen of half- a-dozen demagogues who are forever talking about the dear people, and let no opportunity escape of affronting them. There was an easier way for them to clear out the galleries: let either of them arise to make a speech, and the object is accomplished without a resort to violence. But what a glorious triumph of eloquence! I would have given the world at that moment to have been Preston; but I would have given such worlds to be Crittenden! The latter was greatly moved; those that were near him say that he wept visibly. He is beloved by all parties. Mr. Buchanan, a political opponent, but the most gentlemanly Senator on that side, paid him a handsome personal compliment in a speech in which he opposed his motion. This exhibition of vulgar rage gave occasion to the following jeu d'esprit, which was handed to me the next morning by a Senator:

"'Turn out the blackguards!' If they do,
Friend Benton, what becomes of you?"

As soon as this affair was ended, a new excitement was created, which continued until the adjournment. Mr. Webster having retired from his place, a letter addressed to the Vice-President was read, in which he resigns his seat, and took leave of the Senate; immediately upon which a firebrand from Georgia, Mr. Cuthbert, arose and attacked him. He regretted that the Senator from Massachusetts had not made a verbal valedictory, as he had intended to put certain interrogatories to him touching his doctrines on the subject of the transmission of slaves from one State to another, doctrines which Georgia's Senator denounced as "damnable heresies." He evidently desired to get up a quarrel. His manner and his language were equally insulting, and there was something so discourteous, so unkind in his taking that moment to vent his spleen against the absent Senator, when the tide of generous feeling was flowing so strongly in his favor, that there was not an individual of Cuthbert's Party who, by word, look, or action, seemed disposed either to countenance or support him. Mr. Clay rebuked the ruffian in a manly and eloquent speech, in which the character and principles of his friend were ably defended, and Mr. Rives and Mr. Preston followed in the same strain. The former gentleman came in for an undue share of the wrath of the Hotspur of Georgia; his manner toward him was provoking and insulting and met with haughty scorn and defiance. Mr. Rives, at the commencement of his speech, happened to apply to Cuthbert the parliamentary term, "My honorable friend." "No, sir; no friend," was the uncivil reply. "So be it," retorted Mr. Rives; and it is not likely the term will be repeated very soon. Mr. Rives defended Mr.

Webster with great ability, approving, though a Southern man, his opinions on the exciting subject of slavery.

February 26.

Rufus Choate is elected a Senator from Massachusetts, to fill Mr. Webster's place; and Mr. Morehead, after several ballots, was elected, by the relinquishment of two of his Whig opponents, to fill that of Mr. Crittenden, as Senator from Kentucky. It is a fearful venture for those gentlemen to undertake to supply the void occasioned by the setting of those two "bright particular stars" of the Senate.

I dined with Mr. Barnard; a small and very pleasant party, and an excellent dinner of French cookery and good wine. The party consisted of Mr. John Quincy Adams, Mr. Richard Bayard, Gouverneur Wilkins, Abbott Lawrence, Mr. Jackson of Philadelphia, and myself. Mr. Adams was, as usual, the fiddle of the party. He talked a great deal; was gay, witty, instructive, and entertaining. It is a privilege, and an era in one's life, to see him as he was on this occasion. A man must be stupid, indeed, who can listen to this wonderful man for three or four hours, as I have done today, without being edified and delighted.

We had an account before I left home of some amiable passages of courtesy between the outgoing and the incoming Presidents, in which the former had great credit for courtesy extended to the latter, particularly in inviting him to dine. I have heard since I came here some particulars about this dinner, which have satisfied me that it was not the kind of compliment which we gave him credit for. Instead of inviting to meet the General, his personal and political friends, such as Webster, Clay, Crittenden, Southard, etc., the party consisted, besides General Harrison and Colonel Chambers and Mr. Todd, his personal suite, of the following: the Cabinet Ministers, Mr. Gouveneur Kemble, Silas Wright, and Aaron Vanderpoel, all Loco Focos of the bitterest stamp, and his most decided political opponents. He was in the camp of the Philistines; it seemed as if they were there to take advantage of the old man's kind, benevolent openness of disposition, and treasure up for future use anything which may have fallen from him in an unguarded moment.

They write me from home that times are hard in New York, despondency prevails among men of business, and melancholy forebodings of worse times to come. The State of Illinois will not pay the interest of her debt, and doubts are entertained of the great State of Pennsylvania. Stocks have fallen very much; Delaware and Hudson down to eighty per cent.

March 1.

I went yesterday to St. John's Church, where I caused some remarks to be made by my sitting in the President's pew, for which I had afterwards to stand some shots from the Whigs, who have not the taste to understand how a man may continue on good terms with a gentleman whose election he has worked hard to defeat. The truth is, the President passed me in his carnage on his way to church, and when I arrived I found his son Smith waiting for me at the door, to take me to his father's pew, a civility which I accepted most willingly, and did not find my devotions interfered with, nor my political principles contaminated, by the company I had the honor to be placed in.

March 2.

Broadway on a fine Sunday, when the churches are emptied, does not present a more animated spectacle than Pennsylvania Avenue on this bright and beautiful morning; there are men here from every State in the Union. Our good city of New York has its full proportion. I have remarked, and heard it remarked by others, that there is not a country in the world where in such a crowd, so gotten together, there could be found so large a proportion of good-looking and well-behaved persons.

I was talking about it with Mr. Bell yesterday, and he remarked that he was here at the time of General Jackson's inauguration, when the same objects and motions brought together a greater crowd, and the difference in appearance and deportment of the people is most striking; but now they are Whigs and gentlemen, then Loco Focos and . . . .

I was forcibly stricken this morning by a characteristic circumstance, of which an American may well be proud. Passing through the crowd of which I was just speaking was to be seen an elderly gentleman dressed in black, and not remarkably well dressed, with a mild, benignant countenance, a military air, but stooping a little, bowing to one, shaking hands with another, and cracking a joke with a third; and this man was William H. Harrison, the President-elect of this great empire, whose elevation has been produced by a severe throe which has been felt in the most remote corners of the land, which has destroyed and elevated the hopes of hundreds of thousands, and which is destined to effect a change of principles and policy to which the whole world looks with interest; and there he was, unattended, and unconscious of the dignity of his position, the man among men, the sun of the political firmament. People may say what they will about the naked simplicity of Republican institutions; it was a sublime moral spectacle.

March 3.

This city is an immense mass of animated Whig matter; every hole and corner are filled; thousands have arrived today, and happy is the man who finds "where to lay his head." A large building has been erected in the court at Gadsby's, in which four hundred breakfast, dine, and sup; and the dining-room is a vast camp-bed. This has been a day of confusion; everybody running against his neighbor, all full of business, and nobody accomplishing any.

I witnessed the last moments of the 26th Congress. At twelve o'clock the refractory old lady terminated the career which she so naughtily began. The Speaker sang a requiem to her departing moments in a very respectable speech, somewhat too long and a little too school-boyish. He is an amiable man, and has acted with impartiality, but no more fit to be Speaker than I to dance on the tight rope. On the whole, the scene was imposing, and more orderly and decorous than I had anticipated. The aforesaid old lady behaved with propriety, "and, like immortal Caesar, died with dignity."

March 4.

The affair is consummated. General Harrison has taken the oaths and is President of the United States. The day was fine. A great procession, consisting of several militia companies in uniform, Tippecanoe clubs, and citizens from different States, under the orders of Marshals on horseback, with sashes and batons, escorted the President to the Capitol. He was mounted, and passed through the streets amidst the shouts and hurrahs of fifty thousand men, and almost as many women waving their handkerchiefs, whilst he, like the haughty Bolingbroke:

"Mounted upon a hot and fiery steed,
Which his aspiring rider seemed to know,
With slow but stately pace kept on his course,
While all tongues cried, 'God save thee, Bolingbroke!'
You would have thought the very windows spoke."

As for Van Buren, "No man cried, God save him!" He was snug at the house of the Attorney-General, Gilpin.

I attended the great inauguration ball last evening, at the National Theatre. The crowd was very great; all the great men of the nation were there; an exceedingly brilliant collection of ladies, of whom Mrs. Reverdy Johnson of Baltimore, a mother of nine children, was preeminent. The President came in about half-past ten o'clock, with a numerous escort, and was marched through files of ladies up and down the room. This ceremony, with his previous visits to two other public balls, added to the severe labors of the day, has tried the old soldier's stamina; but he appears to stand it very well. If the opponents of the administration expect to make capital out of his imbecility of either body or mind, they make a woeful mistake. He'll do his duty well and faithfully. The gentlemen had a supper in the lower regions of the theatre, from which in former times ghosts and hobgoblins and infernal spirits made their "exits and their entrances." I was escorted by the managers to this subterranean banquet-hall, where I found Senators, Cabinet Ministers, military officers, and common men like myself, eating, drinking, laughing, and joking in a strain somewhat uproarious.

The nominations of the new Cabinet have, it is said, been confirmed, all but that of Mr. Granger, against whom charges of that crying sin, abolitionism, having been brought by the opposition, his friends consented to let it lie over until tomorrow. This is a base and ungentlemanly proceeding; but it will have no other effect than that of misrepresenting his principles, for he will certainly be confirmed tomorrow.

Adolphe Fourier de Bacourt

The French diplomat Adolphe Fourier de Bacourt (1801-1865) began his career at twenty-one years of age in Turin and would be involved in diplomacy at the highest levels for the rest of his life. His *Souvenirs* (*Private Letters*) were translated for publication by his niece, whose mother was an executrix of Talleyrand (Charles-Maurice de Talleyrand-Périgord) and in part responsible for the eventual publication of his papers years after his death.

The author served only briefly as Minister to the United States, perhaps due to the failure of Martin Van Buren to secure a second terms as President. The brevity and urgency of his *Souvenirs* seems altogether appropriate in describing the situation in Washington, D.C. during the era of the 10th President of the United States, William Henry Harrison.

"Just One Month"

Washington, November 2, 1840.

We are now in the exciting week preceding the election and will know in eight days who will be President of the United States. You cannot imagine what a fever everyone is in: it is political excitement, boiling over with rage! The day before yesterday in Philadelphia the Van Buren Party demolished the house which was the headquarters of the opposite Party. There is no organized civil force in the United States, so the populace can go to any imaginable excess without fear of repression; time will probably make them feel the need of an armed force, and the day when this armed force shall have the preponderance in the country will be the end of the present Constitution. So, I think if they are right in saying that kings will eventually be done away with, they will be able to say the same thing of Republics in America. I console myself better with the one than the other.

Washington, November 10, 1840.

My friend Van Buren is beaten and General Harrison is victorious. The election will not, however, be decided for fifteen days yet, and the new President will not enter upon his duties until March 4, 1841. I am sorry on my own account at the result, which, besides, will be prejudicial to the country. The Democratic Party, which is in power now, has been directed by Mr. Van Buren and his friends with moderation and wisdom, but when it becomes the Opposition Party it will put no bounds to its violence. The Whig Party (which is called that of the aristocracy; my God, what aristocracy!) will split as soon as they come into power, and the governmental machine will find itself opposed by a furious democracy. To give you an idea of the American Constitution, this is what is to take place after the new election. From this time to the 4th of March next Mr. Van Buren will hold the office of President, which puts him in a very ridiculous position in face of those who have taken the power away from him. Congress, in which he has a majority, will meet in December. Of course, nothing will be done to aid the coming Administration, who in coming into power on March 4 will find, in the first place, the Treasury empty, and be able to do nothing until the following December, for Congress is irrevocably dissolved on the 4th of March, and they cannot call a new one until December, because new members must be elected during the interval. It seems to me that the old maxim, "The King is dead: long live the King," is better than these intervals, which open the door so wide to all sorts of disorder. Such a Constitution is vicious in its consequences as in its principle, in spite of the theories, more or less specious, of M. de Tocqueville.

Mr. Van Buren bears his defeat with dignity, and as they say here, with *fortitude*. General Harrison was born in the State of Virginia, which is thought the model State as regards pure republican principles, joined with good education and good manners. It is, in one word, the birthplace of *gentlemen*. Take notice, I beg of you, that I am only the reporter of public opinion, and that I do not guarantee the quality of these so-called *gentlemen*. Mr. Harrison left Virginia very early, as all these poor devils in that State do, to seek his fortune in the West. He settled in Ohio, and later entered the army, and was distinguished enough to be made a General, which does not signify much in America. He served without success from 1812 to 1814 against the English; afterward against the Indians, and his great exploit was a victory he gained over them at a place called Tippecanoe. He lost one hundred and fifty men and killed three hundred of the enemy. And for that this conqueror has received the brilliant title of "The Hero of Tippecanoe;" and it is the refrain of all the songs, of all the pieces of prose and of poetry, in his honor, which have been plentiful during this past year. General Jackson, the predecessor of Mr. Van Buren, sent General Harrison back to his home, where, a new Cincinnatus, he has conducted his plough; he has also been notary in his village. The Party opposed to Mr. Van Buren not daring to bring forward their most distinguished men, who are more brilliant than the Democrats, brought General Harrison from his obscurity to make him a candidate for the Presidency, and from that time he has become a great personage, and his sayings and doings are looked upon as important, *Americanly* speaking.

Thus, he said that he preferred his log-cabin, a house built with trunks of trees, to the palace of a king; and his *log-cabin* has become an emblem of the Party: it is painted on all their flags; it serves as their banner everywhere; they have built one in the middle of Washington. And there, for the last six months, the partisans of the new President have met and yelled speeches and songs. He also said that he drank nothing but hard cider, and not the foreign wines of the aristocrats. Since then, it is not the proper thing to get drunk on anything but *hard cider*, and they have vaunted this drink in prose and in verse. He also said that his log-cabin had no lock, and that all good Democrats could come in and be welcome at any time; then Harrisonian hospitality became proverbial! To tell you all the stupidities that have been inspired by these poor sayings I have cited, during the last year, would be impossible. I have seen nothing, heard nothing, read nothing, in which the log-cabin or hard cider did not appear. The newest style in dress is called Tippecanoe, and the American women in everything they wear seek to do honor to the illustrious conqueror. Thanks to all these truly ridiculous proceedings, this General, not heard of yesterday, is elected today; and solely on account of his mediocrity, which they judge inoffensive, he is to occupy the first position, and govern the country during the next four years. Opinions are divided on the course he will follow. Some say that, like Sixtus V., he will throw away his crutches, and putting aside those who have brought him into power, will rule with an ability that will astonish the universe. But most persons say that he is a vain man, without mind or talent, who will be a puppet in the hands of flatterers, and those who wish to control him will ruin the country while quarrelling amongst themselves. However, they say he is an amiable man, rather vulgar, and having the mania of quoting the Greeks and Romans, whom he knows nothing about, but thinks it good taste to appear to know.

We are buried in snow: in the same degree of latitude as Lisbon, we have the temperature of Sweden in winter and of the tropics in summer.

Washington, April 2, 1841.

Our new President is sick and is so much worse today that his life is in danger. No President has ever died whilst in power; the post of Vice-President has always been looked upon as insignificant, and the man who occupies this supposed sinecure was only nominated after the refusal of several others. Now he will find himself President for the next four years, as ordained by the Constitution; and this unlooked-for change causes great excitement in the country. It will have no influence on our relations and will not prevent the extra session of Congress. The Vice-President is Mr. Tyler of Virginia, where the Administration of General Harrison has met with opposition, but the general opinion is that Mr. Tyler's tendencies are more Harrisonian than Virginian.

Washington, April 5, 1841.

General Harrison died yesterday. He commenced his term on the 4th of March. His reign has lasted just one month, and the poor old man has had nothing but cares and worries during this month of responsibility. His death unsettles all that had been decided upon by the leaders of the victorious Party, and the conquered, Mr. Van Buren's Party, will begin to agitate again. The funeral takes place on the day after tomorrow, and of course the Diplomatic Corps are invited.

Washington, April 12, 1841.

The funeral took place on the 7th. The procession started from the President's House and proceeded on a walk four miles to the cemetery. The ceremonies and the funeral oration passed off in the most proper manner, which is to be noticed in this country, where everything else is very strange. The obsequies lasted altogether about five hours.

Mr. John Tyler is a widower, but has a son who is married, and his wife will do the honors of the Presidency. This young woman was formerly an actress and has played in the theatre in Washington under the name of Miss Cooper; I had the imprudence to say that she would represent very well. The next day it was repeated to her. What a singular country, where a woman can pass from the boards of a theatre to a kind of scaffolding which serves as a republican throne!

I paid a visit to Mr. Southard, Vice-President of the Senate, who, according to the Constitution of the United States, will replace Mr. Tyler in case of his death; he is a man of middle age, whose manners are better than those of the present generation.

Washington, April 25, 1841.

All the Diplomatic Corps went to present their respects to the President for the first time. In the absence of Mr. Fox, who was sick, Mr. Bodisco made the address. Mr. Tyler made a very appropriate reply, then came forward, and gave a shake hand to each of us, accompanied with a short speech. What he said to me I will repeat in as near his own words as possible:

"I am delighted to make the acquaintance of the French Minister, who comes from a country to which we owe much, and to which we are united by the bonds of gratitude. I shall endeavor to establish intimate and friendly relations with you, sir, who have had the advantage of living in intimate relations with the most distinguished diplomat in the whole world and of all time. King Louis Philippe and Prince Talleyrand while living here obtained the right of citizenship, and America is proud to count them amongst her citizens."

I give you the exact words of the President, and I hope that you will be satisfied. As to me, I am always happy to find myself under the protection of a name and a souvenir that I cherish and respect. Mr. Tyler conducted himself during this audience in a manner to satisfy everyone; without being a man of genius, he is thought to be greatly superior to General Harrison.

Solomon Northup

African American author and abolitionist Solomon Northup (c1807-c1864) was born a free man in New York during the first decade of the 19th century. He later married, started a family, and worked in various capacities in Saratoga Springs. In 1841, Northup's life was turned upside down when during a visit to Washington, D.C. he was kidnapped by slave traders and sold into bondage in Louisiana. His memoir of the experience, *Twelve Years a Slave*, appeared after he regained his freedom in 1853. Northup's story was revealed to modern audiences in the Academy Award-winning 2013 film of the same title.

The following excerpt from Northup's memoir recounts his travels to Washington, D.C., during the era when slavery was legal in the Nation's Capital, and his kidnapping by a pair of slave traders, men who deceived Northup into believing they would provide him with work as a musician in a traveling circus.

"I Gave Them My Confidence"

With the evidence of freedom in my possession, the next day after our arrival in New York, we crossed the ferry to Jersey City, and took the road to Philadelphia. Here we remained one night, continuing our journey towards Baltimore early in the morning. In due time, we arrived in the latter city, and stopped at a hotel near the railroad depot, either kept by a Mr. Rathbone, or known as the Rathbone House. All the way from New York, their anxiety to reach the circus seemed to grow more and more intense. We left the carriage at Baltimore, and entering the cars, proceeded to Washington, at which place we arrived just at nightfall the evening previous to the funeral of General Harrison, and stopped at Gadsby's Hotel on Pennsylvania Avenue.

After supper they called me to their apartments and paid me forty-three dollars, a sum greater than my wages amounted to, which act of generosity was in consequence, they said, of their not having exhibited as often as they had given me to anticipate during our trip from Saratoga. They moreover informed me that it had been the intention of the circus company to leave Washington the next morning, but that on account of the funeral, they had concluded to remain another day. They were then, as they had been from the time of our first meeting, extremely kind. No opportunity was omitted of addressing me in the language of approbation; while, on the other hand, I was certainly much prepossessed in their favor. I gave them my confidence without reserve and would freely have trusted them to almost any extent. Their constant conversation and manner towards me, their foresight in suggesting the idea of free papers, and a hundred other little acts, unnecessary to be repeated, all indicated that they were friends indeed, sincerely solicitous for my welfare. I know not but they were. I know not but they were innocent of the great wickedness of which I now believe them guilty. Whether they were accessory to my misfortunes, subtle and inhuman monsters in the shape of men, designedly luring me away from home and family, and liberty, for the sake of gold, those who read these pages will have the same means of determining as myself. If they were innocent, my sudden disappearance must have been unaccountable indeed, but revolving in my mind all the attending circumstances, I never yet could indulge towards them so charitable a supposition.

After receiving the money from them, of which they appeared to have an abundance, they advised me not to go into the streets that night, inasmuch as I was unacquainted with the customs of the city. Promising to remember their advice, I left them together, and soon after was shown by a colored servant to a sleeping room in the back part of the hotel on the ground floor. I laid down to rest, thinking of home and wife, and children, and the long distance that stretched between us, until I fell asleep. But no good angel of pity came to my bedside, bidding me to fly. No voice of mercy forewarned me in my dreams of the trials that were just at hand.

The next day there was a great pageant in Washington. The roar of cannon and the tolling of bells filled the air, while many houses were shrouded with crape, and the streets were black with people. As the day advanced, the procession made its appearance, coming slowly through the Avenue, carriage after carriage in long succession, while thousands upon thousands followed on foot, all moving to the sound of melancholy music. They were bearing the dead body of Harrison to the grave.

From early in the morning, I was constantly in the company of Hamilton and Brown. They were the only persons I knew in Washington. We stood together as the funeral pomp passed by. I remember distinctly how the window glass would break and rattle to the ground, after each report of the cannon they were firing in the burial ground. We went to the Capitol and walked a long time about the grounds. In the afternoon, they strolled towards the President's House, all the time keeping me near to them, and pointing out various places of interest. As yet, I had seen nothing of the circus. In fact, I had thought of it but little, if at all, amidst the excitement of the day.

My friends several times during the afternoon entered drinking saloons and called for liquor. They were by no means in the habit, however, so far as I knew them, of indulging to excess. On these occasions, after serving themselves, they would pour out a glass and hand it to me. I did not become intoxicated, as may be inferred from what subsequently occurred. Towards evening, and soon after partaking of one of these potations, I began to experience most unpleasant sensations. I felt extremely ill. My head commenced aching; a dull, heavy pain, inexpressibly disagreeable. At the supper table, I was without appetite; the sight and flavor of food was nauseous. About dark the same servant conducted me to the room I had occupied the previous night. Brown and Hamilton advised me to retire, commiserating me kindly, and expressing hopes that I would be better in the morning. Divesting myself of coat and boots merely, I threw myself upon the bed. It was impossible to sleep. The pain in my head continued to increase, until it became almost unbearable. In a short time, I became thirsty. My lips were parched. I could think of nothing but water, of lakes and flowing rivers, of brooks where I had stooped to drink, and of the dripping bucket, rising with its cool and overflowing nectar, from the bottom of the well. Towards midnight, as near as I could judge, I arose, unable longer to bear such intensity of thirst. I was a stranger in the house and knew nothing of its apartments. There was no one up, as I could observe. Groping about at random, I knew not where, I found the way at last to a kitchen in the basement. Two or three colored servants were moving through it, one of whom, a woman, gave me two glasses of water. It afforded momentary relief, but by the time I had reached my room again, the same burning desire of drink, the same tormenting thirst, had again returned. It was even more torturing than before, as was also the wild pain in my head, if such a thing could be. I was in sore distress, in most excruciating agony! I seemed to stand on the brink of madness! The memory of that night of horrible suffering will follow me to the grave.

In the course of an hour or more after my return from the kitchen, I was conscious of someone entering my room. There seemed to be several, a mingling of various voices, but how many, or who they were, I cannot tell. Whether Brown and Hamilton were among them, is a mere matter of conjecture. I only remember, with any degree of distinctness, that I was told it was necessary to go to a physician and procure medicine, and that pulling on my boots, without coat or hat, I followed them through a long passageway, or alley, into the open street. It ran out at right angles from Pennsylvania Avenue. On the opposite side there was a light burning in a window. My impression is there were then three persons with me, but it is altogether indefinite and vague, and like the memory of a painful dream. Going towards the light, which I imagined proceeded from a physician's office, and which seemed to recede as I advanced, is the last glimmering recollection I can now recall. From that moment I was insensible. How long I remained in that condition, whether only that night, or many days and nights, I do not know; but when consciousness returned, I found myself alone, in utter darkness, and in chains.

The pain in my head had subsided in a measure, but I was very faint and weak. I was sitting upon a low bench, made of rough boards, and without coat or hat. I was handcuffed. Around my ankles also were a pair of heavy fetters. One end of a chain was fastened to a large ring in the floor, the other to the fetters on my ankles. I tried in vain to stand upon my feet. Waking from such a painful trance, it was some time before I could collect my thoughts. Where was I? What was the meaning of these chains? Where were Brown and Hamilton? What had I done to deserve imprisonment in such a dungeon? I could not comprehend. There was a blank of some indefinite period, preceding my awakening in that lonely place, the events of which the utmost stretch of memory was unable to recall. I listened intently for some sign or sound of life, but nothing broke the oppressive silence, save the clinking of my chains, whenever I chanced to move. I spoke aloud, but the sound of my voice startled me. I felt of my pockets, so far as the fetters would allow, far enough, indeed, to ascertain that I had not only been robbed of liberty, but that my money and free papers were also gone! Then did the idea begin to break upon my mind, at first dim and confused, that I had been kidnapped. But that I thought was incredible. There must have been some misapprehension, some unfortunate mistake. It could not be that a free citizen of New York, who had wronged no man, nor violated any law, should be dealt with thus inhumanly. The more I contemplated my situation, however, the more I became confirmed in my suspicions. It was a desolate thought, indeed. I felt there was no trust or mercy in unfeeling man; and commending myself to the God of the oppressed, bowed my head upon my fettered hands, and wept most bitterly.

Charles Dickens

Charles Dickens (1812-1870), accompanied by his wife, departed England bound for America aboard the Cunard steamer *Britannia* on January 3rd, 1842. The celebrated English novelist was just shy of thirty years of age and had already authored *The Pickwick Papers, Oliver Twist* and *Nicholas Nickleby*. His *American Notes* would be published before year's end with the following Dedication:

I dedicate this book to those friends of mine in America, who, giving me a welcome I must ever gratefully and proudly remember, left my judgment free; and who, loving their country, can bear the truth, when it is told good humouredly, and in a kind spirit.

In this excerpt from his *American Notes*, Dickens reveals his good humor and kind spirit in his observations on Congress.

"Dishonest Faction"

It is sometimes called the City of Magnificent Distances, but it might with greater propriety be termed the City of Magnificent Intentions; for it is only on taking a bird's-eye view of it from the top of the Capitol, that one can at all comprehend the vast designs of its projector, an aspiring Frenchman. Spacious avenues, that begin in nothing and lead nowhere; streets, mile long, that only want houses, roads, and inhabitants; public buildings that need but a public to be complete; and ornaments of great thoroughfares, which only lack great thoroughfares to ornament, are its leading features. One might fancy the season over, and most of the Houses gone out of town forever with their masters. To the admirers of cities, it is a Barmecide Feast; a pleasant field for the imagination to rove in; a monument raised to a deceased project, with not even a legible inscription to record its departed greatness.

Such as it is it is likely to remain. It was originally chosen for the seat of government as a means of averting the conflicting jealousies and interests of the different States; and very probably, too, as being remote from mobs, consideration not to be slighted, even in America. It has no trade or commerce of its own; having little or no population beyond the President and his establishment, the Members of the legislature who reside there during the session, the government clerks and officers employed in the various departments, the keepers of the hotels and boarding-houses, and the tradesmen who supply their tables. It is very unhealthy. Few people would live in Washington, I take it, who were not obliged to reside there; and the tides of emigration and speculation, those rapid and regardless currents, are little likely to flow at any time towards such dull and sluggish water.

The principal features of the Capitol are, of course, the two Houses of Assembly. But there is, besides, in the center of the building, a fine rotunda, ninety-six feet in diameter, and ninety-six high, whose circular wall is divided into compartments, ornamented by historical pictures. Four of these have for their subjects prominent events in the Revolutionary struggle. They were painted by Colonel Trumbull, himself a member of Washington's staff at the time of their occurrence; from which circumstance they derive a peculiar interest of their own. In this same hall Mr. Greenough's large statue of Washington has been lately placed. It has great merits, of course, but it struck me as being rather strained and violent for its subject. I could wish, however, to have seen it in a better light than it can ever be viewed in where it stands.

There is a very pleasant and commodious library in the Capitol; and from a balcony in front the bird's-eye view of which I have just spoken may be had, together with a beautiful prospect of the adjacent country. In one of the ornamented portions of the building there is a figure of Justice; whereunto, the Guide Book says, "the artist at first contemplated giving more of nudity, but he was warned that the public sentiment in this country would not admit of it, and in his caution he has gone, perhaps, into the opposite extreme." Poor Justice! She has been made to wear much stranger garments in America than those she pines in, in the Capitol. Let us hope that she has changed her dressmaker since they were fashioned, and that the public sentiment of the country did not cut out the clothes she hides her lovely figure in just now.

The House of Representatives is a beautiful and spacious hall of semicircular shape, supported by handsome pillars. One part of the gallery is appropriated to the ladies, and there they sit in front rows, and come in and go out, as at a play or concert. The chair is canopied and raised considerably above the floor of the House; and every member has an easy-chair and a writing-desk to himself; which is denounced by some people out of doors as a most unfortunate and injudicious arrangement, tending to long sittings and prosaic speeches. It is an elegant chamber to look at, but a singularly bad one for all purposes of hearing. The Senate, which is smaller, is free from this objection, and is exceedingly well adapted to the uses for which it is designed. The sittings, I need hardly add, take place in the day; and the parliamentary forms are modeled on those of the old country.

I was sometimes asked, in my progress through other places, whether I had not been very much impressed by the *heads* of the lawmakers at Washington; meaning not their chiefs and leaders, but literally their individual and personal heads, whereon their hair grew, and whereby the phrenological character of each legislator was expressed; and I almost as often struck my questioner dumb with indignant consternation by answering, "No, that I didn't remember being at all overcome." As I must, at whatever hazard, repeat the avowal here, I will follow it up by relating my impressions on this subject in as few words as possible.

In the first place, it may be from some imperfect development of my organ of veneration, I do not remember having ever fainted away, or having even been moved to tears of joyful pride, at sight of any legislative body. I have borne the House of Commons like a man and have yielded to no weakness but slumber in the House of Lords. I have seen elections for borough and county and have never been impelled (no matter which Party won) to damage my hat by throwing it up into the air in triumph, or to crack my voice by shouting forth any reference to our Glorious Constitution, to the noble purity of our independent voters, or the unimpeachable integrity of our independent Members. Having withstood such strong attacks upon my fortitude, it is possible that I may be of a cold and insensible temperament, amounting to iciness, in such matters; and therefore, my impressions of the live pillars of the Capitol at Washington must be received with such grains of allowance as this free confession may seem to demand.

Did I see in this public body an assemblage of men bound together in the sacred names of Liberty and Freedom, and so asserting the chaste dignity of those twin goddesses, in all their discussions, as to exalt at once the Eternal Principles to which their names are given, and their own character, and the character of their countrymen, in the admiring eyes of the whole world?

It was but a week since an aged, gray-haired man, a lasting honor to the land that gave him birth, who has done good service to his country, as his forefathers did, and who will be remembered scores upon scores of years after the worms bred in its corruption are but so many grains of dust, it was but a week since this old man had stood for days upon his trial before this very body, charged with having dared to assert the infamy of that traffic which has for its accursed merchandise men and women and their unborn children. Yes. And publicly exhibited in the same city all the while, gilded, framed, and glazed, hung up for general admiration, shown to strangers not with shame, but pride, its face not turned towards the wall, itself not taken down and burned, is the Unanimous Declaration of The Thirteen United States of America, which solemnly declares that All Men are created Equal, and are endowed by their Creator with the Inalienable Rights of Life, Liberty, and the Pursuit of Happiness!

It was not a month since this same body had sat calmly by, and heard a man, one of themselves, with oaths which beggars in their drink reject, threaten to cut another's throat from ear to ear. There he sat among them; not crushed by the general feeling of the assembly, but as good a man as any.

There was but a week to come, and another of that body, for doing his duty to those who sent him there; for claiming in a Republic the Liberty and Freedom of expressing their sentiments, and making known their prayer; would be tried, found guilty, and have strong censure passed upon him by the rest. His was a grave offense; indeed, for years before, he had risen up and said, "A gang of male and female slaves for sale, warranted to breed like cattle, linked to each other by iron fetters, are passing now along the open street beneath the windows of your Temple of Equality! Look!" But there are many kinds of hunters engaged in the Pursuit of Happiness, and they go variously armed. It is the Inalienable Right of some among them, to take the field after their Happiness, equipped with cat and cart-whip, stocks and iron collar, and to shout their view halloa! (always in praise of Liberty) to the music of clanking chains and bloody stripes.

Where sat the many legislators of coarse threats, of words and blows such as coal-heavers deal upon each other, when they forget their breeding? On every side. Every session had its anecdotes of that kind, and the actors were all there.

Did I recognize in this assembly a body of men who, applying themselves in a new world to correct some of the falsehoods and vices of the old, purified the avenues to Public Life, paved the dirty ways to Place and Power, debated and made laws for the Common Good, and had no Party but their Country?

I saw in them the wheels that move the meanest perversion of virtuous Political Machinery that the worst tools ever wrought. Despicable trickery at elections; underhanded tamperings with public officers; cowardly attacks upon opponents, with scurrilous newspapers for shields, and hired pens for daggers; shameful trucklings to mercenary knaves, whose claim to be considered is, that every day and week they sow new crops of ruin with their venal types, which are the dragon's teeth of yore, in everything but sharpness; aidings and abettings of every bad inclination in the popular mind, and artful suppressions of all its good influences: such things as these, and, in a word, Dishonest Faction in its most depraved and most unblushing form, stared out from every corner of the crowded hall.

Did I see among them the intelligence and refinement, the true, honest, patriotic heart, of America? Here and there were drops of its blood and life, but they scarcely colored the stream of desperate adventurers which sets that way for profit and for pay. It is the game of these men, and of their profligate organs, to make the strife of politics so fierce and brutal, and so destructive of all self-respect in worthy men, that sensitive and delicate-minded persons shall be kept aloof, and they, and such as they, be left to battle out their selfish views unchecked. And thus, this lowest of all scrambling fights goes on, and they who in other countries would, from their intelligence and station, most aspire to make the laws, do here recoil the furthest from that degradation.

That there are among the Representatives of the people in both Houses, and among all Parties, some men of high character and great abilities, I need not say. The foremost among those politicians who are known in Europe have been already described, and I see no reason to depart from the rule I have laid down for my guidance, of abstaining from all mention of individuals. It will be sufficient to add, that to the most favorable accounts that have been written of them I more than fully and most heartily subscribe; and that personal intercourse and free communication have bred within me, not the result predicted in the very doubtful proverb, but increased admiration and respect. They are striking men to look at, hard to deceive, prompt to act, lions in energy, Crichtons in varied accomplishment, Indians in fire of eye and gesture, Americans in strong and generous impulse, and they as well represent the honor and wisdom of their country at home as the distinguished gentleman who is now its minister at the British Court sustains its highest character abroad.

I visited both Houses nearly every day during my stay in Washington. On my initiatory visit to the House of Representatives, they divided against a decision of the chair; but the chair won. The second time I went, the Member who was speaking, being interrupted by a laugh, mimicked it, as one child would in quarreling with another, and added, "that he would make honorable gentlemen opposite sing out a little more on the other side of their mouths presently." But interruptions are rare; the speaker being usually heard in silence. There are more quarrels than with us, and more threatenings than gentlemen are accustomed to exchange in any civilized society of which we have record; but farmyard imitations have not as yet been imported from the Parliament of the United Kingdom. The feature in oratory which appears to be the most practised and most relished is the constant repetition of the same idea or shadow of an idea in fresh words; and the inquiry out of doors is not, "What did he say?" but, "How long did he speak?" These, however, are but enlargements of a principle which prevails elsewhere.

The Senate is a dignified and decorous body, and its proceedings are conducted with much gravity and order. Both houses are handsomely carpeted; but the state to which these carpets are reduced by the universal disregard of the spittoon with which every honorable member is accommodated, and the extraordinary improvements on the pattern which are squirted and dabbled upon it in every direction, do not admit of being described. I will merely observe that I strongly recommend all strangers not to look at the floor; and if they happen to drop anything, though it be their purse, not to pick it up with an ungloved hand on any account.

It is somewhat remarkable too, at first, to say the least, to see so many honorable members with swelled faces; and it is scarcely less remarkable to discover that this appearance is caused by the quantity of tobacco they contrive to stow within the hollow of the cheek. It is strange enough, too, to see an honorable gentleman leaning back in his tilted chair, with his legs on the desk before him, shaping a convenient "plug" with his penknife, and when it is quite ready for use, shooting the old one from his mouth, as from a popgun, and clapping the new one in its place.

I was surprised to observe that even steady old chewers of great experience are not always good marksmen, which has rather inclined me to doubt that general proficiency with the rifle of which we have heard so much in England. Several gentlemen called upon me who, in the course of conversation, frequently missed the spittoon at five paces, and one (but he was certainly short-sighted) mistook the closed sash for the open window, at three. On another occasion, when I dined out, and was sitting with two ladies and some gentlemen 'round a fire before dinner, one of the company fell short of the fireplace, six distinct times. I am disposed to think, however, that this was occasioned by his not aiming at that object, as there was a white marble hearth before the fender, which was more convenient, and may have suited his purpose better.

Caleb Atwater

Caleb Atwater (1778-1867) was an influential politician and noted historian in Ohio, his adoptive state. Atwater was also an early enthusiast in the study of archaeology and of the state's indigenous peoples. Writing anonymously as "A Citizen of Ohio," Atwater published his *Mysteries of Washington City* in 1844. The book recounts Atwater's impressions of the city upon his return to Washington, D.C. after a fourteen-year absence. *Mysteries of Washington City* may be considered an exposé, revealing characteristics about the Nation's Capital that Atwater apparently hesitated to attribute to his own pen.

"Speaking of Clerks"

Leaving Baltimore in the cars at 8 o'clock, A. M., we reached Washington City at 10 o'clock in the morning on New Year's Day. I had expected to have seen, at least, one hundred thousand people in Pennsylvania Avenue on New Year's Day, as I saw on that day fourteen years before. Now, I saw no crowd, no bustle, and heard no noise, and saw no stir. There was, however, as I learned at supper from some clerks who boarded where I put up, a levee of clerks and officers, who were dependents on the heads of Departments, and they called it "a crowd" of officers and office seekers? The nation had increased in numbers, greatly, since 1830, but only one thousand officers attended at the White House that day, whereas one hundred thousand people thronged the Avenue fourteen years before! Such was my impression from what I saw and heard that day. The change was striking and told the different feelings of the people towards the Captain from those formerly evinced towards the old General. I leave it to the reader to decide on the cause, but the fact made an impression at the time, and forced the comparison on my own mind, on the first day of the year 1844. Both days, that is, the first day of January 1830, and New Year's Day 1844, were equally fair, and the Avenue was now in a better condition than formerly, made so, at a large expense, by the nation. The officers of the government had doubled in numbers around the Chief Magistrate, but *the people* were not here now.

I had been absent from the city ever since early in August 1832, and it had undergone a change in its exterior appearance, in the meantime, of some magnitude. Its vacant lots had been built on, in many places; old buildings had been removed, and new ones, many of them large and elegant ones, had been erected in their stead. The improvements about the public buildings: the Capitol, the War Office, the President's House, &c., were considerable, and had cost the nation large sums of money. Besides these improvements, a new building of large dimensions had been built instead of the old Post Office, that fire had destroyed, since I had been here. A new Patent Office, of dimensions quite too large for any use to which the nation ought to devote it, had been built. The structure of this building seemed to me to be such that it will fall down in a few years, A new Treasury Office of vast dimensions, had also been built, since I had visited the city. Washington had now assumed more of a city-like aspect, instead of its old one, of a long straggling village. More churches had been built, in various parts of the city, and no disgusting sights of beggars and prostitutes met the eye. These circumstances added much to my satisfaction on my first day's visit to the seat of Government. I met and shook hands with many old friends, residing either here or in Georgetown. Washington no longer presents the outside of vice, and that circumstance speaks highly of those, who have so zealously labored to improve the morals, and mend the hearts, of the great mass of the citizens. Their labors must have been great, otherwise such success would not have followed their works.

I attended, afterwards, divine service in several of their churches in the city, and once in the Episcopal Church, with General Archibald Henderson's family, at the Navy Yard; but I always found good preaching, and orderly, and even devout congregations attending church. In the streets of the city, I have never seen an intoxicated person, whereas, twelve years since, I have seen fifty such sights in a day. Many of them were Members of Congress! During this long visit of several months, constantly visiting all the public places, I have not seen one Member of Congress, either intoxicated or in any wise misbehaving himself, on any occasion.

There may be vice here, but it no longer exhibits its disgusting front in public, and I have not sought for it, nor wished to find it. It is true, the passengers see signs in several places on the Avenue, with the words "BILLIARDS" or "BILLIARD SALOON" printed on them, but otherwise, the stranger would not know without inquiry where the gamblers resort for gaining what they call an "honest livelihood." The reflections I drew from such premises assure me of an improved state of morals, in the nation itself, in many respects. We may hope that moral feelings and moral principles will one day govern this great Republic, through its representatives, in our legislative assemblies.

Let us hope, too, that the day is not far off, when our highest officers, civil, naval, and military, will be sober, honest, and moral men. Many, perhaps all, or nearly all, of our older officers are such men even now, such men as General Henderson, Col. Abert, General Bomford, General Gibson, Col. Totten, General Towson, Maj. Lewis, Judge Blake, M. St. Clair Clarke, and many others, are such men now. The high respect in which these men are held by all who know them, will have a good effect on all their subordinates. The low estimation, likewise, in which men in high places, of an opposite character, are held here and elsewhere, will produce its good effects also. They stand out as beacons on the ocean of life, to warn off every mariner from such an iron bound coast. The success which has always attended the sons and daughters of such good men, and the total ruin which has followed, and overwhelmed the children of wicked officers of government, teach the same lessons of prudence, wisdom, and virtue.

It argues but poorly in favor of an aristocracy in this country, to see, in the offices, as minor clerks, the sons of highly respectable fathers, unless it be in cases, where a man with a family is reduced by misfortunes and losses, by untoward events, without any fault of his; or he may have been a literary man, like William Darby. In such a case, the government may, on the purest principles of morals, give such a man some easy place as a shelter in his old age. Such an act ought to rescue such a head of department from oblivion. Judge Blake deserves and receives his reward in the good opinion of all good men.

Speaking of clerks, it is to be regretted that the young men of this district should, early in life, accept of a clerkship, instead of setting out at once for themselves, whereby they can be more independent and have a better prospect of rising in the world as respectable men and useful ones too, than a clerkship can ever afford them. I was told that it was no very uncommon sight to see in a day one hundred such young men in office hours, walking the streets, standing in refectories, drinking spirits, or lounging about the lobbies of the two Houses, or sauntering about the rotundo with an umbrella over their heads, leading about some female friend! I was told also that while these loafers were thus engaged, the older clerks and older men with families to support, were over worked in their several offices. One hundred such clerks with high salaries, (often the highest ones) ought to be dismissed in a day, and substitutes found in the western states, who have almost nothing here in the departments. Such a state of things would sink any administration in the estimation of all the West.

I give this story for what it is worth, and for the sake of unity, in relation to the appointment of clerks, whose residence is in the District, we relate here another anecdote, which, in order of time belongs to a more recent era than the early part of our present visit. On the morning of the day when Messrs. Gilmer and Wilkins were nominated to the Senate, for the purpose of getting those nominations made that day, I called at the White House very early in the morning, and being the first on the spot by half an hour, the President, in accordance with his usual politeness towards me, directed the messenger to give to me, as the first one that morning whom he would see, the key of the door that led to the President's room, upstairs. I took the key and opened the door, putting my hand against the door case to prevent an ugly old woman getting ahead of me, on my way to see the President; but the old lady stooping under my arm and running before me, cried out aloud, "W . . . . . . ought to be clerk, W . . . . . . ought to be clerk." She kept before me, running a race, thus proclaiming, at the top of her voice, until she reached the President's room, where seating herself without leave or license, she continued her clamor for some minutes. Finally, finding no opportunity to be alone with the Chief Magistrate, I opened to him my business, notwithstanding the presence of this old witch of Endor. She declared that "although they had lived in the District almost one whole year, yet during all that long period they had procured no office yet." They had kept boarders, for which they had received only thirteen dollars a week for each boarder! They had been compelled, it seems, to hire a man at ten dollars a month, to wait on the boarders! Yet neither her husband nor her son-in-law had received any office. Hearing that two Secretaries were to be nominated that day she modestly insisted on "her husband's being a clerk under one of them." The President told her, "that he had nothing to do with such appointments, which he left to the Secretaries to make." It seems, from the best information I could obtain, that women, belonging to this District, and parts of Maryland and Virginia near Washington, come here constantly soliciting offices for their sons, husbands and other relatives. That they have often succeeded, is evident enough to the public injury, and to the injury of the public officers themselves. Were the same rules adopted now, that Jefferson and Madison adhered to formerly, a vast deal of personal inconvenience to the President would be avoided. The Presidents, to whom I have referred, required that all applications for offices should be made in writing. If the office was derived from the President and Senate, the application had to be made to the President; but if the office applied for came from a Secretary, then he only was addressed, but it must be in writing. A story has been for some time past running around the whole Union, during the last year, in relation to the appointment of a clerk. The tale itself is derived, we presume, from some officer here, yet is doubtless wholly untrue. Could that officer be believed, a woman residing in or near the District frequently called to see the President in order to get her husband appointed a clerk. After many vain attempts to accomplish her wishes, she is represented as having succeeded at last by informing the Chief Magistrate "that her husband was entirely helpless in his bed from sickness, and that she and her children must come to want unless her husband was appointed a clerk!"

Daniel Drayton

The American abolitionist Daniel Drayton (1802-1857) was born in New Jersey and spent most of his life as a waterman, working on various ships along the eastern seaboard of the United States. In 1847, Drayton was instrumental in helping an enslaved family from Washington, D.C. escape by ship northward and to freedom. The following year, Drayton was involved in a more ambitious attempt to assist over seventy enslaved people in escaping their bondage aboard the schooner *Pearl*. The effort was betrayed, and Drayton, crew members Edward Sayres and Chester English, and all the passengers aboard the *Pearl* were captured by authorities. For his actions, Drayton was condemned to spend over four years in prison in Washington. In this excerpt from his *Memoir*, Daniel Drayton recalls his arrival in the Nation's Capital after the capture of the *Pearl*.

"The Mob Made the Rush Upon Us"

When we landed at the steamboat-wharf in Washington, which is a mile and more from Pennsylvania Avenue and in a remote part of the city, but few people had yet assembled. We were marched up in a long procession, Sayres and myself being placed at the head of it, guarded by a man on each side; English following next, and then the negroes. As we went along, the mob began to increase; and, as we passed Gannon's slave-pen, that slave-trader, armed with a knife, rushed out, and with horrid imprecations, made a pass at me, which was very near finding its way through my body. Instead of being arrested, as he ought to have been, this slave-dealer was politely informed that I was in the hands of the law, to which he replied, "D — n the law! I have three negroes, and I will give them all for one thrust at this *d — d* scoundrel!" and he followed along, waiting his opportunity to repeat the blow. The crowd by this time was greatly increased. We met an immense mob of several thousand persons coming down Four-and-a-Half Street with the avowed intention of carrying us up before the Capitol and making an exhibition of us there. The noise and confusion was very great. It seemed as if the time for the lynching had come. When almost up to Pennsylvania Avenue, a rush was made upon us. "Lynch them! Lynch them! the *d — n* villains!" and other such cries, resounded on all sides. Those who had us in charge were greatly alarmed; and, seeing no other way to keep us from the hands of the mob, they procured a hack, and put Sayres and myself into it. The hack drove to the jail, the mob continuing to follow, repeating their shouts and threats. Several thousand people surrounded the jail, filling up the enclosure about it.

Our captors had become satisfied, from the statements made by Sayres and myself, and from his own statements and conduct, that the participation of English in the affair was not of a sort that required any punishment; and when the mob made the rush upon us, the persons having him in charge had let him go, with the intention that he should escape. After a while he had found his way back to the steamboat wharf; but the steamer was gone. Alone in a strange place, and not knowing what to do, he told his story to somebody whom he met, who put him in a hack and sent him up to the jail. It was a pity he lacked the enterprise to take care of himself when set at liberty, as it cost him four months' imprisonment and his friends some money. I ought to have mentioned before that, on arriving within the waters of the District, Sayres and myself had been examined before a Justice of the Peace, who was one of the captors, and who had acted as their leader. He had made out a commitment against us, but none against English; so that the persons who had him in charge were right enough in letting him go.

Sayres and myself were at first put into the same cell, but towards night we were separated. A person named Goddard, connected with the police, came to examine us. He went to Sayres first. He then came to me, when I told him that, as I supposed he had got the whole story out of Sayres, and as it was not best that two stories should be told, I would say nothing. Goddard then took from me my money. One of the keepers threw me in two thin blankets, and I was left to sleep as I could. The accommodations were not of the most luxurious kind. The cell had a stone floor, which, with the help of a blanket, was to serve also for a bed. There was neither chair, table, stool, nor any individual piece of furniture of any kind, except a night-bucket and a water-can. I was refused my overcoat and valise, and had nothing but my water-can to make a pillow of. With such a pillow, and the bare stone floor for my bed, looked upon by all whom I saw with apparent abhorrence and terror, as much so to all appearance, as if I had been a murderer, or taken in some other desperate crime, remembering the execrations which the mob had belched forth against me, and uncertain whether a person would be found to express the least sympathy for me (which might not, in the existing state of the public feeling, be safe), it may be imagined that my slumbers were not very sound.

Meanwhile the rage of the mob had taken, for the moment, another direction. I had heard it said while we were coming up in the steamboat that the abolition press must be stopped; and the mob accordingly, as the night came on, gathered about the office of the *National Era* with threats to destroy it. Some little mischief was done; but the property-holders in the city, well aware how dependent Washington is upon the liberality of Congress, were unwilling that anything should occur to place the District in bad odor at the north. Some of them, also, it is but justice to believe, could not entirely give in to the slave-holding doctrine and practice of suppressing free discussion by force; and, by their efforts, seconded by a drenching storm of rain that came on between nine and ten o'clock, the mob were persuaded to disperse for the present. The jail was guarded that night by a strong body of police, serious apprehensions being entertained, lest the mob, instigated by the violence of many southern Members of Congress, should break in and lynch us. Great apprehension, also, seemed to be felt at the jail, lest we might be rescued; and we were subject, during the night, to frequent examinations, to see that all was safe. Great was the terror, as well as the rage, which the abolitionists appeared to inspire. They seemed to be thought capable, if not very narrowly watched, of taking us off through the roof, or the stone floor, or out of the iron-barred doors; and, from the half-frightened looks which the keepers gave me from time to time, I could plainly enough read their thoughts, that a fellow who had ventured on such an enterprise as that of the *Pearl* was desperate and daring enough to attempt anything. For a poor prisoner like me, so much in the power of his captors, arid without the slightest means, hopes, or even thoughts of escape, it was some little satisfaction to observe the awe and terror which he inspired.

Fredrika Bremer

By the time the Swedish feminist and political reformer Fredrika Bremer (1801-1865) made her lengthy visit to the United States in 1849-1851, she was already an established author and well-known in the English-speaking world for her *Sketches of Everyday Life*, published in the 1840s.

In the following excerpt from Bremer's *Homes of the New World*, published in the 1850s, she reflects upon the debate in Congress over the Compromise Bill, perhaps the most contentious political issue in America during her visit. It is a vivid portrayal of the high drama that increasingly played out in the Nation's Capital during the decade prior to the American Civil War.

"'No! No!' to the Compromise Bill"

I have visited every day the Senate and the Assembly of Representatives, though generally the former, because I hear well there, and because as a parliamentary assembly it seems, in every case, to stand above the other.

In the House of Representatives, no speaker may occupy more than an hour of time. As soon as the hour is at an end, and a little bell rings, another speaker has a right to interrupt him, even should it be in the very midst of his most profound argument, or in the highest flight of his genius, and demand general attention for *his* speech, which may occupy another hour, after which he again must give place to someone else, and as the speakers in a general way speak with great ease, and have a [great] deal to say, they are anxious to make good use of their power, and that I suppose is the reason for the headlong speed with which the speech is hurled forth, like an avalanche, into the House, at least it has been so every time I have been there. A certain kind of hurry-hurry seems to prevail in this House, which contrasts strongly with the decorum of the Senate. There, each Senator may speak as long as he will, nay even through the whole of the session if he chose, without anyone having a right to interrupt him except to make an observation or with his consent.

During this talking however, whether in the Senate or the House of the Representatives, I am often enough minded of Mr. Poinsett's words when I praised the American talent for talking. "It is a great misfortune!" But is it better as regards this misfortune in other countries assemblies where people make speeches? And if I do sigh now and then as I listen to a speech, yet I am interested by many on account of their straightforwardness, on account of the subjects upon which they touch, or on account of the speakers themselves. I like both to see and to hear parliamentary assemblies. Human nature seems to me great when it stands forth and does battle for some high purpose or principle, and if it be possessed of power or of genius, it wins great victories; and I love to see human nature great and important, to see it from its private little world, its isolated point, labor for the whole World. And even without genius, human nature represents, as a moral power, an interesting sight, merely by its *"yes"* or *"no."* Such an assembly is in its operation a grand dramatic scene, and there sometimes occur in it scenes and episodes of much more vital effect than many a one which we witness on the stage.

Some such, at which I have been present here, I will mention to you. But first a word about the scene itself; that is to say, the Senate, because it has an especial interest for me, inasmuch as all the Senators represent States, and the characteristic and poetic features of these present themselves to my imagination in picturesque groups, in the men who represent them. Each State in the Union sends two Senators to Congress.

These stand up in the Senate and are addressed not as Mr. this or that, but as the Senator of Kentucky, or Massachusetts, or Mississippi, or Louisiana, and so on; and I then immediately see before me an image of Kentucky, or Massachusetts, or Mississippi, or Louisiana, according to what I know of the life and temperament of the States, as well in spirit as in natural scenery, even though the human representative may not answer to it; and the whole fashion and form of this hemisphere stands before me like a great drama, in which Massachusetts and Louisiana, Carolina and Pennsylvania, Ohio and Alabama, and many others, are acting powers with definite individuality. Individuality is again supplied by the surname, which chance, or the humor of the people, have given to some of the States, and according to which it would be easy to christen all. Thus, I behold here the Emperor State (New York), the Granite State (New Hampshire); the Keystone State (Pennsylvania); the Wolverines (Michigan); and many other tilt and combat with the Giant State (Kentucky); with the Palmetto State (Carolina); the French State (Louisiana), and so on. And the warfare that goes on about the Gold State, called also the Pacific State (California), calls forth all those marked features and circumstances which distinguish and separate the Northern and the Southern States, and which set them in opposition one to the other. I will now tell you what the great apple of contention looks like, which has been here fought for during the last seven months. Behold!

THE COMPROMISE BILL.

The admission of California as a State into the Union, the arrangement of Territorial Administration for Utah (the Mormon State) *and New Mexico, as well the project for determining the western and north-western boundary of Texas.*

And now a word in explanation: in order that a State can have a right to be admitted as such into the Union it is necessary for it to have a population of at least 55,000 souls. Until then every separate portion of the United States' land is called [a] Territory and is governed, during the period of its development and minority, more immediately by the Federal Administration which appoints a Governor and other officials and furnishes troops to defend the inhabitants against the Indians or other enemies, whatever they may be, of whom the population of the Territory may complain. Every State in the Union has a right to form its own laws, on condition that they do not encroach upon the enactments of the other Federal States, as well as that the form of government be republican. The Territory again has not the privileges of the State, and people are not yet agreed as to how far its privileges of self-government ought to extend. Well now; California, the population of which became suddenly augmented to above 150,000 souls, principally by emigration from the free northeastern States, desires to be admitted into the Union as a Free State. New Mexico, which in consequence of the Mexican law is free from slavery, and Utah which calls its young population. "Latter-Day Saints," desire also, as Territories, resolutely to oppose the introduction of slavery.

But as these three States, that which has attained its majority as well as those which yet remain in their minority, are situated below a geographical line called the Missouri Line, which accordingly to ancient agreement is to constitute the line of separation between the Free States and the Slave States, so that all the States north of this line shall have a right to be free from slaves, and all States lying to the south of it have a right to slaves and slave-labor; and as three new States would disturb the balance of political power between the North and the South and give the preponderance to the North and the Free States, therefore do all the men of the South, yet not all!, cry "No! No!" to this; and the ultras amongst them add, "rather will we break with the North and form ourselves into a separate Union, the Southern States' Union! We will declare war against the North!"

The Southerners insist upon it that both California and New Mexico shall be open to receive their slave institutions, and beyond this they insist that Congress shall pass a law forbidding the Free States to give harborage and protection to fugitive slaves, and that it shall give to them, the Southerners, the right to demand and obtain the aid of the legislative power in the Free States for the recovery of their human property.

To this the men of the North shout "No! No!" with all their might. And the ultras of their Party add, "Rather, bloody war! We will never consent to Slavery! Away with Slavery! We will remain a free people! Congress shall pass a law to forbid slavery in every new State."

Many of the Southerners admit in the meantime the right of California to enter the Union as a Free State but deny to the Territories any right to legislate for themselves on the question of slavery. The Southerners in general maintain that they do not contend for the cause of slavery, but for States' Rights and the cause of the Constitution. Many are right in this assertion, but with many others it is easy to see that the interests of slavery color their opposition.

Other questions of contention belong to the same category, as, for instance, whether Columbia, the District in which Washington stands, shall continue to hold slaves or not. There is at the present time, within sight of the Capitol, a gloomy, gray building, half-buried in trees, as if ashamed of itself, that is a slave-pen, where slaves are brought up or kept for sale. Washington is situated in the Slave State of Maryland. One portion of the Southerners are anxious to maintain, even here, their beloved domestic institutions, as the phrase is. Another point of contention is the question about the boundaries between Texas and Mexico, and about a strip of land between the Slave State and the yet Free Territory, or which shall have and which shall give up this piece; and Freedom and Slavery get to fighting anew on this ground about this piece of land.

Such is the aspect which this great apple of discord presents, an actual gordian knot which seems to demand the sword of an Alexander to sever.

Henry Clay's scheme of compromise says California shall be introduced into the Union as a Free State, according to her wishes, because her population of nearly 200,000 have a right to determine their measures. New Mexico shall wait for the determination of the law until she is possessed of a population large enough to constitute a State. She shall, in the meantime, continue to be a Territory without slaves. And the same with regard to Utah.

On the contrary, the Slave States shall possess the right to demand the restoration of their fugitive slaves, and if it be necessary, to regain them by the aid of law as the Constitution has decreed.

Columbia shall be a Free District, from which slavery shall be banished.

These, I believe, are the principal points of Clay's scheme to bring about peace between the North and South. Both North and South, however, demand greater concession, each on his own side, and exclaim "No! No!" to the Compromise Bill.

John F. Weishampel

John Frederick Weishampel, Jr. (1832-1904), born a century to the year after George Washington, was a Baltimore-based publisher of guidebooks to his native city and of various religious tracts, including *The Man Christ Jesus* and *A Narrative of the Life of Reverend Noah Davis, a Colored Man*. Early in his career, Weishampel published the text of an address he had given in Philadelphia on Washington's birthday in 1852. Weishampel's address focused on an issue of growing concern regarding the Nation's Capital and the construction of the Washington Monument. The address is reprinted here and in full.

"Feared by Many"

Fellow Countrymen:

Permit me, a humble citizen of one of these United States, to call your attention to a subject that, as far as I have been able to learn, has failed to elicit the investigation of the Pulpit or the Press, and that to me appears to be one of no ordinary import, as touching the future destiny of our beloved Country. It behooves us, as friends of that Country, to watch, with a jealous eye, every effort that is made by the enemies of its free institutions, under whatever pretense, to subvert its government and destroy its liberties. I have reference to the proffer, by the *Pope of Rome*, of a *block of marble for the Washington National Monument*, now in course of erection at the City of Washington, the Capital of the United

States, which is intended to bear the inscription: "Rome to America." This proffer should wake up in every Protestant the spirit of inquiry as to the probable motives that actuate the Pope, and the object he may have in view. And let me seriously ask you, in the face of the history of Popery, *Is there no cause to induce suspicion and alarm?* Let us look into the matter.

The first thing that claims our attention, is the inscription upon the block: "Rome to America." Is this inscription appropriate? What, I ask, is the design of erecting the Monument? I understand it to be to perpetuate the memory of the illustrious and immortal Washington, and to transmit to posterity a worthy memorial of the high honor which the American people have always conferred upon him, as a pure patriot, a good man, and (as he is justly termed) the "Father of his Country," the deliverer, under God, of his Country from the galling yoke of foreign bondage and oppression. And this Monument is to be *American*, erected by the American people, a *National* and not a Universal memorial. But how does the inscription "Rome to America" correspond to this view? In the first place, it is a *foreign* contribution, thrust upon us without an invitation or a precedent; and secondly, with an inappropriate inscription. "Rome to America." Is it not the language of greeting from the one Country to the other? And does our Country require such a greeting from the Pope that an amicable relation may be continued? Or does America need such a token of pretended respect from Rome, the Roman Power? No! Then the inscription is not appropriate; and therefore, the block has no claim to a place in the Monument.

The inscription is now "Rome to America." Suppose we ask whether the Pope designs that it shall ever be altered to *Rome in America*. It is feared by many that the Papal throne will be removed to America. Indeed, there was much talk of it in 1849. If it ever be located here, those significant words will be referred to, by his adherents, as an inspired prophecy of the change of location of that holy Power! Then the Monument would cease to be a Washington memorial, it would be converted into a trophy of Roman Papal victory, a pillar of triumph of *Rome in America*. For it is a fact that our Country is being every year more densely populated by the Pope's zealous followers, and his menials; and when we take into consideration that the Roman Power moves with deliberation, and looks far ahead, making calculations upon successes hundreds of years hence, and that it spares no means, nor "leaves one stone unturned" to accomplish its despotic designs, we have sufficient reasons to scan its apparent friendly approaches and guard against its encroachments in every shape and form. We have already one Cardinal, a foreigner, a man who would, unquestionably, betray our Country into the hands of the holy *Papa*, if it were in his power to do so; soon we will have more; for his subjects are increasing here so rapidly that it will be graciously granted as a measure of *justice* to *America*! To have a greater representation in the holy conclave in Rome! Next, we may hear of his Holiness flying (under false pretense) "*to* America" for safety; and ultimately, he may modestly erect his heaven-on-earth throne in Father Mathew's Cathedral in Washington, near by the base of the Monument bearing the predictive inscription "Rome to America." Query. Had Father Mathew an eye to that when traveling through the U[nited] States, often in great poverty! Who received many gifts of charity to relieve his embarrassed situation, but who in the end was rich enough to buy the lot at a tremendous price and present it for the great Cathedral to be erected upon it?

When the great holy Potentate
Removes from Rome in royal state,
And "to America" shall come,
Where else but here will then be Rome?

So far as I have learned no other foreign power has made any similar proffer, and the likelihood is that none will, for the very good reason that the Monument is an *American* affair altogether. Especially do I suppose that none of the Emperors, Kings, or Queens of other despotic or even limited monarchies will offer to do so, from the additional reason that it would be inconsistent with their character, and thus perhaps detrimental to their existing dignity at home. Their system of government is despotic, absolute, or, at best, anti-republican; ours is republican and democratic; they all, more or less, play the lord over the people, while here the people are their own lords; they curtail the people's liberties wherever they can, while our magnanimous Washington fought to *give the people liberty*; and when he had it in his power to play the game of the Bonapartes and other usurpers, he proved himself the people's true friend, by not only filling the office of President with a father's care, and with honor to his Country and himself, but by laying down precepts and examples for the future welfare of the new Republic, over which he was the first man that was called to preside, and among those precepts and examples were these: To beware of foreign influence, not to meddle with the affairs of other nations, and not to have any man to serve more than two terms in the presidential chair. Their positions are so vastly different to these principles, that the thought does not probably occur to them to send blocks of stone for the Monument.

Such a man, although the monarchs of the world must do him the justice to admit his greatness and goodness, such a man they cannot so signally and perpetually honor (with *consistency*) as to place blocks of stone in the Monument, which is designed to stand to the end of time for the admiration of the people of all the nations under the sun, which shall be to our future generations the rainbow token of salvation from foreign bondage. No, they offer no such hypocritical offerings. But the subtle Pope, he passes over this inconsistency, and as though the world were blind to it, offers to place one there. But he adopts an inscription that shall not convict him of duplicity, and one that shall for the present appear as a gracious token of friendship from "Rome to America." It says nothing of Washington, nothing of liberty, nothing of human rights. And our Monument Committee, like a certain kind of fish, that catches at anything red, even if it be a bit of flannel on a hook, accept the proffer in great haste, and return thanks to this "god on earth" for his condescending consideration, for his hypocritical contribution. I consider that they had no right to accept it until the people had an opportunity to express their opinion upon the subject. I repeat again, that it is an *American* National Monument, and we should be jealous as to who shall be permitted to place blocks in its structure; and no despots ought to be allowed to do so under any pretense whatever.

Now let it be understood that I am not opposing the Roman Catholic Church, but the *Politico-Religious policy of the Roman Power.* I have no objections to any church, as such, or all Protestant churches together, or Catholic and Protestant churches conjointly, in our whole Country, contributing blocks or one general block of marble for this Monument. Indeed, I think it would be in good keeping with the Christian character we desire to maintain as a Nation, if they did so. Might they not all, or singly, with great propriety, furnish a block, with the inscription "To God be all the glory!" To be placed above all those bearing inscriptions? This would not detract one iota of honor from Washington. On the contrary, it would throw around his immortal name the hallowed glory of the Christian Religion, in the faith of which he lived and died. We as a people believe that God raised up our Washington to lead us out of bondage, and we look to that God with gratitude, and thank him for all his good providence, by which we have been made and preserved a free and happy Nation. It becomes us, but especially the people professing to be worshippers of that God, to say, in the language of the devout David of old: "Not unto us, O Lord! Not unto us, but unto Thy name give glory for thy mercy's sake."

Yes, fellow citizens, I desire to oppose the approaches, under the garb of friendship, of a Power that will, when it gains the designed and desired ascendency, burn our Bibles, bind our consciences, make slaves of us, and put us to the stake, the rack, or the dungeon, for attempting to exercise the free minds with which a gracious Creator has gifted us. It is true, we may not live to suffer these things; but our descendants, not many generations hence, may have cause to lament the supineness and imprudence of their too easily duped ancestors. If I should succeed in arousing you to the consideration of this subject and cause you to save the Country from the insult referred to, I shall feel that I have done the cherished land of my birth a noble service, upon which my descendants may look with pride.

The effects of this block, if placed in the Monument, will be a mortification to nearly every American Protestant who looks upon it; and its influence upon the zealous supporters of the Roman hierarchy will be tremendous, especially with foreigners. They will look through it *at the Pope*, and not at Washington. I fancy I see a foreign papist winding his way up the quadrangular stairs, and he passes the hundreds of inscriptions with but little emotion; but suddenly his eyes rest upon "Rome to America." Instantly he makes the sign of the cross, bows, and perhaps, exclaims, "Holy mother! Here is the blessed gift of his Holiness!" When he descends, he will remember that inscription, though he should forget all the rest, and he will remember it for life, and ever communicate to his children and others, that the holy Pope has *honored* Washington with a sacred block of marble, taken from the ancient Temple of Peace at Rome. And upon that assumed fact will they base the erroneous presumption, that the Roman Power (dwelling in the Pope) is generous, liberal, and friendly to human freedom and human rights. This will forever shut the ears of all the American descendants of the papist against every argument and fact relative to the despotism and tyranny of the Roman Power, and blind their eyes, so as to prevent them from seeing any danger, danger of losing *American liberty* and *human rights*, such liberty and rights as no country ever enjoys when the Papal influence sways it.

What is to be done? What can be done in this matter? Can we prevent the reception and placing the block in the sacred walls of the Monument? Perhaps not: seeing that the Committee have accepted the proffer. But we can enter our solemn protest against it. Let the Protestants everywhere in the whole Land hold meetings and send to the Committee the protestations of those meetings against that measure; and if that will not induce the Committee to recall their acceptance, then let a protest block be furnished by us, to be placed by the side of the objectionable stone, bearing an inscription by which all men may see that we are awake to the hypocrisy and schemes of that designing, crafty, subtle, far-seeing and far-reaching Power, which is ever grasping after the whole World, to sway its iron scepter, with blood-stained hands, over the millions of its inhabitants.

Will the Monument Committee heed such a protest? I am fully persuaded they would sooner incur the displeasure of the Pope, by recalling their letter, than that of a great majority of their fellow countrymen, by placing the objectionable stone in the building, which has Justice for its foundation, Freedom for its crowning stone, and Human Happiness for its glory. No, they will not, they dare not so insult the American people. I repeat, let the American Catholics put in a block of stone as a church testimonial, if they choose, and so every other church; but O keep the foreign influence, especially of avowed deadly enemies to human rights, and above all, the Roman Power, from desecrating that pure pillar, so sacredly dedicated to the memory of the good and great Washington! The friend of human rights, and the foe to despotism and tyranny! Fellow Countrymen, in the name of all that you hold dear in this world, let its high-towering column not be blemished by a foreign, despotic, and tyrannical hypocrite's hand, or a hypocrite's gift!

Philadelphia, near *Independence Hall*,
Washington's Birthday, Feb. 22, 1852.

Let every true friend to our common Country aid in speedily circulating this warning throughout the land, that all may be roused before the Pope shall have placed his block in the Freedom Monument. Be wide awake! Watch!

Casimir Bohn

Casimir Bohn (1816-1883) was a German immigrant to the United States who operated a bookstore on Pennsylvania Avenue. Bohn also published popular guidebooks to Washington, D.C. during the 1850s. Editions of his *Hand-Book of Washington* included steel engravings illustrating the city's public buildings, statuary, and other popular tourist destinations. Later editions of Bohn's *Hand-Book* were revised and updated by Charles Lanman. The following selections excerpted from the 1860 edition of Bohn's *Hand-Book* describe for visitors what they might expect to see in the Nation's Capital on the eve of the Civil War.

"The Capitol"

The New Hall of Representatives

The new Hall of Representatives is 139 feet long, 93 feet wide, and 36 feet high.

It is in the form of a parallelogram, with galleries on three sides, affording room for 1,200 persons, comfortably seated. Upon the floor are seats for 260 Representatives, arranged upon a semicircular plan, the seat and desk of the Speaker of the House being at the center of the semicircle, and in the middle of the south side of the Hall, which is one of the longer sides of the room.

The ceiling is of cast-iron, with large skylights. The cast-iron ceiling is deeply coffered with sunk panels, relieved with enriched moldings.

A richly decorated cornice along the upper part of the wall, above the galleries, unites the wall and ceiling.

The skylights are glazed with ornamented glass, having in the center of each skylight the arms of a State or Territory, emblazoned in colored glass.

The room is lit at night by means of about 1,500 jets of gas, which are placed above the glass of the ceiling, and which throw down a soft and agreeable light, scarcely to be distinguished from that of a bright day.

The area of this room is 12,927 square feet. It contains 465,372 cubic feet of space. About five thousand persons could stand in it if crowded, as is not uncommon in public meetings.

The room is ventilated by numerous openings in the walls and floor, through which air, warmed in cold weather, by steam pipes in the basement, is forced by a revolving fan of sixteen feet in diameter. This fan is driven by a steam engine and is capable of supplying one hundred thousand cubic feet of air per minute, and thus of renewing the whole of the air in the Hall every five minutes.

This engine and fan are placed in the cellar under the northwest corner of the south wing of the Capitol. The steam pipes, of which ten miles are used, to be able at any time, in the severest weather, to control the temperature of the Hall, are placed in a room behind the western stairway of the south wing.

The boilers are in vaults under the western terrace, outside of the building. These things are well worth a visit, and the people employed by the House to manage them and keep them in order will always be found ready and obliging to give any information or explanation in regard to them.

The decoration of the Hall is yet far from complete. Panels on the gallery fronts have been provided, which it is expected will be filled with pictures of American History, under the orders to be given by Congress; and the upper part of the walls is filled with niches, empty as yet, but which will, at some future day, be tenanted by the effigies in marble of our worthiest citizens.

The walls and ceiling of the Hall have been richly colored, and, when the panels are filled with paintings, and the niches with statues, the room will have a much more finished appearance. At present, the design of the architect being incomplete, the effect he arrived at can scarcely be appreciated.

The New Senate Chamber

The new Senate Chamber is built on the same general plan as that of the Representative Chamber. It is in the north wing, in the center of the second or principal floor. Like the other, it is ceiled with iron and glass, lighted from above, and surrounded by galleries, under which are cloak and hat and dressing rooms for the use of Senators.

The style of decoration is rich, but in lighter color than those used in the Representative Chamber.

Panels for pictures, and niches for statues, as yet empty, occupy the walls.

The lighting, heating, and ventilation are arranged upon the same general plan as those of the House.

The size of the room is 80 feet 7 inches by 113 feet 3 inches; the height is 36 feet. The galleries seat comfortably 1,200 persons.

The heating and ventilating apparatus is under the southwest corner of the north wing and is approached by a small staircase under the principal western stairway. The boilers are under the exterior western terrace.

The New Dome

The old Dome of the Capitol was built of wood. The outer and inner shells were not concentric, and while the inner was in proportion a copy of that of the Pantheon of Agrippa at Rome, though much inferior in size, the outer dome was higher in proportion than that of the Pantheon.

Its inflammable nature, and its narrow escape at the time the library was burnt, in 1851, called attention to it, and it was finally resolved to replace it by a Dome of iron, entirely fire-proof.

The new Dome, in its proportions, resembles the modern rather than the antique structures of this character. Instead of the low and flat outlines of the Pantheon of Rome, and the Saint Sophia of Constantinople, we see in the design a light structure, decorated with columns and pilasters, rich cornices and entablatures, springing up towards the sky, and supporting, at the height of three hundred feet above the ground of the eastern square, and 372 feet above the western gate of the park, a colossal Statue of Freedom in bronze, from the studio of the lamented [Thomas] Crawford.

The interior diameter of the Dome is 96 feet. The height from floor of rotunda to the ceiling, which closes it in, is 220 feet in the clear. Galleries at various heights will afford fine views of the interior and of the exterior, the views stretching many miles down the Potomac.

The structure is double and between the exterior and interior shells, a staircase winding spirally around the whole, affording access to the very summit.

The general outline of this structure resembles that of the Dome of St Peter's of Rome, of St. Paul's of London, and of St. Genevieve and the Invalides of Paris, and of the last great work of the kind erected in modern times, that of the Hussian National Church, the Cathedral of St. Isaac's at St. Petersburg, which is also partly built of iron.

The interior diameter of the Dome is, as stated above, 96 feet. The exterior diameter of the peristylian circular colonnade is 124 feet 9½ inches. The height of the whole 300 feet above the ground, or 230 feet above the roof of the Capitol.

The height of the Statue of Freedom which will crown the pinnacle is 20 feet.

"Churches"

The Metropolis is well supplied with Churches, and considering its extent is quite as well supplied with eloquent preachers, as any city in the Union. Of Baptist Churches there are four, one on Tenth Street, one on E, and two on Virginia Avenue; their Congregations are all large and their pastors popular. Of Roman Catholic Churches there are four, St. Matthew's, on H Street, St. Peter's, on Second, St. Patrick's, on F, and St. Mary's on Fifth. Of Episcopal Churches there are five, viz. Christ Church, on G Street, St. John's, on H, Trinity on Third, Epiphany, on G, and Ascension, on H. The Trinity Church edifice is one of the handsomest, devoted to religion, in the City. It is after the Gothic style of architecture. It is the Church where Mr. Webster and Mr. Clay were in the habit of attending, when in Washington. In this Church, as indeed in all the other Churches of the City, a certain number of pews are assigned to strangers. St. John's Church stands directly in front of the President's House, and when the President happens to attend there, is considered the meeting place of the town. There is also one Quaker meeting held in the City, on I Street; and two Lutheran Churches, the English on H Street, and the German on G Street. Of Methodist Churches there are seven in the City: one on 4th, one on 14th, one on 5th, one on Massachusetts Avenue, one on Maryland Avenue, one on 9th Street, and one on Virginia Avenue. Of Presbyterian Churches there are six, one on F Street, one on 8th Street, one on 4th Street, one on H, and two on 9th Street. There is also one Unitarian Church in the City, on D Street; and of colored Churches there are some half dozen scattered about the City. In Georgetown there are two Episcopalian Churches, one Presbyterian, one Roman Catholic, and several Methodist and Baptist Churches.

"Columbian College"

This Institution, which was incorporated in 1821, is beautifully situated on an eminence, adjoining the City Corporation on the North, and on 14th Street West. It is a fine brick edifice, four stories high, and overlooks the City, Capitol, and other Public Buildings; and commands a fine view of the Potomac, with the surrounding country, for many miles in extent. In beauty and healthfulness of position, it is unsurpassed; and its local advantages are such as no other situation in the country can afford.

Its proximity to the National Metropolis gives to young men the opportunity of observing distinguished public characters; of becoming acquainted with the nature and operations of our Government, and of witnessing the highest exhibitions of talent in the halls of Congress and in the Supreme Court of the United States. This is a great advantage, especially to those who are destined to public life; and its practical effects are seen in the number of its Alumni who are now filling important and useful stations in society.

The College has a good Library, a valuable Philosophical Apparatus, and other means and facilities for pursuing a thorough and liberal course of studies. The last Catalogue (1850) embraces a President, and twelve Professors and Teachers, including those of the National Medical College, which is under the same Corporation, one hundred students, and between two and three hundred Alumni.

The expenses of a student, including board, tuition, and all College charges, are about $180 per annum; for those who do not board in the College, it is about $65 or $70 per annum.

"Hotels"

Hotels are quite numerous, but not sufficiently so, even now, to accommodate the public. With one or two unimportant exceptions, they are all situated on Pennsylvania Avenue. The names of the principal ones are the National Hotel, Brown's Hotel, Willard's Hotel, the United States Hotel, the Kirkwood House, the Washington Hotel (formerly Gadsby's), and the American Hotel. All these hotels are supplied with the best of a first-rate market, and with numerous and generally accommodating servants. From the doors of each, the stranger may at almost any moment step into a convenient and elegant omnibus and go to almost any part of the city he may desire. The prices charged for board are not uniform, but the expenses generally are by no means lower than in such cities as Philadelphia, New York, and Boston. Of private boarding houses there are a great number, and by lovers of quiet these are frequently preferred to the more public establishments. The Washington Club have their quarters in a spacious building on President Square.

"Markets"

From hotels the transition to the markets of the town is natural. Of market houses there are four, but the largest and most important is Center Market on Pennsylvania Avenue. In describing this, we describe them all. A greater variety of good things can nowhere be found collected under one roof, than may at all times be found in Center Market. The highlands of Maryland and Virginia supply it with beef and mutton that cannot be excelled, while the adjoining country pours into it a variety of vegetables that makes one wonder where they all come from. In the way of fish, the Potomac yields a great variety, the shad, rock fish or bass and the oysters, having no superior in the country: and no market is better supplied with venison, wild turkey, ortolan, reed-birds and the famous canvas-back ducks. And then again, although the Center Market building is by no means a classical one, yet no market in this land has been frequented by so many illustrious men, such men for example as Marshall and Jackson, Webster, Clay, and John Quincy Adams; and those who take pleasure in studying the peculiarities of an interesting negro population cannot fail to be amused by a morning walk in and about the Center Market when business is in full blast.

"National Cemetery"

The National or Congressional Burial Ground is situated about one mile east of the Capitol, embraces about ten acres, commands an extensive view of the country, is well enclosed with a brick wall, laid out with taste, and beautified with trees and shrubbery. It was located in 1807 and ever since been in the keeping of an incorporated company. The Monuments are manifold and many of them beautiful; and in addition to several private vaults is one spacious and well-constructed, enclosed by a neat railing, built by the order and at the expense of Congress, as a place of deposit for the dead whose remains it may be the purpose of friends subsequently to remove.

Measures have recently been adopted to enlarge this Cemetery, and some twenty additional acres will soon be brought within its limits. The number of interments which have taken place up to the present time is six thousand.

A visit to the "City of the Dead" cannot but prove interesting to the stranger visiting the Metropolis, and among the few and picturesque monuments which will attract his attention, are those to the memory of George Clinton, Elbridge Gerry, Major General Jacob Brown, Joseph Lovel, Commodore Rogers' son, A. P. Upsher, Commodore Beverly Kennon, Lieut. G. M. Bache, Capt. B. A. Terrett, the wife of Peter von Schmidt, Judge Pendleton Barbour, and Peter Lenox. Quite a large number of Members of Congress have been buried here, and there is a mournful interest in wandering among the monuments which commemorate their names.

"Smithsonian Institution"

This Institution was founded upon a bequest of more than half a million of dollars, made to the United States by an Englishman named James Smithson, a man of good family, and of sufficient learning to have published in the Transactions of the Royal Society and other Journals no less than twenty-four scientific treatises, the majority of which were on Mineral Chemistry. The object of the bequest, according to his will, was "To found at Washington, under the name of the Smithsonian Institution, an Establishment for the increase and diffusion of knowledge among men." On the 1st of July 1836, Congress solemnly accepted this important trust, and the money was paid into the Treasury of the United States in 1838. The Act of Congress establishing the Institution as it now exists, was passed in 1846. By this Act, the President, Vice President, all the Members of the Cabinet, the Chief Justice, the Commissioner of the Patent Office and the Mayor of Washington, during the time for which they should hold their offices, were made the personnel of the Institution; and they are to be assisted by a Board of Regents, who were to be empowered to elect a Chancellor, a Secretary, and an Executive Committee.

The Institution is situated on the Mall below the Capitol, and though the edifice is yet in an unfinished state, it presents a noble appearance, and is unquestionably one of the great attractions of the Metropolis. The style of the Architecture is the Romanesque, the material a reddish free-stone of fine grain, its extreme length is four hundred and fifty feet, its width one hundred and forty feet, and it has nine towers varying in height from seventy-five to one hundred and fifty feet. The grounds which surround it are very extensive, and are now in progress of being beautified by Mr. Downing.

The Secretary of the Institution is *Professor Joseph Henry*, who has the reputation of being one of the most accomplished scientific men of the age, and the property of the Institution and its general operations are in his charge, and among his assistants are several gentlemen of high scientific and literary acquirements.

To describe minutely the interior economy of this important establishment is not our intention in this place. We can only say that its beneficial influence upon the world at large has already been felt; it has already printed and circulated a number of valuable volumes, acquired collections in the way of natural history and scientific as well as general literature which are very valuable and very interesting, and engaged distinguished men to deliver lectures. The great library room when completed will be capable of holding one hundred thousand volumes. The building is supplied with a lecture room, which will scat twelve hundred persons; and its Museum, when completed, will be two hundred feet long, and filled with the wonders of nature and art from all parts of the world; its rooms for Chemical experiments will be more spacious and convenient than any to be found in the country: and in the western wing which is one hundred and twenty feet long, will hereafter be located a gallery of Art. The collection of Indian pictures now on exhibition there is the property of Mr. Stanley the artist.

"Washington Monument"

As this Structure is not yet finished, we will not describe it as it is, but as it will be when completed, according to the design adopted by the Board of Managers. It stands on the Mall, between the President's House and the Potomac, and embraces the idea of a grand circular colonnaded building two hundred and fifty feet in diameter, one hundred feet high, from which springs an obelisk shaft seventy feet in diameter at the base and five hundred feet high, making a total elevation of six hundred feet.

The vast rotundo, forming the grand base of the Monument, will be surrounded by thirty columns of massive proportions, twelve feet in diameter and forty-five feet high, elevated upon a base of twenty feet in height and three hundred feet square, surmounted by an entablature twenty feet high, and crowned by a massive balustrade fifteen feet in height. The terrace outside the colonnade will be twenty-five feet wide, and the walk within the colonnade twenty-five feet. The front portico will be adorned with a triumphal car and Statue of the Illustrious Chief; and over each column around the entire building will be sculptured escutcheons, coats of arms of each State of the Union, surrounded by bronze civic wreaths, banded together by festoons of oak leaves, while the center of the portico will be emblazoned with the coat of arms of the United States. Around the rotundo will be stationed statues of the Signers of the Declaration of Independence: in niches prepared for the purpose, statues of the Fathers of the Revolution contemporary with Washington; and directly opposite to the entrance will be placed a statue of Washington himself. The interior of the shaft will be embellished with a great variety of inscriptions; at one point it will be ornamented with four of the leading events of Washington's career sculptured in *basso relievo*, above which will be placed a single star, emblematic of the glory which the name of Washington has attained; and in the center of the Monument will be placed the Tomb of the Father of his country.

"The White House"

The plan of this building was made by James Hoban, and the cornerstone was laid on the 13th of October 1792; but having been partially destroyed during the last war, the same architect was employed to rebuild it in 1815. It is situated at the "west end" of the city, at the intersection of Pennsylvania, New York, Connecticut, and Vermont Avenues. It occupies the center of a plat of ground containing twenty acres, and at an elevation of forty-four feet above the waters of the Potomac. For several years past the grounds both in front and in the rear of the President's House have been in a neglected condition, but under the management of competent persons the grounds lying south of the Mansion are being transformed into a magnificent park, which when completed, will afford a fine carriage drive of three or four miles, the Potomac at one end, and the Capitol at the other; the Smithsonian Institute and the Washington Monument being situated in its midst. Besides this, the same persons are planning the improvement of Lafayette and Franklin Squares into fine pleasure grounds. In the center of Lafayette Square has been placed Mr. Mills' colossal equestrian statue of General Jackson.

The Mansion in question is 170 feet front and 86 deep, is built of white freestone with Ionic pilasters comprehending two lofty stories of rooms, crowned with a stone balustrade. The north front is ornamented with a lofty portico, of four Ionic columns in front, and projecting with three columns. The outer inter-columniation is for carriages to drive under, and place company under shelter: the middle space is for those visitors who come on foot; the steps from both leading to a broad platform in front of the door of entrance. The garden front is varied by having a rusticated basement story under the Ionic ordonnance, and by a semi-circular projecting colonnade of six columns, with two flights of steps leading from the ground to the level of the principal story.

The interior arrangements of the Executive Mansion are of course elegant and convenient, well adapted to the various purposes for which the building was designed; and as the rooms, both public and private, are newly furnished with the coming in of every new Administration, we deem it unnecessary to trouble the reader with elaborate descriptions. All the public rooms may be examined by strangers at any time, but His Excellency the President can only be seen during those hours which he is pleased to designate. During the sessions of Congress, the President usually has two reception evenings, on which occasions the public at large are privileged to pay him their respects and promenade the famous East Room. In addition to this it is generally expected of him that during each winter he will entertain at dinner all the members of both Houses of Congress and the Diplomatic Corps, so that official dinners have to be given by him as often as twice a week. The grounds immediately around the Mansion are quite beautiful in themselves, but they present a particularly fine appearance during those summer afternoons when the citizens of Washington assemble there by hundreds and thousands for the purpose of enjoying the music of the Marine Band and the pleasures of a fashionable promenade.

In the center of the small square immediately in front of the President's House, stands a bronze statue of Thomas Jefferson, executed by whom we know not, but presented to the Government by Capt. Levy of the United States Navy, the present proprietor of Monticello, the former abode of Mr. Jefferson. It is a handsome piece of statuary, and in its present position has quite a commanding appearance. A resolution of acceptance, however, was never passed by Congress, so that this statue may be considered as still the private property of Capt. Levy. Directly across Pennsylvania Avenue from the above-mentioned square, is Lafayette Square, which, as before intimated, has recently been laid out in fashionable style, and planted with new shrubbery. Mills' Equestrian Statue of General Jackson occupies its center and is a work of superior merit. It is in bronze and was cast from certain cannon captured by General Jackson in some of his military engagements. The cost of this statue was $50,000, and a duplicate was ordered to be executed for the city of New Orleans, which commission has been duly executed by the successful artist.

Anthony Trollope

Anthony Trollope (1815-1882) was the son of that earlier and by now notoriously well-known visitor to the United States, Mrs. Francis Trollope. While the son is surely the better novelist (see *Barchester Towers* and the *Palliser* novels), he must have learned the value of prodigious output from his mother.

Anthony Trollope indicated in the Introduction to his *North America* that writing a book about the United States was a life-long ambition, and that he intended to describe the social and political state of the country as he found it. Perhaps by way of distinction, he also referred to his mother's *Domestic Manners of the Americans* as "essentially a woman's book." Whether or not his work is "a man's book" remains a subject for debate. Trollope covers some familiar ground in his critique of Washington, D.C., but upon his departure, his final observations on the city become less critical and more melancholy.

"No Neutrality Possible"

The President's House, or the White House as it is now called all the world over, is a handsome mansion fitted for the chief officer of a great Republic, and nothing more. I think I may say that we have private houses in Loudon considerably larger. It is neat and pretty, and with all its immediate outside belongings calls down no adverse criticism. It faces on to a small garden, which seems to be always accessible to the public, and opens out upon that everlasting Pennsylvania Avenue, which has now made another turn. Here in front of the White House is President's Square, as it is generally called. The technical name is, I believe, Lafayette Square. The houses 'round it are few in number, not exceeding three or four on each side, but they are among the best in Washington, and the whole place is neat and well kept. President's Square is certainly the most attractive part of the city. The garden of the square is always open and does not seem to suffer from any public ill-usage; by which circumstance I am again led to suggest that the gardens of our London squares might be thrown open in the same way. In the center of this one at Washington, immediately facing the President's House, is an equestrian statue of General Jackson. It is very bad; but that it is not nearly as bad as it might be is proved by another equestrian statue, of General Washington, erected in the center of a small garden-plat at the end of Pennsylvania Avenue, near the bridge leading to Georgetown. Of all the statues on horseback which I ever saw, either in marble or bronze, this is by far the worst and most ridiculous. The horse is most absurd, but the man sitting on the horse is manifestly drunk. I should think the time must come when this figure at any rate will be removed.

I did not go inside the President's House, not having had while at Washington an opportunity of paying my personal respects to Mr. Lincoln. I had been told that this was to be done without trouble, but when I inquired on the subject, I found that this was not exactly the case. I believe there are times when anybody may walk into the President's House without an introduction; but that, I take it, is not considered to be the proper way of doing the work. I found that something like a favor would be incurred, or that some disagreeable trouble would be given, if I made a request to be presented, and therefore I left Washington without seeing the great man.

The President's House is nice to look at, but it is built on marshy ground, not much above the level of the Potomac, and is very unhealthy. I was told that all who live there become subject to fever and ague, and that few who now live there have escaped it altogether. This comes of choosing the site of a new city and decreeing that it shall be built on this or on that spot. Large cities, especially in these latter days, do not collect themselves in unhealthy places. Men desert such localities, or at least do not congregate at them when their character is once known. But the poor President cannot desert the White House. He must make the most of the residence which the nation has prepared for him.

Of the other considerable public building of Washington, called the Smithsonian Institution, I have said that its style was bastard Gothic; by this, I mean that its main attributes are Gothic, but that liberties have been taken with it, which, whether they may injure its beauty or no, certainly are subversive of architectural purity. It is built of red stone and is not ugly in itself. There is a very nice Norman porch to it, and little bits of Lombard Gothic have been well copied from Cologne. But windows have been fitted in with stilted arches, of which the stilts seem to crack and bend, so narrow are they and so high. And then the towers with high pinnacled roofs are a mistake, unless indeed they be needed to give to the whole structure that name of Romanesque which it has assumed. The building is used for museums and lectures, and was given to the city by one James Smithson, an Englishman. I cannot say that the City of Washington seems to be grateful, for all to whom I spoke on the subject hinted that the Institution was a failure. It is to be remarked that nobody in Washington is proud of Washington, or of anything in it. If the Smithsonian Institution were at New York or at Boston, one would have a different story to tell.

There has been an attempt made to raise at Washington a vast obelisk to the memory of Washington, the first in war and first in peace, as the country is proud to call him. This obelisk is a fair type of the city. It is unfinished, not a third of it having as yet been erected, and in all human probability ever will remain so. If finished it would be the highest monument of its kind standing on the face of the globe, and yet, after all, what would it be even then as compared with one of the great pyramids? Modern attempts cannot bear comparison with those of the old world in simple vastness. But in lieu of simple vastness, the modern world aims to achieve either beauty or utility. By the Washington

Monument, if completed, neither would be achieved. An obelisk with the proportions of a needle may be very graceful; but an obelisk which requires an expanse of flat-roofed, sprawling buildings for its base, and of which the shaft shall be as big as a cathedral tower, cannot be graceful. At present some third portion of the shaft has been built, and there it stands. No one has a word to say for it. No one thinks that money will ever again be subscribed for its completion. I saw somewhere a box of plate-glass kept for contributions for this purpose, and looking in, perceived that two half-dollar pieces had been given; but both of them were bad. I was told also that the absolute foundation of the edifice is bad; that the ground, which is near the river and swampy, would not bear the weight intended to be imposed on it.

A sad and saddening spot was that marsh, as I wandered down on it all alone one Sunday afternoon. The ground was frozen, and I could walk dry-shod, but there was not a blade of grass. Around me on all sides were cattle in great numbers, steers and big oxen, lowing in their hunger for a meal. They were beef for the army, and never again I suppose would it be allowed to them to fill their big maws and chew the patient cud. There, on the brown, ugly, undrained field, within easy sight of the President's House, stood the useless, shapeless, graceless pile of stones. It was as though I were looking on the genius of the city. It was vast, pretentious, bold, boastful with a loud voice, already taller by many heads than other obelisks, but nevertheless still in its infancy, ugly, unpromising, and false. The founder of the monument had said, "Here shall be the obelisk of the world!" And the founder of the city had thought of his child somewhat in the same strain. It is still possible that both city and monument shall be completed; but at the present moment nobody seems to believe in the one or in the other. For myself I have much faith in the American character, but I cannot believe either in Washington City or in the Washington Monument. The boast made has been too loud, and the fulfilment yet accomplished has been too small!

Have I as yet said that Washington was dirty in that winter of 1861-1862? Or, I should rather ask, have I made it understood that in walking about Washington one waded as deep in mud as one does in floundering through an ordinary ploughed field in November? There were parts of Pennsylvania Avenue which would have been considered heavy ground by most hunting-men, and through some of the remoter streets none but light weights could have lived long. This was the state of the town when I left it in the middle of January. On my arrival in the middle of December, everything was in a cloud of dust. One walked through an atmosphere of floating mud; for the dirt was ponderous and thick, and very palpable in its atoms. Then came a severe frost and a little snow; and if one did not fall while walking, it was very well. After that we had the thaw; and Washington assumed its normal winter condition. I must say that, during the whole of this time, the atmosphere was to me exhilarating; but I was hardly out of the doctor's hands while I was there, and he did not support my theory as to the goodness of the air. "It is poisoned by the soldiers," he said, "and everybody is ill." But then my doctor was perhaps a little tinged with southern proclivities.

I have said that Washington was at that time, the Christmas of 1861-1862, a melancholy place. This was partly owing to the despondent tone in which so many Americans then spoke of their own affairs. It was not that the northern men thought that they were to be beaten, or that the southern men feared that things were going bad with their party across the river; but that nobody seemed to have any faith in anybody. Maclellan had been put up as the true man, exalted perhaps too quickly, considering the limited opportunities for distinguishing himself which fortune had thrown in his way; but now belief in Maclellan seemed to be slipping away. One felt that it was so from day to day, though it was impossible to define how or whence the feeling came. And then the character of the ministry fared still worse in public estimation. That Lincoln, the President, was honest, and that Chase, the Secretary of the Treasury, was able, was the only good that one heard spoken. At this time two Jonahs were specially pointed out as necessary sacrifices, by whose immersion into the comfortless ocean of private life the ship might perhaps be saved. These were Mr. Cameron, the Secretary of War, and Mr. Welles, the Secretary of the Navy. It was said that Lincoln, when pressed to rid his Cabinet of Cameron, had replied, that when a man was crossing a stream, the moment was hardly convenient for changing his horse; but it came to that at last, that he found he must change his horse, even in the very sharpest run of the river. Better that than sit an animal on whose exertions he knew that he could not trust. So, Mr. Cameron went, and Mr. Stanton became Secretary at War in his place. But Mr. Cameron, though put out of the Cabinet, was to be saved from absolute disgrace by being sent as Minister to Russia. I do not know that it would become me here to repeat the accusations made against Mr. Cameron, but it had long seemed to me that the maintenance in such a position, at such a time, of a gentleman who had to sustain such a universal absence of public confidence, must have been most detrimental to the army and to the Government.

Men whom one met in Washington were not unhappy about the state of things, as I had seen men unhappy in the North and in the West. They were mainly indifferent, but with that sort of indifference which arises from a breakdown of faith in anything. "There was the army! Yes, the army! But what an army! Nobody obeyed anybody. Nobody did anything! Nobody thought of advancing! There were, perhaps, two hundred thousand men assembled round Washington; and now the effort of supplying them with food and clothing was as much as could be accomplished! But the contractors, in the meantime, were becoming rich. And then as to the Government! Who trusted it? Who would put their faith in Seward and Cameron? Cameron was now gone, it was true; and in that way the whole of the Cabinet would soon be broken up. As to Congress, what could Congress do? Ask questions which no one would care to answer, and finally get itself packed up and sent home." The President and the Constitution fared no better in men's mouths. The former did nothing, neither harm nor good; and as for the latter, it had broken down and shown itself to be inefficient. So, men ate, and drank, and laughed, waiting till chaos should come, secure in the belief that the atoms into which their world would resolve itself, would connect themselves again in some other form without trouble on their part.

And at Washington I found no strong feeling against England and English conduct towards America. "We men of the world," a Washington man might have said, "know very well that everybody must take care of himself first. We are very good friends with you, of course, and are very glad to see you at our table whenever you come across the water; but as for rejoicing at your joys, or expecting you to sympathize with our sorrows, we know the world too well for that. We are splitting into pieces, and of course that is gain to you. Take another cigar." This polite, fashionable, and certainly comfortable way of looking at the matter had never been attained at New York or Philadelphia, at Boston or Chicago. The northern provincial world of the States had declared to itself that those who were not with it were against it; that its neighbors should be either friends or foes; that it would understand nothing of neutrality. This was often mortifying to me, but I think I liked it better on the whole than the *laisser-aller* indifference of Washington.

Everybody acknowledged that society in Washington had been almost destroyed by the loss of the southern half of the usual sojourners in the city. The Senators and Members of Government, who heretofore had come from the Southern States, had no doubt spent more money in the capital than their northern brethren. They and their families had been more addicted to social pleasures. They are the descendants of the old English Cavaliers, whereas the northern men have come from the old English Roundheads. Or if, as may be the case, the blood of the races has now been too well mixed to allow of this being said with absolute truth, yet something of the manners of the old forefathers has been left. The southern gentleman is more genial, less dry, I will not say more hospitable, but more given to enjoy hospitality than his northern brother; and this difference is quite as strong with the women as with the men. It may therefore be understood that secession would be very fatal to the society of Washington. It was not only that the Members of Congress were not there. As to very many of the Representatives, it may be said that they do not belong sufficiently to Washington to make a part of its society. It is not every Representative that is, perhaps, qualified to do so. But secession had taken away from Washington those who held property in the South, who were bound to the South by any ties, whether political or other, who belonged to the South by blood, education, and old habits. In very many cases, nay, in most such cases, it had been necessary that a man should select whether he would be a friend to the South, and therefore a rebel, or else an enemy to the South, and therefore untrue to all the predilections and sympathies of his life. Here has been the hardship. For such people there has been no neutrality possible. Ladies even have not been able to profess themselves simply anxious for peace and goodwill, and so to remain tranquil. They who are not for me are against me, has been spoken by one side and by the other. And I suppose that in all Civil War it is necessary that it should be so. I heard of various cases in which father and son had espoused different sides in order that property might be retained both in the North and in the South. Under such circumstances it may be supposed that society in Washington would be considerably cut up. All this made the place somewhat melancholy.

Though I had felt Washington to be disagreeable as a city, yet I was almost sorry to leave it when the day of my departure came. I had allowed myself a month for my sojourn in the capital, and I had stayed a month to the day. Then came the trouble of packing up, the necessity of calling on a long list of acquaintances one after another, the feeling that bad as Washington might be, I might be going to places that were worse, a conviction that I should get beyond the reach of my letters, and a sort of affection which I had acquired for my rooms. My landlord, being a colored man, told me that he was sorry I was going. Would I not remain? Would I come back to him? Had I been comfortable? Only for so and so or so and so, he would have done better for me. No white American citizen, occupying the position of landlord, would have condescended to such comfortable words. I knew the man did not in truth want me to stay, as a lady and gentleman were waiting to go in the moment I went out; but I did not the less value the assurance. One hungers and thirsts after such civil words among American citizens of this class. The clerks and managers at hotels, the officials at railway stations, the cashiers at banks, the women in the shops; ah!, they are the worst of all. An American woman who is bound by her position to serve yon, who is paid in some shape to supply your wants, whether to sell you a bit of soap or bring you a towel in your bedroom at a hotel is, I think, of all human creatures, the most insolent. I certainly had a feeling of regret at parting with my colored friend, and some regret also as regards a few that were white.

As I drove down Pennsylvania Avenue, through the slush and mud, and saw, perhaps for the last time, those wretchedly dirty horse sentries who had refused to allow me to trot through the streets, I almost wished that I could see more of them. How absurd they looked, with a whole kit of rattletraps strapped on their horses' backs behind them, blankets, coats, canteens, coils of rope, and, always at the top of everything else, a tin pot! No doubt these things are all necessary to a mounted sentry, or they would not have been there; but it always seemed as though the horse had been loaded gipsy-fashion, in a manner that I may perhaps best describe as higgledy-piggledy, and that there was a want of military precision in the packing. The man would have looked more graceful, and the soldier more warlike, had the pannikin been made to assume some rigidly fixed position, instead of dangling among the ropes. The drawn sabre, too, never consorted well with the dirty outside woolen wrapper which generally hung loose from the man's neck. Heaven knows, I did not begrudge him his comforter in that cold weather, or even his long, uncombed shock of hair; but I think he might have been made more spruce, and I am sure that he could not have looked more uncomfortable. As I went, however, I felt for him a sort of affection, and wished in my heart of hearts that he might soon be enabled to return to some more congenial employment.

I went out by the Capitol, and saw that also, as I then believed, for the last time. With all its faults it is a great building, and, though unfinished, is effective; its very size and pretension give it a certain majesty. What will be the fate of that vast pile, and of those other costly public edifices at Washington, should the South succeed wholly in their present enterprise? If Virginia should ever become a part of the Southern Republic, Washington cannot remain the capital of the Northern Republic. In such case it would be almost better to let Maryland go also so that the future destiny of that unfortunate city may not be a source of trouble, and a stumbling block of opprobrium. Even if Virginia be saved, its position will be most unfortunate.

Rose O'Neal Greenhow

Rose O'Neal Greenhow (1813-1864) was a southern sympathizer and a spy in the Nation's Capital during the Civil War. The mother of four children, Greenhow was widowed in 1854 when her husband was involved in an accident in San Francisco during his posting with the Department of State. Given her well-established social connections and her southern sympathies, Greenhow was ideally suited to conduct espionage on behalf of the Confederacy. She initially proved successful in her efforts but was eventually discovered and put under house arrest at her residence in Washington, D.C.

When house arrest failed to discourage her espionage activities, Greenhow was transferred to the Old Capitol, a building which once served as its name suggests after the War of 1812 and at that time stood in the vicinity of the current Supreme Court building. The Old Capitol served as a prison during the Civil War, and when Greenhow was transferred there, she brought her youngest daughter "Little Rose" with her. In this excerpt from her memoir, *My Imprisonment*, Greenhow reflects on her first impressions of prison life.

"Endowed with Constitutional Rights"

[January] 25th [1862]. I have been one week in my new prison. My letters now all go through the Detective Police, who subject them to a chemical process to extract the treason. In one of the newspaper accounts, prepared under the direction of the Secret Police, I am

supposed to use sympathetic ink. I purposely left a preparation very conspicuously placed in order to divert attention from my real means of communication, and they have swallowed the bait and fancy my friends are at their mercy.

How I shrink from the notoriety which these dastards force upon me: for five months I have had a daily paragraph. One would think that curiosity would have been satiated; but not so. And I have the uneasy consciousness that every word I utter will appear with exaggeration in the newspapers. Even my child of eight years is deemed of importance enough to have her childish speeches recorded. Well! I bide my time, confident in the retributive justice of Heaven. Rose is subject to the same rigorous restrictions as myself. I was fearful at first that she would pine, and said, "My little darling, you must show yourself superior to these Yankees and not pine." She replied quickly, "Oh mamma, never fear; I hate them too much. I intend to dance and sing 'Jeff Davis is coming,' just to scare them!"

January 28. This day, as I raised my barred windows, and stood before one of them to get out of the smoke and dust, &c., the Guard rudely called, "Go away from that window!" and raised his musket and levelled it at me. I maintained my position without condescending to notice him, whereupon he called for the Corporal of the Guard. I called also for the Officer of the Guard, who informed me that I "must not go to the window." I quietly told him that, at whatever peril, I should avail myself of the largest liberty of the four walls of my prison. He told me that his guard would have orders to fire upon me. I had no idea that such monstrous regulations existed. Today the dinner for myself and [my] child consists of a bowl of beans swimming in grease, two slices of fat junk, and two slices of bread. Still, my consolation is, "Every dog has his day."

January 30. I wonder what will happen next. My child has been ill for several days, brought on by close confinement and want of proper food. Just now I went to the door and rapped, that being the prescribed manner of making known my wants. The Guard came. "What do you want?" "Call the Corporal of the Guard," I said. "What do you want with him?" "That is no business of yours; call him?" "I won't call him." "You shall" (rap, rap, rap). The Guard; "G— d d — n you, if you do that again I will shoot you through the door." "Call the Corporal of the Guard!" Here horrid imprecations followed. I thereupon raised the window and called, "Corporal of the Guard." The ruffian called also, finding that I was not to be terrified by his threats. But, when the Corporal came and opened the door, I was seized with laughter, for there stood the Abolitionist blubbering like a child, that he *"had not orders to shoot the d — d Secesh woman, who was not afraid of the devil himself."*

I sent for the Officer of the Guard, who was Lieutenant Carlton, of Zanesville, Ohio, and reported this outrage. He said that the Guard had acted by his orders in refusing to call the Corporal of the Guard, and that he had no idea of allowing his non-commissioned officers to act as servants, &c. I told him that my child was ill, and I demanded the use of a servant; whereupon he told me that a servant should not be allowed me, save morning and night. I replied, "Very well, sir. I will resort to the window, then, as my only expedient." A servant after this was sent but had to perform her functions with a Sergeant of the Guard standing over her. I told Lieutenant Carlton that I would report him to the Provost-Marshal, which I accordingly did, and the following is a copy of my letter:

TO GENERAL PORTER, PROVOST-MARSHAL.
OLD CAPITOL PRISON: Jan. 31.

Sir, I feel it to be my duty to make a representation of certain things done here under sanction and authority of your name.

A few days since I went to my window and leaned against the bars to escape the dust and bad odors with which it was filled, when the Guard below, No. 5, called to me in a rude manner to go away, and threatened to shoot me. This morning, I again went to my window, to escape the dust and atmosphere of a room without ventilation, the windows of which you well know are barred, as I am told that they evidence your mechanical skill, and the Guard called to me in the same fashion, and again levelled his musket at me. A few moments since, I was threatened to be fired upon through the door of my chamber, and your Officer of the Guard justified the outrage, and assumed the responsibility of the act. Sir, I call your attention to these and other gross outrages, and warn you that there is another tribunal, that of the public opinion of the civilized world, to which I will appeal against your acts of inhumanity. And I now formally demand that you cause this Officer, Lieutenant Carlton, to be punished for his brutality; and that you establish rules and regulations here, in accordance with the laws of humanity, and my rights as a prisoner.

I have the honor to be, &c. &c.
ROSE O'N. GREENHOW.

This brought no response, but I was subsequently informed that Lieutenant Carlton was temporarily placed under arrest, although he was, in the order of rotation, again in command at the prison. I can give no idea of the petty annoyances to which I was constantly exposed. I was never allowed to cross my chamber door. If a servant now entered to perform the smallest duty, the door was immediately locked and bolted, so that it was necessary to rap or call some five or ten minutes before they could get out. And when it is remembered that these servants were often negro men, who claimed perfect equality, and would tauntingly tell me that *"Massa Lincoln had made them as good as me, that they would not be called negroes, but gem' men of color,"* some idea may be felt of the vague, undefined feeling of uneasiness that was constantly upon me. It is but justice to the Superintendent of the Prison, Mr. Wood, to state that, whenever the insolence of the negroes came to his knowledge, that he invariably sent them away; and that, so far as he was able to do so, he protected the prisoners from the insolence and outrage of the Guard and Officers.

The rules with regard to my child were barbarously rigid. The act of commitment ran thus: "Miss Rose Greenhow, although not a prisoner, is subject to the same rules and regulations prescribed for a prisoner." She was in fact as much a prisoner as I was. I had never been consulted on the subject. And when occasionally, from very shame, she was allowed to go down in the yard, the child often came up crying, from the effects of the brutality and indecency to which she was exposed. The Superintendent was, as I have above said, disposed to be kind, but there was a constant struggle going on between him and the military authorities for supremacy, by which the comfort of the prisoner was sacrificed, and his liberty abridged. It would seem to have been purposely arranged that these respective jealousies should result in stricter vigilance over the helpless victims.

I can conceive no more horrible destiny than that which was now my lot. At nine o'clock the lights were put out, the roll was called every night and morning, and a man peered in to see that a prisoner had not escaped through the keyhole. The walls of my room swarmed with vermin, and I was obliged to employ a portion of the precious hours of candlelight in burning them on the wall, in order that myself and [my] child should not be devoured by them in the course of the night. The bed was so hard that I was obliged to fold up my clothing and place them under my child. In spite of this she would often cry out in the night, "Oh, mamma, the bed hurts me so much."

The portion of the prison in which I was confined was now almost entirely converted into negro quarters, hundreds of whom were daily brought in, the rooms above and below mine being appropriated to their use; and the tramping and screaming of negro children overhead was most dreadful. The prison-yard, which circumscribed my view, was filled with them, shocking both [in] sight and smell, for the air was rank and pestiferous with the exhalations from their bodies; and the language which fell upon the ear, and sights which met the eye, were too revolting to be depicted, for it must be remembered that these creatures were of both sexes, huddled together indiscriminately, as close as they could be packed. Emancipated from all control, and suddenly endowed with Constitutional rights, they considered the exercise of their unbridled will as the only means of manifesting their equality.

In addition to all other sufferings was the terrible dread of infectious diseases, several cases of smallpox occurring, and my child had already taken the camp-measles, which had broken out amongst them. My clothes, when brought out from the wash, were often filled with vermin; constantly articles were stolen. Complaint on this head, of course, was unheeded. Our free fellow citizens of color felt themselves entitled to whatever they liked. Several times during this period my child was reduced to a bare change of garments; and the supreme contempt with which they regarded a rebel was, of course, very edifying to the Yankees, who rubbed their hands in glee at the signs of the "*irrepressible conflict.*" One day I called for a servant from the window. A negro man, basking in the sun below, called out, "*Is any of you ladies named Laura? Dat woman up dare wants you.*" And, by way of still further increasing the satisfaction with this condition of things, Captain Gilbert, of the 91st Pennsylvania Volunteers, drilled these negroes just below my window.

I protested against these infamies and threatened to make an appeal to the United States Senate to send a committee to enquire into our present hapless condition, as they had done in the case of the negro thieves and felons confined in the gaol, many of whom had been released by *habeas corpus*, and whose cases had been deemed worthy of a Senatorial report. This threat procured the instant removal of the negroes to more comfortable quarters.

Louisa May Alcott

Louisa May Alcott (1832-1888), often remembered by modern readers for her novel *Little Women,* served as a nurse in Washington, D.C. during the winter of 1862-1863. Alcott's experiences as "Nurse Periwinkle" in a Georgetown hospital she called "Hurly-Burly House" were published in the *Commonwealth,* a Boston newspaper. These letters were subsequently revised and expanded by Alcott and published under the title *Hospital Sketches.* While Alcott's *Sketches* tend more toward storytelling than journalism, her writing nevertheless conveys a sense of authenticity about the Nation's Capital during the Civil War. Alcott's Boston-based publisher James Redpath pledged to donate some of the proceeds for the book "to the support of orphans made fatherless or homeless by the war."

"Nurse Periwinkle's Mission"

Washington. It was dark when we arrived; and but for the presence of another friendly gentleman, I should have yielded myself a helpless prey to the first overpowering hackman who insisted that I wanted to go just where I didn't. Putting me into the conveyance I belonged in, my escort added to the obligation by pointing out the objects of interest which we passed in our long drive. Though I'd often been told that Washington was a spacious place, its visible magnitude quite took my breath away, and of course I quoted Randolph's expression, "a city of magnificent distances," as I suppose everyone does when they see it. The Capitol was so like the pictures that hang opposite the staring Father of his Country in boardinghouses and hotels that it did not impress me, except to recall the time when I was sure that Cinderella went to housekeeping in just such a place after she had married the inflammable Prince; though, even at that early period, I had my doubts as to the wisdom of a match whose foundation was of glass.

The White House was lighted up, and carriages were rolling in and out of the great gate. I stared hard at the famous East Room and would have liked a peep through the crack of the door. My old gentleman was indefatigable in his attentions, and I said "Splendid!" to everything he pointed out, though I suspect I often admired the wrong place and missed the right. Pennsylvania Avenue, with its bustle, lights, music, and military, made me feel as if I'd crossed the water and landed somewhere in Carnival time. Coming to less noticeable parts of the city, my companion fell silent, and I meditated upon the perfection which Art had attained in America, having just passed a bronze statue of some hero, who looked like a black Methodist minister, in a cocked hat, above the waist, and a tipsy squire below; while his horse stood like an opera dancer, on one leg, in a high, but somewhat remarkable wind, which blew his mane one way and his massive tail the other.

"Hurly-Burly House, ma'am!" called a voice, startling me from my reverie, as we stopped before a great pile of buildings, with a flag flying before it, sentinels at the door, and a very trying quantity of men lounging about. My heart beat rather faster than usual, and it suddenly struck me that I was very far from home; but I descended with dignity, wondering whether I should be stopped for want of a countersign, and forced to pass the night in the street. Marching boldly up the steps, I found that no form was necessary, for the men fell back, the guard touched their caps, a boy opened the door, and, as it closed behind me, I felt that I was fairly started, and Nurse Periwinkle's Mission was begun.

From *A Day*

All having eaten, drank, and rested, the surgeons began their rounds; and I took my first lesson in the art of dressing wounds. It wasn't a festive scene by any means for Dr. P., whose Aid I constituted myself, fell to work with a vigor which soon convinced me that I was a weaker vessel, though nothing would have induced me to confess it then. He had served in the Crimea, and seemed to regard a dilapidated body very much as I should have regarded a damaged garment; and, turning up his cuffs, whipped out a very unpleasant looking housewife, cutting, sawing, patching and piecing, with the enthusiasm of an accomplished surgical seamstress; explaining the process, in scientific terms, to the patient, meantime; which, of course, was immensely cheering and comfortable There was an uncanny sort of fascination in watching him, as he peered and probed into the mechanism of those wonderful bodies, whose mysteries he understood so well. The more intricate the wound, the better he liked it. A poor Private, with both legs off, and shot through the lungs, possessed more attractions for him than a dozen Generals, slightly scratched in some "masterly retreat;" and had anyone appeared in small pieces, requesting to be put together again, he would have considered it a special dispensation.

The amputations were reserved till the morrow, and the merciful magic of ether was not thought necessary that day, so the poor souls had to bear their pains as best they might. It is all very well to talk of the patience of woman; and far be it from me to pluck that feather from her cap, for, heaven knows, she isn't allowed to wear many; but the patient endurance of these men, under trials of the flesh, was truly wonderful; their fortitude seemed contagious, and scarcely a cry escaped them, though I often longed to groan for them, when pride kept their white lips shut, while great drops stood upon their foreheads, and the bed shook with the irrepressible tremor of their tortured bodies. One or two Irishmen anathematized the doctors with the frankness of their nation, and ordered the Virgin to stand by them, as if she had been the wedded Biddy to whom they could administer the poker if she didn't; but, as a general thing, the work went on in silence, broken only by some quiet request for roller, instruments, or plaster, a sigh from the patient, or a sympathizing murmur from the Nurse.

It was long past noon before these repairs were even partially made; and, having got the bodies of my boys into something like order, the next task was to minister to their minds, by writing letters to the anxious souls at home; answering questions, reading papers, taking possession of money and valuables; for the eighth commandment was reduced to a very fragmentary condition, both by the blacks and whites, who ornamented our hospital with their presence. Pocketbooks, purses, miniatures, and watches, were sealed up, labelled, and handed over to the Matron, till such times as the owners thereof were ready to depart homeward or campward again. The letters dictated to me, and revised by me, that afternoon, would have made an excellent chapter for some future history of the war; for, like that which Thackeray's "Ensign Spooney" wrote his mother just before Waterloo, they were "full of affection, pluck, and bad spelling;" nearly all giving lively accounts of the battle, and ending with a somewhat sudden plunge from patriotism to provender; desiring "Marm," "Mary Ann," or "Aunt Peters," to send along some pies, pickles, sweet stuff, and apples, "to *yourn* in haste," Joe, Sam, or Ned, as the case might be.

My little Sergeant insisted on trying to scribble something with his left hand, and patiently accomplished some half dozen lines of hieroglyphics, which he gave me to fold and direct, with a boyish blush, that rendered a glimpse of "My Dearest Jane," unnecessary, to assure me that the heroic lad had been more successful in the service of Commander-in-Chief Cupid than that of General Mars; and a charming little romance blossomed instanter in Nurse Periwinkle's romantic fancy, though no further confidences were made that day, for Sergeant fell asleep, and, judging from his tranquil face, visited his absent sweetheart in the pleasant land of dreams.

At five o'clock a great bell rang, and the attendants flew, not to arms but to their trays to bring up supper, when a second uproar announced that it was ready. The newcomers woke at the sound; and I presently discovered that it took a very bad wound to incapacitate the defenders of the faith for the consumption of their rations; the amount that some of them sequestered was amazing; but when I suggested the probability of a famine hereafter, to the matron, that motherly lady cried out: "Bless their hearts, why shouldn't they eat? It's their only amusement; so, fill everyone, and, if there's not enough ready tonight, I'll lend my share to the Lord by giving it to the boys." And, whipping up her coffeepot and plate of toast, she gladdened the eyes and stomachs of two or three dissatisfied heroes, by serving them with a liberal hand; and I haven't the slightest doubt that, having cast her bread upon the waters, it came back buttered, as another large-hearted old lady was wont to say.

Then came the doctor's evening visit; the administration of medicines; washing feverish faces; smoothing tumbled beds; wetting wounds; singing lullabies; and preparations for the night. By eleven, the last labor of love was done; the last "good night" spoken; and, if any needed a reward for that day's work, they surely received it, in the silent eloquence of those long lines of faces, showing pale and peaceful in the shaded rooms as we quitted them, followed by grateful glances that lighted us to bed, where rest, the sweetest, made our pillows soft, while Night and Nature took our places, filling that great house of pain with the healing miracles of Sleep, and his diviner brother, Death.

From *A Night*

Being fond of the night side of nature, I was soon promoted to the post of Night Nurse, with every facility for indulging in my favorite pastime of "owling." My colleague, a black-eyed widow, relieved me at dawn, we two taking care of the ward between us like the immortal Sairy and Betsey, "turn and turn about." I usually found my boys in the jolliest state of mind their condition allowed; for it was a known fact that Nurse Periwinkle objected to blue devils, and entertained a belief that he who laughed most was surest of recovery. At the beginning of my reign, dumps and dismals prevailed; the nurses looked anxious and tired, the men gloomy or sad; and a general *"Hark! From the tombs a doleful sound"* style of conversation seemed to be the fashion: a state of things which caused one coming from a merry, social New England town, to feel as if she had got into an exhausted receiver; and the instinct of self-preservation, to say nothing of a philanthropic desire to serve the race, caused a speedy change in Ward No. 1.

More nattering than the most gracefully turned compliment, more grateful than the most admiring glance, was the sight of those rows of faces, all strange to me a little while ago, now lighting up, with smiles of welcome, as I came among them, enjoying that moment heartily, with a womanly pride in their regard, a motherly affection for them all. The evenings were spent in reading aloud, writing letters, waiting on and amusing the men, going the rounds with Dr. P., as he made his second daily survey, dressing my dozen wounds afresh, giving last doses, and making them cozy for the long hours to come, till the nine o'clock bell rang, the gas was turned down, the day nurses went off duty, the night watch came on, and my nocturnal adventure began.

My ward was now divided into three rooms; and, under favor of the Matron, I had managed to sort out the patients in such a way that I had what I called, "my duty room," my "pleasure room," and my "pathetic room," and worked for each in a different way. One, I visited, armed with a dressing tray, full of rollers, plasters, and pins; another, with books, flowers, games, and gossip; a third, with teapots, lullabies, consolation, and, sometimes, a shroud.

Wherever the sickest or most helpless man chanced to be, there I held my watch, often visiting the other rooms, to see that the General Watchman of the ward did his duty by the fires and the wounds, the latter needing constant wetting. Not only on this account did I meander, but also to get fresher air than the close rooms afforded; for, owing to the stupidity of that mysterious "somebody" who does all the damage in the world, the windows had been carefully nailed down above, and the lower sashes could only be raised in the mildest weather, for the men lay just below. I had suggested a summary smashing of a few panes here and there, when frequent appeals to headquarters had proved unavailing, and daily orders to lazy attendants had come to nothing. No one seconded the motion, however, and the nails were far beyond my reach; for, though belonging to the sisterhood of "ministering angels," I had no wings, and might as well have asked for Jacob's ladder, as a pair of steps, in that charitable chaos.

One of the harmless ghosts who bore me company during the haunted hours, was Dan, the Watchman, whom I regarded with a certain awe; for, though so much together, I never fairly saw his face, and, but for his legs, should never have recognized him, as we seldom met by day. These legs were remarkable, as was his whole figure, for his body was short, rotund, and done up in a big jacket, and muffler; his beard hid the lower part of his face, his hat brim the upper; and all I ever discovered was a pair of sleepy eyes, and a very mild voice. But the legs! Very long, very thin, very crooked, and feeble, looking like gray sausages in their tight coverings, without a ray of *pegtopishness* about them, and finished off with a pair of expansive, green cloth shoes, very like Chinese junks with the sails down. This figure, gliding noiselessly about the dimly lighted rooms, was strongly suggestive of the spirit of a beer barrel mounted on corkscrews, haunting the old hotel in search of its lost mates, emptied, and staved in long ago.

Another goblin who frequently appeared to me, was the attendant of the pathetic room, who, being a faithful soul, was often up to tend two or three men, weak and wandering as babies, after the fever had gone. The amiable creature beguiled the watches of the night by brewing jorums of a fearful beverage, which he called coffee, and insisted on sharing with me, coming in with a great bowl of something like mud soup, scalding hot, guiltless of cream, rich in an all-pervading flavor of molasses, scorch, and tin pot. Such an amount of goodwill and neighborly kindness also went into the mess, that I never could find the heart to refuse, but always received it with thanks, sipped it with hypocritical relish while he remained, and whipped it into the slop-jar the instant he departed, thereby gratifying him, securing one rousing laugh in the doziest hour of the night, and no one was the worse for the transaction but the pigs. Whether they were "cut off untimely in their sins," or not, I carefully abstained from inquiring.

It was a strange life; asleep half the day, exploring Washington the other half, and all night hovering, like a massive cherubim, in a red *rigolette* over the slumbering sons of man. I liked it, and found many things to amuse, instruct, and interest me. The snores alone were quite a study, varying from the mild sniff to the stentorian snort, which startled the echoes and hoisted the performer erect to accuse his neighbor of the deed, magnanimously forgive him, and, wrapping the drapery of his couch about him, lie down to vocal slumber. After listening for a week to this band of wind instruments, I indulged in the belief that I could recognize each by the snore alone, and was tempted to join the chorus by breaking out with John Brown's favorite hymn:

"Blow ye the trumpet, blow!"

I would have given much to have possessed the art of sketching, for many of the faces became wonderfully interesting when unconscious. Some grew stern and grim, the men evidently dreaming of war, as they gave orders, groaned over their wounds, or damned the rebels vigorously; some grew sad and infinitely pathetic, as if the pain borne silently all day, revenged itself by now betraying what the man's pride had concealed so well. Often the roughest grew young and pleasant when sleep smoothed the hard lines away, letting the real nature assert itself; many almost seemed to speak, and I learned to know these men better by night than through any intercourse by day. Sometimes they disappointed me, for faces that looked merry and good in the light, grew bad and sly when the shadows came; and though they made no confidences in words, I read their lives, leaving them to wonder at the change of manner this midnight magic wrought in their nurse. A few talked busily; one drummer boy sang sweetly, though no persuasions could win a note from him by day; and several depended on being told what they had talked of in the morning. Even my constitutionals in the chilly halls possessed a certain charm, for the house was never still. Sentinels tramped round it all night long, their muskets glittering in the wintry moonlight as they walked, or stood before the doors, straight and silent, as figures of stone, causing one to conjure up romantic visions of guarded forts, sudden surprises, and daring deeds; for in these war times the humdrum life of Yankeedom has vanished, and the most prosaic feel some thrill of that excitement which stirs the nation's heart, and makes its capital a camp of hospitals. Wandering up and down these lower halls, I often heard cries from above, steps hurrying to and fro, saw surgeons passing up, or men coming down carrying a stretcher, where lay a long white figure, whose face was shrouded and whose fight was done. Sometimes I stopped to watch the passers in the street, the moonlight shining on the spire opposite, or the gleam of some vessel floating, like a white-winged seagull, down the broad Potomac, whose fullest flow can never wash away the red stain of the land.

James J. Williamson

James Joseph Williamson (1834-1915) was born and raised in Baltimore, Maryland. During the Civil War his allegiance was to the Confederacy. Williamson served with Confederate Colonel John Singleton Mosby during the war and would go on to write the popular *Mosby's Rangers*, a history of the partisan military group that operated in Northern Virginia from 1862 until 1865. In his memoir, *Prison Life in the Old Capitol*, published several years before his death, Williamson reflected upon his arrest and imprisonment in Washington, D.C. in January 1863. Williamson spent about two months in the Old Capitol before he was paroled and released in a prisoner exchange the following March.

"The Oath of Allegiance"

On the evening of Saturday, January 31, 1863, between seven and eight o clock, an officer in full uniform, but unarmed, came into a bookstore on Seventh Street, Washington, D. C., where I was then engaged, and asked for the proprietor, Mr. Russell. I pointed out Russell. The officer then asked him if he knew a Mr. Williamson. Russell answered, "Yes."

"Is he a printer?" asked the officer.

"Yes."

"Is he the only one of that name that you know?"

"Yes."

"Where is he?"

"There he is," answered Russell, pointing toward me.

The officer walked over to me and said: "Sir, you will have to come along with me."

"All right," said I.

He then went to the door and called in a soldier he had left standing guard outside and said: "Take charge of that man."

I asked the officer if I would be permitted to call at my home in order to acquaint my family with the cause of my absence. He said I would not; that I must go to the Provost-Marshal's office. I obtained permission to send a note to my wife, stating that I was under arrest. Putting on my hat and coat, I was marched to the corner of Eighth Street and Pennsylvania Avenue. Here we halted, and the officer called out to another soldier, who stood there holding his sword which he took from the man and buckled on. Placing me between the two guards, we all marched up Pennsylvania Avenue to the Provost-Marshal's office. The Marshal was not in, but his assistant said:

"Do you belong in Washington?"

"I do," said I.

"Haven't you been South lately?"

"Yes," I said; "I came from Richmond on the third of last August."

"Have you reported yourself to the military authorities?"

"I have not."

He next asked me if I would take the oath of allegiance to the Government. I told him I would not; that I could not think of doing so. He said I would have time enough to think about it, as it might be necessary to do so before I could obtain my release. That I was charged with having been in Richmond, and also with being [an] accessory to the imprisonment of some Union citizens.

I again asked if I would be permitted to go home under [the] escort of a guard, so as to acquaint my family with the cause of my absence and also to get a change of clothing and some few articles necessary for me during the time I might be kept under arrest. This request was denied, and I was marched off under guard to the Old Capitol Prison at the corner of First and A Streets.

The building known as the Old Capitol had a memorable history. Built in 1800, it was originally designed for a tavern or boarding-house, but owing to bad management it proved a failure and was closed shortly before the War of 1812. In August 1814, when the British troops under General Ross entered Washington, they burned the Capitol and other public buildings, and the Government bought this old tavern or boarding-house, in which Congress should hold their sessions and public business be transacted until the Capitol could be rebuilt.

The interior of the building was completely renovated and reconstructed, and here both Houses sat for a number of years. Within its walls two Presidents were inaugurated, and here some of our most distinguished statesmen began their careers. It was in this building the Honorable John C. Calhoun died.

When it was abandoned by Congress upon the completion of the Capitol, it was called the "Old Capitol," as a distinctive title. After that it underwent a number of changes as boardinghouse, school, etc., until, in 1861, it was taken by the Washington authorities to be used as a prison.

A row of houses on the adjoining block, known as Duff Green's Row, was afterward taken and used as an annex to the Old Capitol, and for the same purpose. It was called the "Carroll Prison."

On arriving at the Old Capitol, we were halted at the entrance by the sentry patrolling the pavement in front of the prison door, who called out with a loud voice, "Corporal of the Guard; Post No. 1." This brought out the Corporal, with his musket at his shoulder, and he escorted us inside.

Entering the prison from First Street, we passed through a broad hallway, which was used as a guardroom, and thence into a room where prisoners were first taken to be questioned and searched. I found the Lieutenant in charge more courteous than any of those in whose custody I had been. After receiving my commitment from the guard who brought me from the Provost-Marshal's office, he inquired if I had any arms or other prohibited goods in my possession. I replied that the only article I had which might come within the forbidden class was a small pocket-knife, which I took from my pocket and handed him. He smiled as he gave it back and made no further search. He asked me if I had been to supper, and receiving a negative reply, led me to a dirty, dismal room, which I afterward learned was the messroom. Here, grouped around a big stove was a gang of negroes, one of whom, at the Lieutenant s command, brought out a chunk of beef, a slice of bread over an inch thick, and a cup of coffee (?), sweetened, but without milk. This was set out on a table, of what material constructed it was impossible to determine on account of the accumulation of dirt. The meat was served in a tin plate which looked as though it might have been through the Peninsula campaign. Though I failed, no doubt, to do full justice to the repast set before me by the good-natured Lieutenant, I certainly appreciated his good intentions and his honest efforts to entertain me with the best at his command.

The Lieutenant sat and talked with me for some time before taking me to my room. He asked me if I would take the oath of allegiance to the Government. I told him I would not. He asked if I would be willing to take an oath to support the Constitution of the United States. "Yes," said I, "but not an oath to support the Government or Administration." He asked if I were living in a Northern city and came to Washington and went into business, would I in that case take the oath. I told him I would not. I said, "If I were in the South, even, and that iron-clad oath" (as it was called) "was offered to me, I would not take it."

THE OATH

District of Columbia,
County of Washington

I, _____, of _____, do solemnly swear on the Holy Evangelist of Almighty God, without any mental reservation, that I will at any and all times hereafter, and under all circumstances, yield a hearty and willing *support to the Constitution of the United States and to the Government thereof; that I will not, either directly or indirectly, take up arms against said Government, nor aid those now in arms against it; that I will not pass without the lines now established by the Army of the United States, or hereafter from time to time to be established by said Army, nor hold any correspondence whatever with any person or persons beyond said lines so established by said Army of the United States during the present rebellion, without permission from the Secretary of War; also, that I will do no act hostile or injurious to the Union of the States; that I will give no aid, comfort or assistance to the enemies of the Government, either domestic or foreign; that I will defend the flag of the United States and the armies fighting under it from insult and injury, if in my power so to do; and that I will in all things deport myself as a good and loyal citizen.*

Subscribed and sworn to before me, this day of _____.

[Signed] _____.

He then accompanied me upstairs to Room No. 16, and here, after the door was unlocked, I was ushered into my future quarters. I was welcomed and introduced by one of my fellow-prisoners to the others of the party, some of whom had been brought in that same day.

Room No. 16 was a spacious room, with one very large arch window opposite the door from which the room was entered. This window was directly over the main entrance to the building on First Street, and in by-gone days it lighted up the former Senate Chamber. In the middle of the room a huge cylinder stove formed the centerpiece, while around and against the walls were twenty-one bunks or berths, arranged in three tiers, one above the other. There were a couple of pine tables, each about five feet long, with a miscellaneous collection of chairs, benches, and home-made apologies for seats.

When the building was used as the Capitol, this floor contained the Senate and House of Representatives, but after its abandonment by Congress the floor was cut up into five rooms, now numbered from 14 to 18, No. 16 being the largest. The doors of all opened into a large hall, from which a broad stairway led to the floor below.

After spending a couple of hours in swapping stories and getting better acquainted, the whole party adjourned to their up-and-downy beds.

Sunday, February 1, 1863. My first night in my new quarters was a very uncomfortable one. An old blanket spread over the hard boards, with a piece of wood morticed in at the head for a pillow, was the bed on which I was expected to sleep. All night the steady tramp of the sentry up and down the hall outside of our room door, with the clanking of arms, the challenging of the guards and the calls of the relief through the night, kept me awake, until at last tired nature gave way and the god of sleep closed my weary eyes. How long I slept I know not, but when I woke it was as if awaking from a troubled dream. I looked around at my surroundings and then lay down again on my bunk, pondering on the events of the past night. After a while I got up and took a wash. There was but little time required for dressing. Soon the door was thrown open and there was a call to breakfast. Being totally unacquainted with the daily routine, I mechanically followed the crowd, without knowing where it would lead me. It led me to the messroom. It might have led me to a worse place, but it would have been difficult to find.

It was a long, dirty, gloomy-looking room, with nothing in its appearance to tempt the appetite, and the food looked as though served at second-hand. The odor which assailed the nostrils seemed as if coming from an ancient garbage heap. The waiter stood at the head of the long board table, with a handful of tin cups filled with a liquid by courtesy called coffee. He would, with a dexterous twist of the wrist, send them spinning along down the table, leaving each man to catch one of the flying cups before it slid past. Fortunately, the waiter had by practice acquired sufficient skill to enable him to shoot a cup in your direction without spilling more than one-half of its contents. With this was served a chunk of beef and a slice of bread. The beef was left untouched by those who had the privilege and the means of providing their own food, but the bread was good, and a generous slice. I saw my companions slipping their quota of bread under the breasts of their coats, and I did the same.

After a half-hour's recreation in the prison yard, we went back to our rooms and were locked in. In our room a table was spread and we had breakfast of ham, sausage, bread, butter and tea.

Room No. 16 faces the east front of the Capitol, and by standing or sitting back a short distance from the window we can look out and see the passers-by. No persons, however, are allowed to show any signs of recognition. If a person is seen loitering in passing the prison or walking at a pace not considered satisfactory by the guard, he soon receives a peremptory command to "pass on," or, "Hurry up, there," and if this warning is not heeded the offending person, whether male or female, is arrested and detained.

This morning, two gentlemen walking down on the opposite side of the street looked across and smiled. One of my roommates raised his hat and bowed. One of the gentlemen did the same. Immediately we heard the sentry under the window call out: "Corporal of the Guard, Post No. I," and an officer coming out, the person was pointed out, with the remark, "That man bowed over here." A guard was instantly dispatched after him, and he was brought over, but was released in a short time.

Dinner today consisted of boiled beans and rusty-looking fat pork, with molasses (the molasses thin as water), served up in a dirty tin plate. There being neither knife, fork nor spoon given out with it, the only way the mixture could be eaten was by dipping it up with the bread and thus conveying it to the mouth.

When we went back to our room we prepared dinner from our own supply of provisions.

This afternoon three young ladies passing the prison looked over very pleasantly at the prisoners, who were in sight at the window, much to the displeasure of the guard, who stopped his walk and stood watching them. Finally, one of them smiled and nodded her head. At this moment came the call "Corporal of the Guard, Post No. I." The young ladies had by this time reached the corner of the street. Turning around and seeing the soldier coming after them, they waved their handkerchiefs and ran down the street. The sentry, after picking his way through the mud across the street, turned back and gave up the chase.

For supper we had a piece of bread, without butter, and a cup of coffee (?), without milk.

The bill of fare here given for the three meals of this day would serve, with but little variation, for the entire time of my detention.

One of the prisoners, a Confederate soldier, whom I met in the yard today, told me that he was just recovering from a fever, and although he had an excellent appetite, his stomach was weak and he could not eat the food set before him; that as he had no money to purchase anything else, he was compelled to go hungry.

With the exception of the bread, which is good (thanks to Superintendent Wood), the food dealt out here is poor in quality and insufficient in quantity. I noticed some of the boxes were marked "White House," from which I inferred the contents were condemned army stores.

Those who can afford to do so club together and, having obtained permission, purchase such articles as the sutler will procure for them. The goods kept in stock by this dignitary are neither very choice nor varied, chiefly tobacco, cigars, cakes, candy, pies, etc. For our mess in Room 16, we select one man as treasurer, and he purchases our supplies, such as coffee, tea, sugar, cheese, and he occasionally has a large ham boiled. All of these articles the sutler furnishes at prices far beyond their market value; but we are glad to get them and compelled from necessity to submit to the extortion.

Prisoners having money of friends outside of the prison can obtain many necessaries and enjoy comforts which are denied those less fortunate. A friend (Mrs. Ennis), living near the prison, sends dinner in to me every day. There is always enough to feed three or four abundantly, and none of it is ever wasted.

We take turns in the household work, cooking and cleaning up, two men being detailed for this duty each day. It is unnecessary to say our cooking arrangements are very simple.

In our room there are two, one, I think, a Yankee deserter, known as "Dutchy" and "Slim Jim," who are unable to contribute their quota to the commissary fund, but as they can make a pot of coffee or tea, and wield a broom or wash a dirty dish, they are always ready to make up their deficit by taking the place of roommates afflicted with hookworm or victims of inertia.

Having our meals in our own room, we can take the whole half-hour allowed at mealtime for recreation in the prison yard, which gives us an opportunity to mingle with prisoners from other rooms than our own. This meeting of old friends and comrades, and the making of new acquaintances, is a source of great pleasure to us and a relief from the monotony of what would otherwise be the dull routine of prison life.

Walt Whitman

Walt Whitman (1819-1892), often ranked among the most important and influential of American poets, is familiar to modern readers as the author of *Leaves of Grass*. Whitman was also a journalist, a newspaper editor, and at times a clerk in various federal government departments. During the Civil War he volunteered as a nurse in hospitals in Washington, D.C. Whitman wrote of his experiences on numerous occasions during and after the war. The following letter to the *New York Times* was published February 26th, 1863, and is excerpted from a later collection of Whitman's hospital writings entitled *The Wound Dresser*.

"The Great Army of the Wounded"

The military hospitals, convalescent camps, etc., in Washington and its neighborhood, sometimes contain over fifty thousand sick and wounded men. Every form of wound (the mere sight of some of them having been known to make a tolerably hardy visitor faint away), every kind of malady, like a long procession, with typhoid fever and diarrhea at the head as leaders, are here in steady motion. The soldier's hospital! How many sleepless nights, how many women's tears, how many long and waking hours and days of suspense, from every one of the Middle, Eastern, and Western States, have concentrated here! Our own New York, in the form of hundreds and thousands of her young men, may consider herself here. Pennsylvania, Ohio, Indiana, and all the West and Northwest the same, and all the New England States the same.

Upon a few of these hospitals I have been almost daily calling as a missionary, on my own account, for the sustenance and consolation of some of the most needy cases of sick and dying men, for the last two months. One has much to learn to do good in these places. Great tact is required. These are not like other hospitals. By far the greatest proportion (I should say five sixths) of the patients are American young men, intelligent, of independent spirit, tender feelings, used to a hardy and healthy life; largely the farmers are represented by their sons, largely the mechanics and workingmen of the cities. Then they are soldiers. All these points must be borne in mind.

People through our Northern cities have little or no idea of the great and prominent feature which these military hospitals and convalescent camps make in and around Washington. There are not merely two or three or a dozen, but some fifty of them, of different degrees of capacity. Some have a thousand and more patients. The newspapers here find it necessary to print every day a directory of the hospitals, a long list, something like what a directory of the churches would be in New York, Philadelphia, or Boston.

The Government (which really tries, I think, to do the best and quickest it can for these sad necessities) is gradually settling down to adopt the plan of placing the hospitals in clusters of one-story wooden barracks, with their accompanying tents and sheds for cooking and all needed purposes. Taking all things into consideration, no doubt these are best adapted to the purpose; better than using churches and large public buildings like the Patent Office. These sheds now adopted are long, one-story edifices, sometimes ranged along in a row, with their heads to the street, and numbered either alphabetically Wards A or B, C, D, and so on or Wards 1, 2, 3, etc. The middle one will be marked by a flagstaff, and is the office of the establishment, with rooms for the ward surgeons, etc. One of these sheds, or wards, will contain sixty cots; sometimes, on an emergency, they move them close together, and crowd in more. Some of the barracks are larger, with, of course, more inmates. Frequently there are tents, more comfortable here than one might think, whatever they may be down in the army.

Each ward has a ward-master, and generally a nurse for every ten or twelve men. A ward surgeon has, generally, two wards, although this varies. Some of the wards have a woman nurse; the Armory-square wards have some very good ones. The one in Ward E is one of the best.

A few weeks ago, the vast area of the second story of that noblest of Washington buildings, the Patent Office, was crowded close with rows of sick, badly wounded, and dying soldiers. They were placed in three very large apartments. I went there several times. It was a strange, solemn, and, with all its features of suffering and death, a sort of fascinating sight. I went sometimes at night to soothe and relieve particular cases. Some, I found, needed a little cheering up and friendly consolation at that time, for they went to sleep better afterwards. Two of the immense apartments are filled with high and ponderous glass cases crowded with models in miniature of every kind of utensil, machine, or invention it ever entered into the mind of man to conceive, and with curiosities and foreign presents. Between these cases were lateral openings, perhaps eight feet wide, and quite deep, and in these were placed many of the sick; besides a great long double row of them up and down through the middle of the hall. Many of them were very bad cases, wounds and amputations. Then there was a gallery running above the hall, in which there were beds also. It was, indeed, a curious scene at night when lit up. The glass cases, the beds, the sick, the gallery above and the marble pavement under foot; the suffering, and the fortitude to bear it in the various degrees; occasionally, from some, the groan that could not be repressed; sometimes a poor fellow dying, with emaciated face and glassy eyes, the nurse by his side, the doctor also there, but no friend, no relative. Such were the sights but lately in the Patent Office. The wounded have since been removed from there, and it is now vacant again.

Of course, there are among these thousands of prostrated soldiers in hospital here all sorts of individual cases. On recurring to my notebook, I am puzzled which cases to select to illustrate the average of these young men and their experiences. I may here say, too, in general terms, that I could not wish for more candor and manliness, among all their sufferings, than I find among them.

Take this case in Ward 6, Campbell hospital: a young man from Plymouth County, Massachusetts; a farmer's son, aged about twenty or twenty-one; a soldierly, American young fellow, but with sensitive and tender feelings. Most of December and January last he lay very low, and for quite a while I never expected he would recover. He had become prostrated with an obstinate diarrhea: his stomach would hardly keep the least thing down; he was vomiting half the time. But that was hardly the worst of it. Let me tell his story; it is but one of thousands.

He had been some time sick with his regiment in the field, in front, but did his duty as long as he could; was in the battle of Fredericksburg; soon after was put in the regimental hospital. He kept getting worse, could not eat anything they had there; the doctor told him nothing could be done for him there. The poor fellow had fever also; received (perhaps it could not be helped) little or no attention; lay on the ground, getting worse. Toward the latter part of December, very much enfeebled, he was sent up from the front, from Falmouth Station, in an open platform car (such as hogs are transported upon North) and dumped with a crowd of others on the boat at Aquia Creek, falling down like a rag where they deposited him, too weak and sick to sit up or help himself at all. No one spoke to him or assisted him; he had nothing to eat or drink; was used (amid the great crowds of sick) either with perfect indifference, or, as in two or three instances, with heartless brutality.

On the boat, when night came and when the air grew chilly, he tried a long time to undo the blankets he had in his knapsack but was too feeble. He asked one of the employees, who was moving around deck, for a moment's assistance to get the blankets. The man asked him back if he could not get them himself. He answered, no, he had been trying for more than half an hour and found himself too weak. The man rejoined, he might then go without them, and walked off. So *H.* lay chilled and damp on deck all night, without anything under or over him, while two good blankets were within reach. It caused him a great injury, nearly cost him his life.

Arrived at Washington, he was brought ashore and again left on the wharf, or above it, amid the great crowds, as before, without any nourishment; not a drink for his parched mouth, no kind hand had offered to cover his face from the forenoon sun. Conveyed at last some two miles by the ambulance to the hospital, and assigned a bed (Bed 49, Ward 6, Campbell Hospital, January, and February 1863), he fell down exhausted upon the bed. But the ward-master (he has since been changed) came to him with a growling order to get up: the rules, he said, permitted no man to lie down in that way with his own clothes on; he must sit up, must first go to the bathroom, be washed, and have his clothes completely changed. A very good rule properly applied. He was taken to the bathroom and scrubbed well with cold water. The attendants, callous for a while, were soon alarmed, for suddenly the half-frozen and lifeless body fell limpsy in their hands, and they hurried it back to the cot, plainly insensible, perhaps dying.

Poor boy! The long train of exhaustion, deprivation, rudeness, no food, no friendly word or deed, but all kinds of upstart airs and impudent, unfeeling speeches and deeds, from all kinds of small officials (and some big ones), cutting like razors into that sensitive heart, had at last done the job. He now lay at times out of his head but quite silent, asking nothing of anyone, for some days, with death getting a closer and a surer grip upon him; he cared not, or rather he welcomed death. His heart was broken. He felt the struggle to keep up any longer to be useless. God, the world, humanity, all had abandoned him. It would feel so good to shut his eyes forever on the cruel things around him and toward him.

As luck would have it, at this time I found him. I was passing down Ward No. 6 one day about dusk (4th January, I think), and noticed his glassy eyes, with a look of despair and hopelessness, sunk low in his thin, pallid-brown young face. One learns to divine quickly in the hospital, and as I stopped by him and spoke some commonplace remark (to which he made no reply), I saw as I looked that it was a case for ministering to the affection first, and other nourishment and medicines afterward. I sat down by him without any fuss; talked a little; soon saw that it did him good; led him to talk a little himself; got him somewhat interested; wrote a letter for him to his folks in Massachusetts (to L. H. Campbell, Plymouth County); soothed him down as I saw he was getting a little too much agitated, and tears in his eyes; gave him some small gifts, and told him I should come again soon. He has told me since that this little visit, at that hour, just saved him. A day more, and it would have been perhaps too late.

Of course I did not forget him, for he was a young fellow to interest anyone. He remained very sick, vomiting much every day, frequent diarrhea, and also something like bronchitis, the doctor said. For a while I visited him almost every day, cheered him up, took him some little gifts, and gave him small sums of money (he relished a drink of new milk, when it was brought through the ward for sale). For a couple of weeks his condition was uncertain. Sometimes I thought there was no chance for him at all; but of late he is doing better, is up and dressed, and goes around more and more (February 21) every day. He will not die but will recover.

The other evening, passing through the ward, he called me; he wanted to say a few words, particular. I sat down by his side on the cot in the dimness of the long ward, with the wounded soldiers there in their beds, ranging up and down. *H.* told me I had saved his life. He was in the deepest earnest about it. It was one of those things that repay a soldiers' hospital missionary a thousandfold, one of the hours he never forgets.

A benevolent person, with the right qualities and tact, cannot, perhaps, make a better investment of himself, at present, anywhere upon the varied surface of the whole of this big world, than in these military hospitals, among such thousands of most interesting young men. The army is very young, and so much more American than I supposed. Reader, how can I describe to you the mute appealing look that rolls and moves from many a manly eye, from many a sick cot, following you as you walk slowly down one of these wards? To see these, and to be incapable of responding to them, except in a few cases (so very few compared to the whole of the suffering men), is enough to make one's heart crack. I go through in some cases, cheering up the men, distributing now and then little sums of money, and, regularly, letter-paper and envelopes, oranges, tobacco, jellies, etc., etc.

Many things invite comment and some of them sharp criticism in these hospitals. The Government, as I said, is anxious and liberal in its practice toward its sick; but the work has to be left, in its personal application to the men, to hundreds of officials of one grade or another about the hospitals, who are sometimes entirely lacking in the right qualities. There are tyrants and shysters in all positions, and especially those dressed in subordinate authority. Some of the ward doctors are careless, rude, capricious, needlessly strict. One I found who prohibited the men from all enlivening amusements; I found him sending men to the guardhouse for the most trifling offence. In general, perhaps, the officials, especially the new ones, with their straps or badges, put on too many airs. Of all places in the world, the hospitals of American young men and soldiers, wounded in the volunteer service of their country, ought to be exempt from mere conventional military airs and etiquette of shoulder-straps. But they are not exempt.

W.W.

Lafayette C. Baker

The reputation of Civil War era Chief of Detectives Lafayette C. Baker (1826-1868) is at least partially self-endowed, as anyone who reads his *History of the United States Secret Service* will likely confirm. Among Baker's formative experiences was a stint with the San Francisco Vigilance Committee which in the 1850s worked aggressively to clean up the gold-rush city. Baker brought this experience and his vigilante style to Washington, D.C. where he was tapped by General Winfield Scott to gather intelligence in Confederate-held Virginia. Although this mission briefly landed Baker in a Richmond prison, he eventually returned to Washington, D.C. and subsequently served as the self-styled Chief of the National Detective Bureau. This rather grandiose bureaucratic title essentially applied to Lafayette C. Baker's service as a Provost Marshal in the War Department, where he proved to be aggressive in combating vice in Washington, D.C., so aggressive that he often found himself engaged with individuals in the very government he served.

"Men of Commanding Position Exposed"

I have made some disclosures respecting the contraband trade in gaming-cards; but it remains now to record the prevalence and ruinous effects of the vice of gambling itself, during the war, pre-eminently in the National Capital. I have no desire to exaggerate the evils that lurk in the high or low places of society; to speak of Washington in a carping tone, as if it had been, or is, a Sodom beyond redemption; nor do I wish to magnify my office at the expense of any man's fair fame, whatever his position.

But I cannot be true to myself, the Bureau I represented, nor yet to the people for whose sake I send forth these annals and omit a narrative which will surprise and sadden thousands. And may the country we love, the families, the youth of the land, profit by the recital. It is well known that there have always been in large cities what are called "gambling hells;" costly houses, fitted up with elegance, and furnished with everything to attract the eye, and lend fascination to the destructive pastime. Indeed, many virtuous citizens earnestly defend the existence of this and other unblushing vices as necessary evils; when, there can be no crime which the law should not reach, and will, if fearlessly wielded by its officers, and they, in turn, are sustained by the people.

In Washington, gambling increased naturally and inevitably, with the progress of the war. It is not a pleasant thing to say that the patronage of the gaming-table had been drawn largely from Members of Congress; to whom were added, with the increasing number of officers gathering to the capital, many high in military command. With the demand for such haunts of "sporting men," their number multiplied until I had a list of more than a hundred houses, many of which were gorgeous beyond description. The fitting up of a single place of this kind cost twenty-five thousand dollars.

The terrible fact which drew my attention to the subject was the discovery that nine in every ten of the defalcations by paymasters, and others in the employment of the Government, were occasioned in every instance by losses at the card table. I recovered forty thousand dollars which had passed into the hands of gamblers from those of a trusted and respected official.

I called on the Military Commander of the District and was discouraged in my purpose of testing the statute on gaming in the capital. The popular acquiescence in this state of things, the patronage of distinguished men, and the character of the proprietors of the "hells," were the arguments used by that officer. Still, I was not convinced, but the more decided to proceed to business.

I, accordingly, mustered my entire force of assistants and detailed to them my plans. We were to move at the same moment, surround the dozen or more gaming-houses on Pennsylvania Avenue, and at the designated time, to prevent any concert of action by the proprietors, or concealment of their business, to enter and break them up. It was half past two o'clock in the morning, when the dash was made, the gamblers arrested, and their houses closed. The next morning brought intense excitement among the sporting gentlemen, some denouncing the interference, and others offering bribes. A number of them raised a sum of more than twenty thousand dollars for me, if I would allow them to resume their lucrative calling. It is scarcely necessary to say that I refused to pause in the reform commenced.

Mr. Lincoln sent for me, and I repaired to the White House, to find him carelessly sitting in shirtsleeves and slippers, ready to receive me. He said:

"Well, Baker, what is the trouble between you and the gamblers?"

I told my story. He laughed, and said:

"I used to play penny-ante when I ran a flat-boat out West, but for many years have not touched a card."

I stated to him the havoc gambling was making with the army, alluded to before, when he approved my course, but reminded me of the difficulties in the way of reform.

I replied: "I cannot fight the gamblers and the Government both."

The President replied: "You won't have to fight *me*."

I added: "It *is* a fight; and all I ask is fair play: that the Government will let me alone, and I will break up the business."

And, with this perfect understanding, we parted for the time.

Remarked one of the gamesters to me: "After all, I don't care; it has cost me five thousand dollars a month to keep officers still."

The result was, the business was effectually spoiled in Washington, and some of the leaders in it removed to other cities; the power of wholesome law was vindicated, the offenders punished, and Washington saved, for the time, from one of its greatest curses; men of commanding position exposed, and young men saved from the serpent's charm and fang.

Another kindred and gigantic vice was unblushingly doing its work of death, which I could not overlook. The most superficial observer of Washington must have noticed the unusual number of drinking places, in every form and under every possible disguise. Wherever soldiers were stationed, or army work in progress, there was seen, at least, the beer barrel and whisky demijohn. Old street corners and vacant lots were occupied with the bar, around which lay the intoxicated victims of their poison, the "boys in blue." In the suburbs, under the shadow of hospitals, and beside bridges, the **liquor** booth was reared, until it was estimated that not less than *thirty-seven hundred* such fountains of ruin were in active operation. In spite of the most stringent municipal and military regulations, the traffic went on unchecked, and daily increasing. The imposition of a fine, or incarceration for a few hours in a guardhouse, was a mere joke to the speculators in the morals and lives of men. But to enter the saloons, and, with the heavy blows of the ax, to crush in the barrelhead, bring decanters in fragments to the floor, and then lay the structure itself in ruins, was too expensive a jest to be often repeated.

In the vicinity of Twenty-Second and G Streets were the headquarters of the Depot Quartermaster. Here were located the Government warehouses, storehouses, workshops, manufactories, and corrals, employing eight thousand men or more. Two sides of an entire square were occupied by the lowest places of intoxication. In many of them, the entire stock in trade was a cask of lager beer and a gallon of unknown and villainous compound called Bourbon whisky, dealt out in an old rusty tin cup, at ten cents per drink. In these dens could be seen, at all hours of the day and night, the common soldier, the teamster, and the mechanic. I distinctly recollect that on the eve of an important battle, when necessary to dispatch to the front, at an hour's notice a train of one hundred wagons, not five Government teamsters were sufficiently sober to move forward.

When all other means, laws, and agents had failed to reach and remedy the frightful evil . . . I officially gave notice to the occupants of these saloons, that they must close them by four o'clock, the next day, or take the consequences of a refusal to comply.

They had so often before been warned that no attention was given to my caution. At the expiration of the appointed time, with my employees, all armed with axes, I proceeded to the dens of Bacchus, and commenced the work of destruction. Soon the long lines of liquor shops were leveled to the ground, and only broken and empty barrels, crushed decanters, and rubbish remained.

In one case, when the demolition began, the proprietor, with pencil and paper, made an inventory of his property. When asked what he proposed to do with it, he replied, "Make a bill," and scratched away.

I replied: "It is hardly worth the while to present to the Government a bill for a few decanters and rattlesnake whisky; I think I will tear down the house over your head, and then you can make out a bill worth your while."

The assembling of a large army at the capital also drew after it those camp-followers who, of all lost humanity, are the most degraded: fallen women. While the gambler and **liquor**-seller's den sprang up at the first sound of war, as if spontaneously from the earth which echoed the tramp of armies, from every city came the painted wreck of womanhood, and hired the room at the fashionable hotel, the dwelling, the abandoned chamber, or the negro cabin, to traffic in the virtue, health, domestic peace, and highest interests of men. Along the Potomac in front of Washington, stretching for fifteen miles along the banks, lay the Union troops.

The horses of staff officers, the ambulance, and orderlies, could be seen during the night, and after the sun had risen even, waiting before the kennels of vice, for those who were within them.

Nor are the instances few, where the pretty, vain wife or daughter has been enticed over the lines, to become the member of the domestic military circle. So notorious had this vice become, that I appealed to the Secretary of War, who issued an order that no commissioned officer or private could enter the city without a written pass from his commanding general. A violation of the order would subject the offender to a lodgment in the guardhouse.

For a time, the order was partially regarded, but soon set aside, and the corruption seemed to gain strength by the temporary check. At length, for the two-fold purpose of enforcing the order and exposing to public contempt the transgressors, I decided to make a descent upon some of the representative houses of this class. The scenes which transpired at the hour of midnight in these dens of corruption beggar language.

At an hour appointed, and with a concerted plan similar in all its details to that which was sprung upon the gamblers, with my force I made a raid upon the disreputable houses.

The moment came, the signal was given, doors were opened, the windows raised, and a scene of confusion and comico-tragic nature followed, which must have been witnessed to have been appreciated. Faces quite covered to avoid recognition, gas turned off, and a general stampede of gentlemen sporting martial emblems, were some of the incidents attending the onset upon the intrenchments of vice in midnight quiet of the Nation's Capital. Between sixty and seventy officers and men were arrested and locked up in the guardhouse, for reflection upon their suddenly interrupted debauchery.

Francis Bicknell Carpenter

The New York artist Francis Bicknell Carpenter (1830-1900) achieved success in his early twenties, maintained a studio in Manhattan, and won commissions for portraits of several well-known political figures of his era. His most memorable work, *First Reading of the Emancipation Proclamation of President Lincoln,* hangs in the rotunda of the United States Capitol. Carpenter's memoir, *Six Months at the White House with Abraham Lincoln,* is itself a portrait, albeit in another medium. It reflects upon on his brief residence in the home of the President of the United States, and his capturing for posterity the bold decision for which Lincoln is so often remembered.

"The Radical and the Conservative"

On the evening of February 4th, 1864, I went to Washington. Shortly after noon of the following day, I rang the bell at Mr. Lovejoy's residence on Fifteenth Street. To my sorrow, I found him very ill; but it was hoped by his friends that he was then improving. Though very feeble, he insisted upon seeing me, and calling for writing materials, sat up in bed to indite a note introducing me to the President. This, handed to me open, I read. One expression I have not forgotten, it was so like Mr. Lincoln himself, as I afterward came to know him. "I am gaining very slowly. It is hard work drawing the sled up-hill." And this suggests the similarity there was between these men. Lovejoy had much more of the agitator, the reformer, in his nature, but both drew the inspiration of their lives from the same source, and it was founded in sterling honesty. Their modes of thought and illustration were remarkably alike. It is not strange that they should have been bosom friends. The President called repeatedly to see him during his illness; and it was on one of these occasions that he said to him, "This war is eating my life out; I have a strong impression that I shall not live to see the end." Mr. Lovejoy's health subsequently improved, and for a change he went to Brooklyn, N. Y., where, it will be remembered, he had a relapse, and died, universally mourned as one of the truest and most faithful of our statesmen. Mr. Lincoln did not hear from him directly after he left Washington. Through a friend I learned by letter that he was lying at the point of death. This intelligence I communicated to the President the same evening, in the vestibule of the White House, meeting him on his way to the War Department. He was deeply affected by it. His only words were, "Lovejoy was the best friend I had in Congress."

To return from this pardonable digression, I took the note of introduction at once to the White House; but no opportunity was afforded me of presenting it during the day. The following morning passed with the same result, and I then resolved to avail myself of Mrs. Lincoln's Saturday afternoon reception, at which, I was told, the President would be present, to make myself known to him. Two o'clock found me one of the throng pressing toward the center of attraction, the "blue" room. From the threshold of the "crimson" parlor as I passed, I had a glimpse of the gaunt figure of Mr. Lincoln in the distance, haggard-looking, dressed in black, relieved only by the prescribed white gloves; standing, it seemed to me, solitary and alone, though surrounded by the crowd, bending low now and then in the process of handshaking, and responding half abstractedly to the well-meant greetings of the miscellaneous assemblage. Never shall I forget the electric thrill which went through my whole being at this instant. I seemed to see lines radiating from every part of the globe, converging to a focus at the point where that plain, awkward-looking man stood, and to hear in spirit a million prayers, "as the sound of many waters," ascending in his behalf. Mingled with supplication I could discern a clear symphony of triumph and blessing, swelling with an ever-increasing volume. It was the voice of those who had been bondmen and bondwomen, and the grand diapason swept up from the coming ages.

It was soon my privilege in the regular succession to take that honored hand. Accompanying the act, my name and profession were announced to him in a low tone by one of the assistant private secretaries, who stood by his side. Retaining my hand, he looked at me inquiringly for an instant, and said, "Oh yes; I know; this is the painter." Then straightening himself to his full height, with a twinkle of the eye, he added, playfully, "Do you think, Mr. C., that you can make a handsome picture of me?" emphasizing strongly the last word. Somewhat confused at this point-blank shot, uttered in a tone so loud as to attract the attention of those in immediate proximity, I made a random reply, and took the occasion to ask if I could see him in his study at the close of the reception. To this he responded in the peculiar vernacular of the West, "I reckon," resuming meanwhile the mechanical and traditional exercise of the hand which no President has ever yet been able to avoid, and which, severe as is the ordeal, is likely to attach to the position, so long as the Republic endures.

The appointed hour found me at the well-remembered door of the official chamber, that door watched daily, with so many conflicting emotions of hope and fear, by the anxious throng regularly gathered there. The President had preceded me, and was already deep in Acts of Congress, with which the writing-desk was strewed, awaiting his signature. He received me pleasantly, giving me a seat near his own armchair; and after having read Mr. Lovejoy's note, he took off his spectacles, and said, "Well, Mr. C., we will turn you in loose here, and try to give you a good chance to work out your idea." Then, without paying much attention to the enthusiastic expression of my ambitious desire and purpose, he proceeded to give me a detailed account of the history and issue of the great proclamation.

"It had got to be," said he, "midsummer, 1862. Things had gone on from bad to worse, until I felt that we had reached the end of our rope on the plan of operations we had been pursuing; that we had about played our last card, and must change our tactics, or lose the game! I now determined upon the adoption of the emancipation policy; and, without consultation with, or the knowledge of the Cabinet, I prepared the original draft of the proclamation, and, after much anxious thought, called a Cabinet meeting upon the subject. This was the last of July, or the first part of the month of August 1862." The exact date he did not remember. "This Cabinet meeting took place, I think, upon a Saturday. All were present, excepting Mr. Blair, the Postmaster-General, who was absent at the opening of the discussion, but came in subsequently. I said to the Cabinet that I had resolved upon this step and had not called them together to ask their advice, but to lay the subject matter of a proclamation before them; suggestions as to which would be in order, after they had heard it read. Mr. Lovejoy," said he, "was in error when he informed you that it excited no comment, excepting on the part of Secretary Seward. Various suggestions were offered. Secretary Chase wished the language stronger in reference to the arming of the blacks. Mr. Blair, after he came in, deprecated the policy, on the ground that it would cost the Administration the fall elections. Nothing, however, was offered that I had not already fully anticipated and settled in my own mind, until Secretary Seward spoke. He said in substance: 'Mr. President, I approve of the proclamation, but I question the expediency of its issue at this juncture. The depression of the public mind, consequent upon our repeated reverses, is so great that I fear the effect of so important a step. It may be viewed as the last measure of an exhausted government, a cry for help; the government stretching forth its hands to Ethiopia, instead of Ethiopia stretching forth her hands to the government.' His idea," said the President, "was that it would be considered our last *shriek*, on the retreat." (This was his precise expression.) "'Now,' continued Mr. Seward, 'while I approve the measure, I suggest, sir, that you postpone its issue, until you can give it to the country supported by military success, instead of issuing it, as would be the case now, upon the greatest disasters of the war!'" Mr. Lincoln continued: "The wisdom of the view of the Secretary of State struck me with very great force. It was an aspect of the case that, in all my thought upon the subject, I had entirely overlooked. The result was that I put the draft of the proclamation aside, as you do your sketch for a picture, waiting for a victory. From time to time, I added or changed a line, touching it up here and there, anxiously watching the progress of events. Well, the next news we had was of Pope's disaster, at Bull Run. Things looked darker than ever. Finally, came the week of the battle of Antietam. I determined to wait no longer. The news came, I think, on Wednesday, that the advantage was on our side. I was then staying at the Soldiers' Home (three miles out of Washington). Here I finished writing the second draft of the preliminary proclamation; came up on Saturday; called the Cabinet together to hear it, and it was published the following Monday."

At the final meeting of September 20th, another interesting incident occurred in connection with Secretary Seward. The President had written the important part of the proclamation in these words:

"That, on the first day of January, in the year of our Lord one thousand eight hundred and sixty-three, all persons held as slaves within any State or designated part of a State, the people whereof shall then be in rebellion against the United States, shall be then, thenceforward, and forever free; and the Executive Government of the United States, including the military and naval authority thereof, will recognize the freedom of such persons, and will do no act or acts to repress such persons, or any of them, in any efforts they may make for their actual freedom." "When 1 finished reading this paragraph," resumed Mr. Lincoln, "Mr. Seward stopped me, and said, 'I think, Mr. President, that you should insert after the word "*recognize*" in that sentence, the words "*and maintain*."' "I replied that I had already fully considered the import of that expression in this connection, but I had not introduced it, because it was not my way to promise what I was not entirely sure that I could perform, and I was not prepared to say that I thought we were exactly able to 'maintain' this."

"But" said he, "Seward insisted that we ought to take this ground; and the words finally went in!"

"It is a somewhat remarkable fact," he subsequently remarked, "that there were just one hundred days between the dates of the two proclamations issued upon the 22nd of September and the 1st of January. I had not made the calculation at the time."

Having concluded this interesting statement, the President then proceeded to show me the various positions occupied by himself and the different members of the Cabinet, on the occasion of the first meeting. "As nearly as I remember," said he, "I sat near the head of the table; the Secretary of the Treasury and the Secretary of War were here, at my right hand; the others were grouped at the left."

At this point, I exhibited to him a pencil sketch of the composition as I had conceived it, with no knowledge of the facts or details. The leading idea of this I found, as I have stated on a previous page, to be entirely consistent with the account I had just heard. I saw, however, that I should have to reverse the picture, placing the President at the other end of the table, to make it accord with his description. I had resolved to discard all appliances and tricks of picture-making, and endeavor, as faithfully as possible, to represent the scene as it actually transpired; room, furniture, accessories, all were to be painted from the actualities. It was a scene second only in historical importance and interest to that of the Declaration of Independence; and I felt assured, that, if honestly and earnestly painted, it need borrow no interest from imaginary curtain or column, gorgeous furniture, or allegorical statue. Assenting heartily to what is called the "realistic" school of art, when applied to the illustration of historic events, I felt in this case, that I had no more right to depart from the facts, than has the historian in his record.

When friends said to me, as they frequently did, "Your picture will be bald and barren," my reply was, "If I cannot make the portraiture of the scene itself sufficiently attractive without the false glitter of tapestry hangings, velvet tablecloths, and marble columns, then I shall at least have the satisfaction of having failed in the cause of truth." I reasoned in this way: The most important document submitted to a Cabinet during our existence as a nation is under discussion. A spectator permitted to look in upon that scene would give little thought and small heed to the mere accessories and adjuncts of the occasion. His mind would center upon the immortal document, its anxious author, conscious of his solemn responsibility, announcing his matured and inflexible purpose to his assembled councilors. He would listen with unparalleled eagerness to the momentous sentences uttered for the first time in the ears of men, and to the discussion upon them, impatient of mere formalities and technicalities. Should a thought be sprung of important bearing, or an overlooked contingency be brought forward, how intently would its effect be watched. What varying emotions, consequent upon peculiarities of temperament and character, would be expressed in the countenances of the different individuals composing the group. How each in turn would be scanned. Above all, the issues involved: the salvation of the Republic, the freedom of a Race. "Surely," I said, "such a scene may be painted, and abiding if not absorbing interest secured, without the aid of conventional trappings. The republican simplicity of the room and furniture, with its thronging associations, will more than counterbalance the lack of splendor, and the artistic mania for effect. I will depend solely for my success upon the interest of the subject, and its truthfulness of representation." And this purpose I carried with me to the end.

The first sketch of the composition, as it was afterward placed upon the canvas, was matured, I believe, the same afternoon, or the following Monday after the interview recorded above, upon the back of a visiting card; my pockets affording evidence of the employment of all loose material at hand in leisure moments, in the study of the work. The final arrangement of the figures was the result of much thought and many combinations, though the original conception as to the moment of time and incident of action was preserved throughout. The general arrangement of the group, as described by the President, was fortunately entirely consistent with my purpose, which was to give that prominence to the different individuals which belonged to them respectively in the Administration. There was a curious mingling of fact and allegory in my mind as I assigned to each his place on the canvas. There were two elements in the Cabinet, the radical and the conservative. Mr. Lincoln was placed at the head of the official table, between two groups, nearest that representing the radical, but the uniting point of both. The chief powers of a government are War and Finance: the ministers of these were at his right, the Secretary of War, symbolizing the great struggle, in the immediate foreground; the Secretary of the Treasury, actively supporting the new policy, standing by the President's side. The Army being the right hand, the Navy may very properly be styled the left hand of the government. The place for the Secretary of the Navy seemed, therefore, very naturally to be on Mr. Lincoln's left, at the rear of the table. To the Secretary of State, as the great expounder of the principles of the Republican Party, the profound and sagacious statesman, would the attention of all at such a time be given. Entitled to precedence in discussion by his position in the Cabinet, he would necessarily form one of the central figures of the group. The four chief officers of the government were thus brought, in accordance with their relations to the Administration, nearest the person of the President, who, with the manuscript proclamation in hand, which he had just read, was represented leaning forward, listening to, and intently considering the views presented by the Secretary of State. The Attorney-General, absorbed in the constitutional questions involved, with folded arms, was placed at the foot of the table opposite the President. The Secretary of the Interior and the Postmaster-General, occupying the less conspicuous positions of the Cabinet, seemed to take their proper places in the background of the picture.

When, at length, the conception as thus described was sketched upon the large canvas, and Mr. Lincoln came in to see it, his gratifying remark, often subsequently repeated, was, "It is as good as it can be made."

Noah Brooks

The American author and journalist Noah Brooks (1830-1903) is remembered today for his 19th century novel *Our Base Ball Club and How it Won the Championship*, published in 1884. Two decades earlier, Brooks was working as a reporter for the *Sacramento Daily Union*, covering Washington, D.C. under the byline "Castine," after his hometown in Maine. Noah Brooks was already well-acquainted with Abraham Lincoln when he began reporting on the President and the White House during the first years of the Civil War. Brooks' dispatches for the *Sacramento Daily Union* were later collected and edited as *Washington in Lincoln's Time*, published a generation after the war and still highly regarded for its intimate portrayal of Lincoln and his presidency.

"Profound Silence"

The afternoon and evening of April 14, 1865, were cold, raw, and gusty. Dark clouds enveloped the capital, and the air was chilly with occasional showers. Late in the afternoon I filled an appointment by calling on the President at the White House, and was told by him that he "had had a notion" of sending for me to go to the theater that evening with him and Mrs. Lincoln; but he added that Mrs. Lincoln had already made up a party to take the place of General and Mrs. Grant, who had somewhat unexpectedly left the city for Burlington, New Jersey. The party was originally planned for the purpose of taking General and Mrs. Grant to see "Our American Cousin" at Ford's

Theater, and when Grant had decided to leave Washington, he (the President) had "felt inclined to give up the whole thing;" but as it had been announced in the morning papers that this distinguished party would go to the theater that night, Mrs. Lincoln had rather insisted that they ought to go, in order that the expectant public should not be wholly disappointed. On my way home I met Schuyler Colfax, who was about leaving for California, and who tarried with me on the sidewalk a little while, talking about the trip, and the people whom I knew in San Francisco and Sacramento and whom he wished to meet. Mr. Lincoln had often talked with me about the possibilities of his eventually taking up his residence in California after his term of office should be over. He thought, he said, that that country would afford better opportunities for his two boys than any of the older States; and when he heard that Colfax was going to California, he was greatly interested in his trip, and said that he hoped that Colfax would bring him back a good report of what his keen and practiced observation would note in the country which he (Colfax) was about to see for the first time.

The evening being inclement, I stayed within doors to nurse a violent cold with which I was afflicted; and my roommate *McA---* and I whiled away the time chatting and playing cards. About half-past ten our attention was attracted to the frequent galloping of cavalry, or the mounted patrol, past the house which we occupied on New York Avenue, near the State Department building. After a while quiet was restored, and we retired to our sleeping-room in the rear part of the house. As I turned down the gas, I said to my roommate: "Will, I have guessed the cause of the clatter outside tonight. You know Wade Hampton has disappeared with his cavalry somewhere in the mountains of Virginia. Now, my theory of the racket is that he has raided Washington, and has pounced down upon the President, and has attempted to carry him off." Of course, this was said jocosely and without the slightest thought that the President was in any way in danger; and my friend, in a similar spirit, banteringly replied, "What good will that do the rebs unless they carry off Andy Johnson also?" The next morning, I was awakened in the early dawn by a loud and hurried knocking on my chamber door, and the voice of Mr. Gardner, the landlord, crying, "Wake, wake, Mr. Brooks! I have dreadful news." I slipped out, turned the key of the door, and Mr. Gardner came in, pale, trembling, and woebegone, like him who "drew Priam's curtain at the dead of night," and told his awful story. At that time, it was believed that the President, Mr. Seward, Vice-President Johnson, and other members of the Government, had been killed; and this was the burden of the tale that was told to us. I sank back into my bed, cold and shivering with horror, and for a time it seemed as though the end of all things had come. I was aroused by the loud weeping of my comrade, who had not left his bed in another part of the room.

When we had sufficiently collected ourselves to dress and go out of doors in the bleak and cheerless April morning, we found in the streets an extraordinary spectacle. They were suddenly crowded with people, men, women, and children thronging the pavements and darkening the thoroughfares. It seemed as if everybody was in tears. Pale faces, streaming eyes, with now and again an angry, frowning countenance, were on every side. Men and women who were strangers accosted one another with distressed looks and tearful inquiries for the welfare of the President and Mr. Seward's family. The President still lived, but at half-past seven o'clock in the morning the tolling of the bells announced to the lamenting people that he had ceased to breathe. His great and loving heart was still. The last official bulletin from the War Department stated that he died at twenty-two minutes past seven o'clock on the morning of April 15.

Instantly flags were raised at half-mast all over the city, the bells tolled solemnly, and with incredible swiftness Washington went into deep, universal mourning. All shops, government departments, and private offices were closed, and everywhere, on the most pretentious residences and on the humblest hovels, were the black badges of grief. Nature seemed to sympathize in the general lamentation, and tears of rain fell from the moist and somber sky. The wind sighed mournfully through streets crowded with sad-faced people, and broad folds of funeral drapery flapped heavily in the wind over the decorations of the day before. Wandering aimlessly up F Street toward Ford's Theater, we met a tragical procession. It was headed by a group of army officers walking bareheaded, and behind them, carried tenderly by a company of soldiers, was the bier of the dead President, covered with the flag of the Union, and accompanied by an escort of soldiers who had been on duty at the house where Lincoln died. As the little cortege passed down the street to the White House, every head was uncovered, and the profound silence which prevailed was broken only by sobs and by the sound of the measured tread of those who bore the martyred President back to the home which he had so lately quitted full of life, hope, and cheer.

On the night of the 17th the remains of Lincoln were laid in the casket prepared for their reception and were taken from the large guest-chamber of the House to the famous East Room, where so many brilliant receptions and so many important public events had been witnessed; and there they lay in state until the day of the funeral (April 19). The great Room was draped with crape and black cloth, relieved only here and there by white flowers and green leaves. The catafalque upon which the casket lay was about fifteen feet high, and consisted of an elevated platform resting on a dais and covered with a domed canopy of black cloth which was supported by four pillars and was lined beneath with fluted white silk. In those days the custom of sending "floral tributes" on funereal occasions was not common, but the funeral of Lincoln was remarkable for the unusual abundance and beauty of the devices in flowers that were sent by individuals and public bodies. From the time the body had been made ready for burial until the last services in the House, it was watched night and day by a guard of honor, the members of which were one Major-General, one Brigadier-General, two field officers, and four line-officers of the army and four of the navy. Before the public were admitted to view the face of the dead, the scene in the darkened Room, a sort of *chapelle ardente*, was most impressive. At the head and foot and on each side of the casket of their dead Chief stood the motionless figures of his armed warriors.

When the funeral exercises took place, the floor of the East Room had been transformed into something like an amphitheater by the erection of an inclined platform, broken into steps, and filling all but the entrance side of the apartment and the area about the catafalque. This platform was covered with black cloth, and upon it stood the various persons designated as participants in the ceremonies, no seats being provided. In the northwest corner were the pall-bearers: Senators Lafayette S. Foster of Connecticut, E. D. Morgan of New York, Reverdy Johnson of Maryland, Richard Yates of Illinois, Benjamin F. Wade of Ohio, and John Conness of California; Representatives Henry L. Dawes of Massachusetts, A. H. Coffroth of Pennsylvania, Green Clay Smith of Kentucky, Schuyler Colfax of Indiana, E. B. Washburne of Illinois, and H. G. Worthington of Nevada; Lieutenant-General Grant, Major-General Halleck, and Brevet Brigadier-General Nichols; Vice-Admiral Farragut, Rear-Admiral Shubrick, and Colonel Zeilin, of the Marine Corps; civilians O. H. Browning, George Ashmun, Thomas Corwin, and Simon Cameron. The New York Chamber of Commerce was represented by its officers, and the New York Associated Merchants by Simeon Draper, Moses Grinnell, John Jacob Astor, Jonathan Sturges, and Hiram Walbridge, Next to them, at the extreme southern end of the Room, were the Governors of the States; and on the east side of the coffin, which lay north and south, and opposite the main entrance of the East Room, stood Andrew Johnson, President of the United States. He was supported on each side by his faithful friend Preston King and ex-Vice-President Hamlin. Behind these were Chief Justice Chase and his Associates on the Supreme Bench, and near them were the members of the Cabinet and their wives, all of whom were in deep mourning. On the right of the Cabinet officers, at the northern end of the Room were the diplomatic corps, whose brilliant court costumes gleamed in strange contrast with the somber monotony of the rest of the spectacle. The Members of the Senate and House of Representatives were disposed about the Room and adjoining apartments, and at the foot of the catafalque was a little semicircle of chairs for the family and friends. Robert T. Lincoln, son of the President, was the only one of the family present, Mrs. Lincoln being unable to leave her room, where she remained with Tad. General Grant, separated from the others, sat alone at the head of the catafalque, and during the solemn services was often moved to tears. The officiating clergymen were the Rev. Dr. Gurley, Pastor of the President, who preached the funeral sermon; the Rev. Dr. Hall, of the Epiphany Episcopal Church; the Rev. Dr. Gray, who was then Chaplain of the Senate; and Bishop Simpson, who was an intimate friend of Lincoln. A singular omission, whether intentional or not I do not know, was that no music of any sort was mingled with the exercises.

The sight of the funeral pageant will probably never be forgotten by those who saw it. Long before the services in the White House were over, the streets were blocked by crowds of people thronging to see the procession, which moved from the House precisely at two o'clock, amid the tolling of bells and the booming of minute-guns from three batteries that had been brought into the city, and from each of the many forts about Washington. The day was cloudless, and the sun shone brilliantly upon cavalry, infantry, artillery, marines, associations, and societies, with draped banners, and accompanied in their slow march by mournful dirges from numerous military bands. The Ninth and Tenth Regiments of Veteran Reserves headed the column; next came a battalion of Marines in gorgeous uniforms; then the Sixteenth New York and the Eighth Illinois Cavalry Regiments; then eight pieces of United States Light Artillery in all the pomp and panoply peculiar to that branch of the service; next several mounted Major-Generals and Brigadiers, accompanied by their staffs; then army and naval officers on foot by the hundred, more mounted officers, and pall-bearers in carriages; then the funeral car, a large structure canopied and covered with black cloth, somewhat like the catafalque which had been erected in the White House. The casket rested on a high platform eight or ten feet above the level of the street. As it passed many shed tears, and all heads were uncovered. The car was enclosed in a hollow square formed by a guard of honor consisting of mounted non-commissioned officers of various light artillery companies from Camp Barry, among them being the Independent Pennsylvania (Hampton's) Artillery, and the First West Virginia Battery, and the company of cavalry known as the President's Bodyguard; then came the carriages for the family, and then the President, the Cabinet, the diplomatic corps, both houses of Congress, and others.

One noticeable feature of the procession was the appearance of the colored societies which brought up the rear, humbly, as was their wont; but just before the procession began to move, the Twenty-Second United States Colored Infantry (organized in Pennsylvania), landed from Petersburg and marched up to a position on the avenue, and when the head of the column came up, played a dirge, and headed the procession to the Capitol. The coffin was taken from the funeral car and placed on a catafalque within the rotunda of the Capitol, which had been darkened and draped in mourning.

The coffin rested in the rotunda of the Capitol from the 19th of April until the evening of the 20th. During that time many thousands of people from every part of the United States paid to the dead form of the beloved President their last tearful tribute of affection, honor, and respect. The center of the building was temporarily in charge of the military. Congress not being in session, and the arrangements were admirable for the preservation of order, while all who came were allowed every reasonable facility in the carrying out of their melancholy errand. Guards marshaled the vast procession of sightseers into a double line which separated at the foot of the coffin, passed on either side, was reunited again, and was guided out by the opposite door, which opened onto the great portico of the building on its east front.

While this solemn pageant was passing, I was allowed to go alone up the winding stairs that lead to the top of the great dome of the Capitol. Looking down from that lofty point, the sight was weird and memorable. Directly beneath me lay the casket in which the dead President lay at full length, far, far below; and, like black atoms moving over a sheet of gray paper, the slow-moving mourners, seen from a perpendicular above them, crept silently in two dark lines across the pavement of the rotunda, forming an ellipse around the coffin and joining as they advanced toward the eastern portal and disappeared. When the lying in state at the Capitol was over, the funeral procession from Washington to Springfield, Illinois, began, the cortege passing over the same route which was taken by Abraham Lincoln when he left his home for the national capital to assume the great office which he laid down only with his life.

It would be superfluous now to dwell on the incidents of that historic and most lamentable procession, or to recall to the minds of the present and passing generation the impressiveness of the wonderful popular demonstration of grief that stretched from the seaboard to the heart of Illinois. History has recorded how thousands of the plain people whom Lincoln loved came out from their homes to stand bareheaded and reverent as the funeral train swept by, while bells were tolled and the westward progress through the night was marked by campfires built along the course by which the Great Emancipator was borne at last to his dreamless rest.

Sources

The writings that comprise the *Capital City Anthology* were first published in the late 18th and 19th centuries by various publishing companies adhering to different editorial standards, some works appearing in English translations. In selecting works for inclusion, the focus has been, for the most part, on the writings of individuals rather than on the official proceedings of governmental organizations. In the present edition, minor changes have been made to the original texts with respect to capitalization, grammar, punctuation, and spelling. Occasional editorial intrusions appear in [brackets]. However, no substantive alterations have been made to the original works. The following citations are provided for those readers who wish to review the texts as they originally appeared.

[Adams] Abigail Adams: "Keep All This to Yourself." Excerpted from *Letters of Mrs. Adams: the Wife of John Adams, with an Introductory Memoir by Her Grandson Charles Francis Adams*. Boston: C. C. Little and J. Brown, 1840. See pp. 432-435.

[Alcott] Louisa May Alcott: "Nurse Periwinkle's Mission." Excerpted from *Hospital Sketches* by L. M. Alcott. Boston: James Redpath, 1863. See pp. 29-30; pp. 42-45; pp. 46-50.

[Atwater] Caleb Atwater (Citizen of Ohio): "Speaking of Clerks." Excerpted from *Mysteries of Washington City During Several Months* of the Session of the 28th Congress by A Citizen of Ohio. Washington, D.C.: Printed by G. A. Sage, E Street Near Ninth, 1844. See pp. 16-27.

[Bacourt] Adolphe Fourier de Bacourt: "Just One Month." Excerpted from *Souvenirs of a Diplomat* by the Chevalier de Bacourt. New York: Henry Holt, 1885. See Letters LV-LVI: pp. 164-170 and Letters LLXVII-LLXX, pp. 208-212.

[Baker] Lafayette C. Baker: "Men of Commanding Position Exposed." Excerpted from *History of the United States Secret Service* by General L. C. Baker. Philadelphia: Published by L. C. Baker, 1867. See Chapter XIX: "Gigantic Vices of the National Capital," pp. 241-243; pp. 245-246; pp. 251-252.

[Bohn] Casimir Bohn: "The New Dome." Excerpted from *Bohn's Hand-Book of Washington . . . With a Supplement Prepared by Charles Lanman*. Washington: Published by Casimir Bohn, 1860. See Index and various selections as identified.

[Bremer] Fredrika Bremer: "'No! No!' to the Compromise Bill." Excerpted from *The Homes of the New World: Impressions of America* by Fredrika Bremer. Translated by Mary Howitt. London: Arthur Hall, Virtue, & Co., 1853. See Volume II: pp. 58-64.

[Brooks] Noah Brooks: "Profound Silence." Excerpted from *Washington in Lincoln's Time* by Noah Brooks. New York: The Century Co., 1896. See pp. 257-266.

[Carpenter] Francis Bicknell Carpenter: "The Radical and the Conservative." Excerpted from *Six Months at the White House with Abraham Lincoln: The Story of a Picture* by F. B. Carpenter. New York: Hurd and Houghton, 1866. See pp. 17-28.

[Chambers] William Chambers: "I Am a Public Officer." Excerpted from *Things as They Are in America* by William Chambers. London and Edinburgh: William and Robert Chambers, 1854. See pp. 257-265.

[Constitution] Constitution of the United States: "Article I, Section 8, Clause 17."

[Cooper] James Fenimore Cooper: "The Manners of the Country." Excerpted from *Notions of the Americans: Picked Up by a Travelling Bachelor*. Philadelphia: Carey, Lea and Carey, 1828. See Volume II: pp. 56-61.

[Dickens] Charles Dickens: "Dishonest Faction." Excerpted from *American Notes for General Circulation* by Charles Dickens. Boston: Ticknor and Fields, 1867. See pp. 60-67.

[District] District of Columbia Corporation Laws. "Thirty-Nine Lashes." Excerpted from *Historical Sketches of the Ten Miles Square Forming the District of Columbia* by Jonathan Elliot [Elliott]. Washington: Printed by J. Elliot Jr., 1830. See pp. 509-510.

[Drayton] Daniel Drayton: "The Mob Made the Rush Upon Us." Excerpted from *Personal Memoir of Daniel Drayton: For Four Years and Four Months a Prisoner (for Charity's Sake) in Washington Jail* by Daniel Drayton. Boston: Published by Bela Marsh, 1853. See pp. 39-43.

[Dwight] Theodore Dwight, Jr.: "Such Things are Salutary." Excerpted from *Things as They Are: Or, Notes of a Traveler Through Some of the Middle and Northern States*. New York: Harper & Brothers, 1834. See Chapter II: pp. 17-20.

[Fearon] Henry Bradshaw Fearon: "Human Beings are Sold in the Streets." Excerpted from *Sketches in America* by Henry Bradshaw Fearon. London: Longman, Hurst, Rees, Orme, and Brown, 1818. See pp. 285-295.

[Gleig] George Robert Gleig: "An Elegant Dinner." Excerpted from *A Narrative of the Campaigns of the British Army at Washington and New Orleans, Under Generals Ross, Pakenham, and Lambert, in the Years 1814 and 1815* by George Robert Gleig. London: John Murray, 1826. 2nd Edition. See pp. 114-123 and pp. 124-131.

[Greenhow] Rose O'Neal Greenhow: "Endowed with Constitutional Rights." Excerpted from *My Imprisonment and the First Year of Abolition Rule at Washington* by Mrs. Greenhow. London: Richard Bentley, 1863. See pp. 215-224.

[Hall, Basil] Captain Basil Hall: "Do You Mean to Buy the Lad, Sir?" Excerpted from *Travels in North America, in the Years 1827 and 1828* by Captain Basil Hall. Edinburgh: Printed for Cadell and Co., 1830. See Volume III: pp. 34-42.

[Hall, Francis] Francis Hall: "Splitting Hairs." Excerpted from *Travels in Canada, and the United States, in 1816 and 1817* by Francis Hall. Boston: Re-Published from the London Edition by Wells and Lilly, 1818. See pp. 196-202.

[Hamilton] Thomas Hamilton: "A Wise Institution." Excerpted from *Men and Manners in America* by the Author of Cyril Thornton, etc. Edinburgh: William Blackwood, 1833. See Volume II: pp. 127-133.

[Harriott] John Harriott: "This Intended City." Excerpted from *Struggles Through Life, Exemplified in the Various Travels and Adventures in Europe, Asia, Africa, & America* by John Harriott. London: Printed for the Author, 1815. See Volume III: Chapter II, pp. 11-17.

[Hone] Philip Hone: "Loco Focos." Excerpted from *The Diary of Philip Hone: 1828-1851.* Edited, with an Introduction by Bayard Tuckerman. New York: Dodd, Mead, 1889. See Volume II: pp. 60-68.

[Jefferson] Thomas Jefferson: "I Avoid Interfering . . ." Excerpted from *The Writings of Thomas Jefferson,* edited by H. A. Washington. New York: John C. Riker, 1854. See Volume III: pp. 236-237.

[Jennings] Paul Jennings: "Beloved by Everybody in Washington." Excerpted from *A Colored Man's Reminiscences of James Madison* by Paul Jennings. Brooklyn: George C. Beadle, 1865. See pp. 7-15.

[L'Enfant] Pierre Charles L'Enfant: "A Grand Plan." Excerpted from *Thomas Jefferson and the National Capital,* edited by Saul K. Padover. Washington, D.C.: Government Printing Office, 1946. See pp. 56-57.

[Levasseur] Auguste Levasseur: "The Name of Lafayette." Excerpted from *Lafayette in America in 1824 and 1825* by Auguste Levasseur. Translated by John D. Godham. Philadelphia: Carey and Lea, 1829. See Volume II: pp. 241-254.

[Marryat] Captain Frederick Marryat: "Long-Winded Speeches About Nothing." Excerpted from *A Diary in America with Remarks on its Institutions* by Capt. Marryat. Paris: A. and W. Galignani, 1839. See pp. 115-119.

[Martineau] Harriet Martineau: "The Great American Lawyer." Excerpted from *Retrospect of Western Travel* by Harriet Martineau. London: Saunders and Otley and New York: Harper & Brothers, 1838. See Volume I: pp. 147-151.

[Melish] John Melish: "Drain the Swamp." Excerpted from *Travels in the United States of America, in the Years 1806 & 1807, and 1809, 1810, & 1811* by John Melish. Philadelphia: Printed for the Author, 1812. See Volume I: Chapter XXXIII, pp. 201-206; "John Melish and his Map of the United States" by Walter Ristow. *Library of Congress Quarterly Journal of Acquisitions* 19 (1962), pp. 159-178.

[Moore] Thomas Moore: "Obelisks in Trees." Excerpted from *Epistles, Odes, and Other Poems* by Thomas Moore. London: Printed for James Carpenter, Old Bond Street, 1806. See pp. 209-215.

[Northup] Solomon Northup: "I Gave Them My Confidence." Excerpted from *Twelve Years a Slave. Narrative of Solomon Northup, a Citizen of New-York, Kidnapped in Washington City in 1841, and Rescued in 1853, from a Cotton Plantation near the Red River in Louisiana* by Solomon Northup. Auburn: Derby and Miller, 1853. See pp. 33-39.

[Poore] Benjamin Perley Poore: "A Noisy Mob." Excerpted from *Perley's Reminiscences of Sixty Years in the National Metropolis*. Philadelphia: Hubbard Brothers, 1886. See Volume I: pp. 92-95.

[Power] Tyrone Power: "Stay Men Turned Loose." Excerpted from *Impressions of America: During the Years 1833, 1834, and 1835* by Tyrone Power. 2nd Edition. Philadelphia: Carey, Lea & Blanchard, 1836. See Volume I: pp. 130-131 and pp. 146-149.

[President] President of the United States, George Washington: "Ten Miles Square." Excerpted from *Historical Sketches of the Ten Miles Square Forming the District of Columbia* by Jonathan Elliot [Elliott]. Washington: Printed by J. Elliot Jr., 1830. See pp. 20-23.

[Rochefoucauld-Liancourt] Duke Rochefoucauld-Liancourt: "A Handsome Tavern." Excerpted from *Travels Through the United States of North America: the Country of the Iroquois, and Upper Canada, In the Years 1795, 1796, and 1797* by François Alexandre Frédéric, duc de La Rochefoucauld-Liancourt. 2nd Edition. London: R. Phillips, 1800. See Volume III: "Federal City," pp. 622-632.

[Trollope, Anthony] Anthony Trollope: "No Neutrality Possible." Excerpted from *North America* by Anthony Trollope. New York: Harper & Brothers, 1863. See pp. 312-315; pp. 321-323; pp. 358-359.

[Trollope, Francis] Francis Trollope: "One Hand Hoisting the Cap of Liberty." Excerpted from *Domestic Manners of the Americans* by Mrs. Trollope. London: Printed for Whittaker, Treacher & Co., 1832. See Volume I: Chapter XX, pp. 305-336.

[Washington] George Washington: "Ardent and Susceptible Minds." Excerpted from *The Writings of George Washington*, Collected and Edited by Worthington Chauncey Ford. New York: G. P. Putnam's Sons, 1889-1893. See Volume 13, pp. 36-38.

[Watterston] George Watterston: *Letters from Washington on the Constitution and Laws; with Sketches of Some of the Prominent Characters of the United States. Written during the Winter of 1817-1818. By a Foreigner.* City of Washington: Printed and Published by Jacob Gideon, 1818. See Letter III: pp. 38-48.

[Weishampel] John F. Weishampel: "Feared by Many." Full text of *The Pope's Stratagem: "Rome to America!" An Address to the Protestants of the United States, Against Placing the Pope's Block of Marble in the Washington Monument.* Baltimore: John F. Weishampel, 1852.

[Weld] Isaac Weld, Jr.: "Drawn by a Frenchman." Excerpted from *Travels Through the States of North America, and the Provinces of Upper and Lower Canada, During the years 1795, 1796, and 1797* by Isaac Weld, Jr. London: Printed for John Stockdale, 1799. See Volume I: Letter IV, pp. 49-53 and pp. 80-89.

[Whitman] Walt Whitman: "The Great Army of the Wounded." Originally published in the *New York Times* on February 26, 1863. Excerpted from *The Wound Dresser: A Series of Letters Written from the Hospitals in Washington During the War of the Rebellion* by Walt Whitman. Edited by Richard Maurice Bucke, M.D. Boston: Small, Maynard & Company, 1898. See pp. 1-10.

[Williamson] James J. Williamson: "The Oath of Allegiance." Excerpted from *Prison Life in the Old Capitol and Reminiscences of the Civil War* by James J. Williamson. West Orange, New Jersey, 1911. See pp. 19-29.

[Wolcott] Oliver Wolcott, Jr.: "In the Company of Crazy People." Excerpted from *Memoirs of the Administrations of Washington and John Adams, Edited from the Papers of Oliver Wolcott, Secretary of the Treasury* by George Gibbs. New York: Printed for the Subscribers, 1846. See Volume II: pp. 376-378; *Fortress of Finance* by Pamela Scott. Washington, D.C.: Treasury Historical Association, 210. See p. 3.

ETHER EDITIONS

Futurum est in aethere...

PUBLISHED BY ETHER EDITIONS

Capital City Anthology
  Christopher Lee Philips

Caricatures
  Gene Markey

In Praise of Folly
  Desiderius Erasmus

Inside Football
  Frank W. Cavanaugh

King of the Black Isles
  J. U. Nicolson

The Arthurian Cycle
  Edwin Arlington Robinson

The Smart Set Conversations
  H. L. Mencken and George Jean Nathan